D1714747

A Functional
Analysis of Political
Television Advertisements

A Functional
Analysis of Political
Television Advertisements

William L. Benoit

LEXINGTON BOOKS
Lanham • Boulder • New York • Toronto • Plymouth, UK

Published by Lexington Books
A wholly owned subsidiary of Rowman & Littlefield
4501 Forbes Boulevard, Suite 200, Lanham, Maryland 20706
www.rowman.com

10 Thornbury Road, Plymouth PL6 7PP, United Kingdom

British Library Cataloguing in Publication Information Available

Library of Congress Cataloging-in-Publication Data

Benoit, William L.
    A functional analysis of political television advertisements / William L. Benoit.
        pages cm
    Includes bibliographical references and index.
    ISBN 978-0-7391-8898-9 (cloth : alk. paper) — ISBN 978-0-7391-8899-6 (electronic)
    1. Advertising, Political—United States. 2. Television in politics--United States. 3. Political campaigns—United States. 4. Presidents—United States—Election. 5. United States—Politics and government—1945–1989. 6. United States--Politics and government—1989–
I. Title.
    JF2112.A4B46 2014
    324.7'30973—dc23
                                                                                    2013050730

∞™ The paper used in this publication meets the minimum requirements of American National Standard for Information Sciences—Permanence of Paper for Printed Library Materials, ANSI/NISO Z39.48-1992.

Printed in the United States of America

Contents

Preface

This book investigates the nature (content) of political television advertising. It focuses on American presidential ads from the general election campaign. However, it also examines presidential primary spots, general election ads from third party candidates, nonpresidential advertisements, and ads from other countries. I thought it would be unwieldy to devote a chapter to each of the sixteen American presidential elections; however, it did not seem right to cram them all into one chapter. When I wrote the first edition of this book (Benoit, 1999), I put two presidential elections in a chapter and it seemed to me that each pair of elections fit together. In this edition, I treat four election campaigns in each of four chapters. This is a compromise between the two extremes of treating American presidential campaigns in sixteen chapters or in one chapter.

First, I wanted to go back to the very beginning, studying every presidential campaign that used television spots. Other research (e.g., Geer, 2006; Kaid and Johnston, 1991; West, 1997) used samples that were limited in different but important ways (as I note in chapter 2). Second, I wanted to include both primary and general spots in the same study. When one of the major party candidates is perceived as weak (e.g., presidents Ford in 1976, Carter in 1980, Bush in 1992, or Obama in 2012), the outcome of the primary contest may essentially determine who will become president. Primary ads can be very important, but have not received the attention they deserve in past books on political advertising. Third, I wanted to include spots by third-party candidates. Although these candidates are occasionally mentioned in reviews of a given election campaign, no study focuses on third-party television spots. I also wanted to include nonpresidential and non-U.S. political TV spots in the sample. This book, therefore, is designed to investigate the content of political television spots.

I would like to express my appreciation to the Central States Communication Association for the Federation Prize, which enabled me to purchase videotapes of hundreds of the spots I analyzed. I also appreciate receipt of a University of Missouri Big Twelve Fellowship, which allowed me to spend two weeks at the University of Oklahoma Political Communication Archive, where I transcribed hundreds of additional spots. I want to thank Lynda Lee Kaid, Charles E. Rand, and Marie Mathos, at the Archive, for assistance and access to those spots. The George Bush Presidential Library sent me videotapes of Bush's television spots without charge. Other presidential libraries sold me tapes, and many spots were obtained courtesy of the Dwight D. Eisenhower, John F. Kennedy, Lyndon Baines Johnson, Jimmy Carter, Ronald Reagan, and Gerald R. Ford presidential libraries. I also want to thank Joseph R. Blaney, who graciously coded spots for this study. Unfortunately, I cannot offer thanks to the Nixon Presidential Library, which outsources videotape duplication, making their cost far too high for my limited resources. I especially regret not having more primary spots from President Nixon for this study.

This book benefitted from the insights and work of many other people. Much of the published data reported here was generated with others who contributed ideas as well as time and effort. Co-authors who worked with me on political campaign research include David Airne, Pam Benoit, Jen Benoit-Bryan, Joe Blaney, LeAnn Brazeal, Sumanna Chattopadhyay, Sooyoung Cho, Yun Son Choi, Jordan Compson, Heather Currie, Corey Davis, Jeff Delbert, Mark Glantz, Allison Harthcock, Glenn Hansen, Kate Hemmer, Jayne Henson, Julio Cesar Herrero, Sungwook Hwang, Andrew Klyukovski, Cheolhan Lee, Glen Leshner, John McGuire, John McHale, John Petrocik, Anji Phillips, Penni Pier, Steve Price, Bryan Reber, Leslie Rill, Tamir Sheafer, Kevin Stein, Leigh Anne Sudbrock, Rebecca Verser, Courtney Vogt, Jack Yu, Bill Wells, John Wen, and Jessica Wilson-Kratzer. I would also like to thank the students in my political campaign communication classes at University of Missouri and Ohio University, who listened to me work out some of these ideas in class and prodded me with questions.

Most importantly, I want to acknowledge my family. Pam, my wife, developed the theory of acclaims on which I rely so heavily. My daughter Jennifer is a constant source of delight. I am lucky to have been able to publish with both Pam and Jennifer, who support me in tangible and intangible ways too numerous to mention.

I

PRELIMINARIES

1

Introduction

Political Television Spots

This chapter provides background on political television advertising. First, I will argue that political spots are an important form of campaign message that we need to understand. Second, I will review past research on political television advertising. Chapter 7 will review research on presidential primary ads and chapter 10 will examine the literature on nonpresidential and non-U.S. political advertising. Finally, I will describe my purpose in conducting this research.

THE IMPORTANCE OF POLITICAL TELEVISION SPOTS

Television spots are an extremely important component of modern political election campaigns. Several arguments support this contention. First, candidates expend huge amounts of money on producing and broadcasting television advertising. Ansolabehere and Iyengar (1995) observed that "The amounts of money spent on political advertising are staggering: Hundreds of millions of dollars are poured into what has become the main means of political communication in the United States" (p. 3). For example, Devlin (1993) reported that in 1992 Bush, Clinton, and Perot together devoted $133 million (three-quarters of their budgets) to television spots. In 1996, for example, Dole, Clinton, and Perot lavished even more money, about $200 million, on television advertising (Devlin, 1997). Over a billion dollars was spent in the 2012 general election campaign by Obama, Romney, and outside groups (Wilson, 2012), almost a half a billion dollars more than was spent on this race just four years earlier. The enormous amount of money candidates devote to television spots is clear evidence of the significance of this kind of political message form. It is also an indication of how many presidential television commercials are broadcast, with many advertisements and ads that are shown over and over. Of course, television spots are also broadcast in presidential primary campaigns and in races for other elective offices, such as governor, mayor, senate, or congress. A vast audience is purchased with this money, and it is exposed repeatedly to these campaign messages. As Jamieson (1996) recognizes, "The spot ad is the most used and most viewed of all available forms of advertising" (p. 517).

A second reason that political advertising merits scholarly attention is the fact that voters obtain substantial amounts of information on the candidates and their policy positions from them. For example, West (1993) analyzed data from eighteen campaigns, concluding that political advertisements affected candidates' images, likability, electability, and assessment of policy positions. Empirical research on both the 1972 (Patterson and McClure, 1976) and the 1984 (Kern, 1989) campaigns concluded that "by a ratio of 4 to 1, Americans received the majority of their information about candidate positions on the issues from ads rather than the news" (Kern, 1989, p. 47; see also Zhao and Bleske, 1995; Weaver and Drew, 1993; cf. Drew and Weaver, 1991). This latter finding, that the electorate obtains more information about the issues in campaigns from commercials than from the news, may seem surprising. However, a closer look at the news media helps us understand why this is the case.

Three different factors are at work here. One reason that voters obtain more information from presidential spots than news is simply that campaign news is only one story topic among many. The nightly network news enjoys a thirty-minute time slot, but after we subtract commercials and stories on non-campaign topics, relatively little time remains for campaign news. Furthermore, the number of campaign stories covered in the news decreased 20 percent from 1968 to 1988 (Steele and Barnhurst, 1996). Exacerbating these trends is the fact that the average length of a political news story decreased by about 20 percent (Hallin, 1992). Thus, the nightly news devotes precious little time to providing coverage of presidential campaigns.

Second, when the presidential campaign does make the news, this coverage has a tendency to focus on the "horse race" elements of the presidential campaign. Patterson (1980) explained that "In its coverage of a presidential campaign, the press concentrates on the strategic game played by the candidates in their pursuit of the presidency, thereby de-emphasizing the questions of national policy and leadership" (p. 21). News stories are likely to report on such questions as: Who is ahead in the polls? Who are the candidates' campaign managers? What campaign strategies are in play for each candidate? What is the status of fundraising efforts? Which states are being actively contested by the candidates? Who will be included in presidential debates? The answers to these questions are clearly news, but they do not really provide information to the electorate about who would make a better president. In fact, Patterson's (1980) investigation of the 1976 campaign concluded that "The election's substance . . . received only half as much coverage as was accorded the game" (p. 24). Benoit, Hemmer, and Stein (2010) content analyzed stories about the presidential primary campaign from 1952–2004 in the *New York Times*: 66 percent of themes (statements) in the sample were about horse race, 16 percent were about the candidates' character, and 12 percent concerned policy. *New York Times* coverage of the general presidential election had similar emphases: 40 percent horse race, 31 percent character, and 25 percent policy (Benoit, Stein, and Hansen, 2005). Thus, the focus on "horse race" coverage of the presidential campaign sharply reduces coverage of the substance of the campaign.

Finally, when the news media do cover the issues in a campaign, in recent years they have devoted less and less of its coverage to the candidates themselves. The news is increasingly likely to offer short sound bites from candidates instead of extended quotations that provide thoughtful consideration of the issues in the campaign. Hallin (1992) reported that the average quotation from presidential candidates included in the news had dropped from forty-three seconds in 1968 to a mere nine seconds in 1988. Although the length of statements from journalists has also diminished, they spoke in campaign stories almost twice as often in 1988 as in 1968: "Journalists inserted their voices more often, by an increment of 0.17 times per report per year" (Steele and Barnhurst, 1996, p. 191). Thus, the stories tend to be fewer in number and shorter in length, they spend far less time quoting the candidates, and they feature the opinions and commentary of journalists (instead of information and arguments from candidates) more frequently. So, it is easy to understand why the electorate obtains more information about the issues in the presidential campaign from televised spots than from the news.

A third reason that campaign spots deserve scholarly attention is that considerable research conducted on the effects of televised political spots shows that such ads can affect viewers. Mulder (1979) found that advertising in a Chicago mayoral campaign correlated positively with attitudes toward the candidates. Studies have established a positive relationship between election outcomes and advertising expenditures (Joslyn, 1981; Palda, 1973). Wanat (1974) found that, for candidates who won elections, broadcast expenditures correlated highly (0.56) with voting outcomes. McClure and Patterson (1974) reported that in the 1972 presidential campaign, "Exposure to political advertising was consistently related to voter belief change" (p. 16; see also Atkin and Heald, 1976). Therefore, empirical research documents the fact that political campaign advertising can influence voters and voting (studies have also examined the effects of political advertising on trust, involvement, and participation: Ansolabehere and Iyengar, 1995; Garramone, Atkin, Pinkleton, and Cole, 1990; Martinez and Delegal, 1990).

Furthermore, experimental research using advertisements actually used by candidates (Atkin, 1977; Basil, Schooler, and Reeves, 1991; Christ, Thorson, and Caywood, 1994; Faber and Storey, 1984; Faber, Tims, and Schmitt, 1993; Garramone, 1984, 1985; Garramone and Smith, 1984; Geiger and Reeves, 1991; Hitchon and Chang, 1995; D.D. Johnston, 1989; Just, Crigler, and Wallach, 1990; Kaid, 1997; Kaid and Boydston, 1987; Kaid, Leland, and Whitney, 1992; Kaid and Sanders, 1978; Lang, 1991; McClure and Patterson, 1974; Merritt, 1984; Newhagen and Reeves, 1991) as well as commercials developed by researchers (Becker and Doolittle, 1975; Cundy, 1986; Donohue, 1973; Garramone, Atkin, Pinkleton, and Cole,

1990; Hill, 1989; Meadow and Sigelman, 1982; Roddy and Garramone, 1988; Rudd, 1989; Thorson, Christ, and Caywood, 1991) demonstrates that televised political advertisements have a variety of effects (recall, attitudes toward candidates, voting intention) on viewers. Gordon and Hartmann (2013), using data from the 2000 and 2004 presidential elections, conclude that "our findings illustrate that advertising is capable of shifting the electoral votes of multiple states and consequently the outcome of an election" (p. 33). Benoit, Leshner, and Chattopadhyay (2007) cumulated existing research with meta-analysis, finding that political spots increased issue knowledge, influenced perceptions of the candidates' character, changed attitudes toward candidates, affected candidate preference (vote choice), and affected vote-likelihood (turnout). Other meta-analyses (Allen and Burrell 2002; Lau, Sigelman, and Rovner, 2007) have found no significant differences in the effects of negative versus positive ads: Both kinds of ads have effects on viewers. Therefore, televised political spots are an important form of messages in political campaigns and these messages definitely merit scholarly attention.

Of course, it is true that other factors—such as political party affiliation, the state of the economy (and other domestic affairs), or significant foreign policy events—can influence voting intention. I would not dispute, for example, the contention that political advertising rarely alters the voting intentions of committed partisans. However, the role political party affiliation plays in elections does not mean campaigns and the messages in those campaigns (like television spots) are unimportant.

First, party affiliation cannot determine (or explain) the outcome of *primary campaigns*, because the candidates who contend with one another for their party's nomination are by definition members of the same party. In 2012, for example, political party affiliation could not help voters choose between Michele Bachmann, Herman Cain, Newt Gingrich, Mike Huckabee, Jon Huntsman, Ron Paul, Tim Pawlenty, Rick Perry, Mitt Romney, and Rick Santorum, because they are all Republicans. Second, the growth in the number of independent voters means that neither political party can win the *general campaign* without persuading other, nonparty members to vote for their candidate. In fact, the number of independent voters has increased from 22.6 percent in 1952 to 38.0 percent in 1992 (Weisberg and Kimball, 1993). Nie, Verba, and Petrocik (1979) observed that voting defections have increased over time: "Even among those who have a partisan identity, the proportion voting for the opposition party has grown" (p. 164). Thus, party affiliation is a significant impact on the voting behavior of many citizens, but it cannot account for the behavior of all voters and it does not determine the outcome of elections. Indeed, the simple fact that we have had six Republicans (Eisenhower, Nixon, Ford, Reagan, Bush [41], and Bush [43]) and five Democrats (Kennedy, Johnson, Carter, Clinton, and Obama) in the White House since 1952 is good evidence that political party does not determine election outcomes. Finally, Iyengar and Kinder's (1988) research on agenda setting indicates that on some issues (although not all), the *actual economic figures* had little or no impact on the perceived importance of an issue—but *presidential speeches* did have a substantial impact on viewers' attitudes. This study did not focus on campaigns or on television spots, but it does demonstrate that politicians can influence people's attitudes on the issues addressed in their messages (and that what they *say* in their messages in some cases can have more impact on attitudes than the *actual economic figures* themselves). Campaign messages do matter (cf. Benoit, Blaney, and Pier [1999] on Lichtman, 1996, who argues the contrary of this claim).

Political TV spots offer candidates a great deal of message control. Candidates can offer information (press releases) to the news media but journalists choose which information to report—and they often comment on that information, sometimes unfavorably. The news may also seek comment from the opposition to provide "balanced" coverage. In election debates a candidate cannot control what questions are asked or what opponents will say. But candidates have complete control over the content of their own political TV spots: They can assure that the ideas they want to express are included and they control exactly how those ideas are presented in these messages.

Furthermore, candidates can target certain groups of voters by buying time on TV stations, networks, and programs viewed by those voters. In a sense, political advertising can be seen as a stealth message. Citizens must choose to watch an election debate, visit a candidate's webpage, or read a newspaper story on the campaign. Voters do not have to choose to watch an ad; ads are run on programs that target audiences are already watching. Of course, viewers could mute the TV, run into the kitchen, or otherwise ignore an ad—but many of the citizens who are tuned in to that program will be exposed to the ad. So, ads send out the candidates' messages without relying on voters to seek out these messages.

Of course, other important forms of campaign messages are employed by candidates to reach voters in addition to television advertisements. Presidential debates, for example, typically attract relatively vast audiences (see Benoit, 2014), and provide viewers with an hour or more of the candidates side-by-side, answering (more or less) the same questions. However, this study is limited to television advertisements, which are an extremely important form of campaign message, as argued above.

For these reasons, television spots are an extremely important component of the modern presidential campaign and merit scholarly attention. This work is designed to provide a comprehensive analysis of the functions of political TV spots. It investigates spots from the first presidential campaign to use television spots—the 1952 contest between Dwight Eisenhower and Adlai Stevenson—through the most recent battle between Barack Obama and Mitt Romney in 2012. Ads from incumbents are contrasted with ones for challengers. This study also contrasts general campaign spots with commercials from primary contests. This book also examines advertisements from several third-party candidates. Nonpresidential (governor, Senate, House, and local) and non-U.S. advertisements are discussed. No work has ever included all three kinds of spots in a single study (chapter 2 describes the sample).

This study applies the functional perspective on political campaigns, analyzing the utterances in spots into acclaims (self-praise or positive remarks), attacks (negative remarks), and defenses (refutations of attacks; see Benoit, 2007a). Chapter 2 elaborates this functional approach. The candidates' statements are divided into those that address policy and those that concern character. Policy comments are further divided into those that address past deeds, future plans, and general goals, whereas character remarks are divided into personal qualities, leadership ability, and ideals. Chapter 9 will investigate political advertising and two other theories—Issue Ownership and Functional Federalism. Together, these analyses will provide the most comprehensive analysis of political television advertisements available.

PAST RESEARCH ON POLITICAL TELEVISION SPOTS

A great deal of research has been conducted on televised spots (see, e.g., Aden, 1989; Kaid, Nimmo, and Sanders, 1986; Louden, 1989). For a history of the spot, see Devlin (1977, 1982, 1987b, 1989, 1993, 1997), Diamond and Bates (1992), Jamieson (1996) or Levine (1995); for a discussion of negative advertisements in particular, see James and Hensel (1991), Johnson-Cartee and Copeland (1991, 1997), or Procter and Schenck-Hamlin (1996). The literature also includes a number of studies of nonpresidential spots (Johnston and White, 1994; Kaid and Davidson, 1986; Latimer, 1984, 1989; Nowlan and Moutray, 1984; Payne and Baukus, 1988; Prisuta, 1972; Rose and Fuchs, 1968; Tinkham and Weaver-Lariscy, 1995; Tucker, 1959; or Weaver-Lariscy and Tinkham, 1987). Several studies compare political advertising in the United States with spots from other countries (Foote, 1991; Griffin and Kagan, 1996; Holtz-Bacha and Kaid, 1995; Holtz-Bacha, Kaid, and Johnston, 1994; A. Johnston, 1991; Kaid, 1991; Kaid and Holtz-Bacha, 1995a, 1995b or Lee and Benoit, 2004). Some research investigates agenda-setting and political advertising (Ghorpade, 1986; Roberts and McCombs, 1994; Schleuder, McCombs, and Wanta, 1991). Several studies adopt more of a rhetorically oriented approach to political advertising (e.g., Cronkhite, Liska, and Schrader, 1991; Descutner, Burnier, Mickunas, and Letteri, 1991; Gronbeck, 1992; Jamieson, 1989; Larson, 1982; Shyles, 1991; or Smith and Johnston, 1991). This next section reviews the literature on the two primary dimensions of televised political spots: function (acclaims, positive ads; attacks, negative ads) and topics (policy or issue; character or image).

Here, I focus on research designed to analyze the nature of political television commercials. This book relies on content analysis, a method that quantifies elements of political TV spot content. Most studies tend to discuss two dimensions: function (negative versus positive spots) and topic (policy/issues versus character/image) ads.

Functions of Political TV Spots

West (1997) studied 379 spots from 1952 to 1996, reporting that 46 percent of the ads were positive and that Democratic ads were more positive than Republican ones. Kaid and Johnston (1991) found that 71 percent of the presidential political commercials from 1960 to 1988 were positive and 29 percent negative. However, the number of negative ads varied over time: negative spots spiked at 40 percent in 1964, dropped to 22–28 percent in the 1970s, and increased to 35–37 percent in the 1980s. Kaid and Johnston (1991) did not find that challengers use more negative ads than incumbents or that Republicans use significantly more negative ads than Democrats. Geer (2006) examines presidential TV spots from 1960–2004. Negative ads ranged from 9 percent in 1960 to 49 percent in 2004; overall 28 percent of ads in his sample were negative, 48 percent positive, and 24 percent contrast (both positive and negative).

Devlin (1989) reported that in 1988 Bush produced thirty-seven ads, fourteen of which were negative (38 percent), whereas Dukakis had forty-seven ads, twenty-three of which were negative (49 percent). In 1992, 63 percent of Clinton's thirty ads were negative and 56 percent of Bush's twenty-four ads were negative (Devlin, 1993). Kaid (1994) reported that 17 percent of the ads in the 1992 primary were negative. In the general election Bush employed 44 percent positive and 56 percent negative ads; Clinton 31 percent positive and 69 percent negative, and Perot had only positive ads. These studies of 1992 suggest that Clinton, the challenger, used more negative ads than Bush—but still more than half of both Bush's and Clinton's ads were negative. In 1996, Clinton and Dole both produced about forty spots for the general campaign. About 10 percent of Clinton's spots were negative, and about 40 percent were comparative (Devlin, 1997). Two-thirds of Dole's spots were negative (and two spots were comparative). Thus, with few exceptions (e.g., Perot), political ads use both acclaims and attacks.

Topics of Political Advertising

Most research on televised political spots has reported a heavier emphasis on issues than on image. Patterson and McClure (1976) found that 42 percent of the television commercials in 1972 focused on issues, and another 28 percent included issue information. Hofstetter and Zukin (1979) reported that 85 percent of the ads by Nixon and McGovern addressed issues. Joslyn (1980) found that 77 percent of the ads discussed issues but only 47 percent focused on images. Kern's study of 1984 ads indicated that "issues were mentioned in 84 percent of such [thirty-second] spots" (1989, p. 51). West (1997), studying 379 spots from 1952 to 1996, reported that 61 percent mentioned issues.

Kaid and Johnston (1991), who examined 830 television spots from 1960 to 1988. They reported that 67 percent of the positive ads and 79 percent of the negative ads provide issue information, and that 65 percent of the positive spots and 64 percent of the negative spots include image information. In the 1992 campaign, Kaid (1994) found that 59 percent of primary television ads addressed image, 24 percent issues, and 17 percent were negative ads. In the general election, Bush's ads were divided evenly between issue and image; Clinton used two-thirds issue and one-third image; whereas Perot used about 60 percent issue and 40 percent image. Geer (2006) also reported that 56 percent of the ads concerned issues (policy) and 44 percent were about character (26 percent of spots were about the candidates' personal characteristics and 18 percent concerned values).

Three studies provide more specifics on issues and image in political advertising. Johnson-Cartee and Copeland (1989) generated a list of topics found in negative political ads, grouped them into ten categories, and asked respondents to rate them as fair or unfair. The topics clustered into two groups, labeled "Political Issues" (political record, stands on issues, criminal record, and voting record) and "Personal Characteristics" (personal life, marriage, family, religion, medical history, and sex life). At least 83 percent rated each political issue as a fair topic for an attack; no more than 36 percent rated any of the personal characteristics as an acceptable topic for political attack. This reveals that there was general, albeit not universal, agreement on which topics are fair for an attack. It also suggests that respondents did not condemn political attacks wholesale, but believed that attacks on some topics were more suitable than others.

Joslyn's (1986) study of 506 political ads from 1960 to 1984 reported that 37 percent of the ads reveal future policy plans, 60 percent evaluate past governmental policy, 57 percent mention candidate qualities (compassion, empathy, integrity, strength, activity, and knowledge). Shyles (1986) analyzed 140 political ads from 1980. He divided his results into issue and image, reporting mentions of these topics: Carter's record, domestic, economy, energy, federalism, foreign policy, government management, national security, and national well-being (issue); altruism, competence, expertise, honesty, leadership, personal, strength, and other qualities (image). It is clear that political advertising addresses both issues and images (see also Benze and Declercq, 1985).

Of course these two topics of political ads are not as discrete as one might assume. Benoit and Wells (1996), in their analysis of the 1992 presidential debates, argue that a candidate's stance on issues shapes that candidate's image, and that a candidate's image probably influences perceptions about his or her issue stances. This relationship between issues and image should hold true in advertising as well. Furthermore, as Devlin (1977) noted in his analysis of advertising in the 1976 presidential campaign, Carter's campaign "used issues or themes as a vehicle for Carter to achieve an image as a legitimate candidate" (p. 244; see also Rudd, 1986; Kern, 1989). Thus, issues and image are interrelated concepts.

Finally, although the distinction between "issues" and "image" is very well established in the literature, I prefer an alternate terminology. Confusion can arise because the term "issue" has two meanings. Generally, it refers to points or topics of conflict in a discussion or conflict. In the context of political discourse, "issue" also is used as a synonym for policy considerations. However, the candidates' character, or qualifications for office (e.g., their experience, their integrity) are certainly legitimate grounds for discussion and dispute during a campaign (whether aspects of a candidate's private life are acceptable topics is another question). This means that "image" is an "issue"—not in the second sense of a policy dispute, but in the first sense as a point of dissention. To try to avoid this possible confusion, I propose an alternative terminology, contrasting utterances on *policy* stands with remarks on the *character* of the candidates.

PURPOSE OF THIS STUDY

It is clear that these scholars have provided important insights into the nature of political advertising. The purpose of this study is to extend this important work in several ways. First, I offer a theoretical framework for understanding the fundamental functions of political advertising—acclaiming, attacking, and defending—articulated in the next section.

Second, unlike some of these studies, I analyze presidential spots on both dimensions used in the literature: functions (acclaim, attack, defend) and topic (policy, character). Other research does not always do so. For example, Kaid (1994) divided 1992 primary ads into image ads, issue ads, and negative ads, a category system that implies that image and issue ads are distinct from negative spots. Surely negative ads can address issues and image (or both), but this classification system does not make that point clear.

Third, most research relies on binary classification of television spots, coding the entire advertisement as enacting *either* one category *or* another (either positive or negative; either policy or character). This assumes that every spot has a single focus. In contrast, my procedure identifies and categorizes each of the appeals (themes) in a given spot. To illustrate the nature of this problem, consider the following Clinton spot from 1996:

> *Ten million new jobs. Family income up $1,600 (since 1993). President Clinton cut the deficit 60 percent. Signed welfare reform—requiring work, time limits. Taxes cut for fifteen million families. Balancing the budget. America's moving forward with an economic plan that works.* Bob Dole: $900 billion in higher taxes. Republicans call him tax collector for the welfare state. His risky tax scheme would raise taxes on nine million families. Bob Dole. Wrong in the past. Wrong for our future.

The italicized portion of this ad is positive, praising Bill Clinton's accomplishments and suggesting future benefits if he is re-elected. The other portion, however, attacks Bob Dole's past deeds and his proposed tax cut. A coding system that classifies this spot as *either* positive *or* negative clearly ignores or misclassifies half of this message.

Some research acknowledges this limitation by adding a third category, comparative ads. However, this move does not really resolve this problem, because ads exist on a continuum from all positive to completely negative. Only if all of the ads that contained both negative and positive appeals had equal amounts of each would addition of a third category, "comparative" (or "contrast") deal with this problem. Therefore, a method that codes *each theme* (each utterance or statement) in a spot as positive or negative (and as concerning policy or character) will provide a more accurate description of the content of TV spots.

Furthermore, some research counts the number of advertisements that "mention" issues. This procedure gives us no idea of how much time was devoted to issues in an ad. Was the entire spot devoted to issues, or was an issue briefly mentioned in passing? More information would be gleaned from counting the number of policy (issue) and character (image) utterances that were contained in each spot.

Fourth, although positive and negative ads may well predominate, some political television spots use defenses, or explicit responses to prior attacks from opponents (Trent and Friedenberg, 1995, acknowledge that such spots exist, but do not study them). Past research (e.g., Benoit, 2007a) found defenses in political TV spots. Although defenses are not nearly as common in television spots as acclaims and attacks (they accounted for 1 percent of the utterances in those spots), they are an option that is used in campaign discourse that should not be ignored by critics and analysts.

Fifth, the sample of spots gathered for this study includes multiple commercials from both major party candidates in every presidential campaign that employed television spots, from 1952 to 2012 (as well as ads from the primary campaign, from third party candidates, nonpresidential candidates, and candidates for prime minister, chancellor, or president in other countries). This will permit an unparalleled description of political television spots.

In this study I will address several topics. Chapters 3–6 will present the results of analysis of general election campaign spots, considered four campaigns at a time (I discuss four campaigns in each chapter as a compromise: I did not want to devote a chapter to each of the sixteen presidential campaigns to use TV spots, but I also did not want to lump together all general spots in a single chapter). My compromise was to discuss four general election presidential campaigns in each of four chapters. In these chapters I begin with a brief background about the situation, the candidates, and their spots. I reproduce the transcripts of several spots from these campaigns to try to give a flavor for each contest. In each of these chapters I take up four topics. First, I describe the functions of presidential television spots (acclaims, attacks, defenses). Second, I consider these spots' treatment of policy and character topics. Third, I will discuss the subdivisions of policy (past deeds, future plans, general goals) and of character (personal qualities, leadership ability, ideals) as delineated in chapter 2. Then I offer chapters on third party presidential ads, primary ads, nonpresidential ads, non-U.S. ads discussing the same basic ideas.

This analysis is followed by a comparative chapter. Chapter 11 discusses trends in general television spots, compares primary with general campaigns, incumbents versus challengers, the advertisements of winners and losers, and a discussion the source of utterances in spots. Chapter 12 discusses the development of several recurring themes in presidential television advertising. Chapter 13 offers a discussion of implications and conclusions derived from this study.

2

Method

The Functional Approach to Political Advertising

This chapter describes the Functional Theory of Political Campaign Discourse (Benoit, 2007a), which was used to produce much of the data discussed in this book (two other theories—Issue Ownership and Functional Federalism—will be discussed in chapter 9). Then I will describe the advantages inherent in this approach to analyzing political television spots. Finally, I will discuss the content analytic method used to generate these data.

A functional analysis is especially appropriate for investigating political campaign advertisements because candidate statements in these messages are intended as a *means* of accomplishing a *goal*: winning the election. Political campaign discourse is therefore inherently instrumental, or functional, in nature. Of course, some candidates campaign in order to espouse a particular point of view. This is presumably the case for some third party candidates; it may also be the case for some of the candidates in the primary who have no realistic chance of winning. However, for those who do have a reasonable chance of winning—which at the presidential level in contemporary campaigns means the Republican or Democratic nominees—campaign messages function as the means to gaining votes and thus winning public office.

ASSUMPTIONS OF FUNCTIONAL THEORY

Functional Theory is based on six key Axioms. Each of these assumptions will be explicated here.

A1. *Voting is a comparative act.*

When voting, citizens face a relatively straightforward decision: For whom should I cast my vote? A vote is a choice between two (or more) competing candidates and it clearly involves a comparison. No candidate for elective office should be expected to be completely without drawbacks; on the other hand, surely no candidate is utterly without redeeming qualities. A voter chooses between two or more candidates, and the candidate who appears most suitable (on the criteria are most important to a given voter) will receive that person's vote (see Downs, 1957; Himmelweit, Humphreys, and Jaeger, 1985; Nie, Verba, and Petrocik, 1979; Pomper, 1975). A candidate does not need to win all votes to win the election; nor must a candidate appear perfect to receive a citizen's voter. All that is required is for a candidate to appear *preferable* to other candidates for the office for a majority (or plurality) of voters. This means that in any contested election, a citizen's vote choice is fundamentally a comparative decision that one candidate appears *preferable* to the other candidate(s) on whatever criterion is most important to that voter. Use of the word "appears" acknowledges that a citizen's evaluation of a candidate is a perception; it is not possible to have objective knowledge of what a candidate would do if elected (policy) or what kind of person (character) he or she "really" is. Some voters, of course, may be so certain that the candidate they prefer is better that they consider this superiority to be a fact rather than a perception, but nevertheless their candidate preference is still a perception. Voters' candidate choices are best understood as perceptions that they form on the basis of their own attitudes and values and the information they possess that appears relevant to them when they make their vote choice. This means that the ultimate goal sought by candidates, winning elections, is achieved by persuading enough voters to believe that he or she is the better candidate in the race. As Popkin explains, "each campaign tries hard to make its side look better and the other side worse" (1994, p. 232). Therefore, political television spots have three basic functions: (1) acclaims, or utterances that enhance their own credentials as a desirable office-holder (positive utterances), (2) attacks, or comments that degrade their opponent's credentials as a potential office-holder (negative utterances), and, if their opponent attacks them, (3) defenses, or remarks that respond to those attacks (rebuttals).

This idea that voting is a choice between *competing candidates* is becoming increasingly important as political parties decline in influence. Popkin observed that "in an environment of diminishing party loyalty, campaigns and candidates exert a greater influence on voters than they did in the elections of 1940 and 1948" (1994, p. 12; see also Menefee-Libey, 2000; Wattenberg, 1991, 1998). In earlier contests, the party nominee was selected at the convention. Patterson (2003) noted that in 1952 Estes Kefauver won

> all but one of the twelve primaries he entered and was the clear favorite of rank-and-file Democrats in the final Gallup Poll before the national nominating convention. Nevertheless, the party's leaders chose Adlai Stevenson as the Democratic presidential nominee. (pp. 145–146)

We cannot know whether Kefauver could have defeated Eisenhower if he had been the Democratic nominee in 1952 (that seems unlikely), but we know Stevenson lost. In 1968 only sixteen Republican and seventeen Democratic primaries were held (Crotty and Jackson, 1985). By 2012, primaries were scheduled across the country, although some occurred after the nominee had been determined through the current delegate count. The candidates do not officially become their party's nominee until after their party's national nominating conventions, but in recent campaigns we have known who would win the nomination well in advance of the conventions.

The increasing prominence of primary contests has changed the nature of politics. One important consequence is an increased importance of individual candidates and their campaign advisors. Although many voters still cast their votes in the general election for whoever represents their political party, the individual candidates, and their apparent preferability to voters, play increasingly important roles in election outcomes. Party loyalty is still important but has less influence on voting decisions today (see Benoit, 2007a; Menefee-Libey, 2000; Wattenberg, 1991, 1998); the individual candidates and their campaign messages are filling the void left by the diminishing role of party identification in vote choice. So, voters choose between the competing candidates, and an increasing number do not do so exclusively by party loyalty, but according to their perceptions of the candidates' preferability, impressions fostered by their TV spots and other messages. Furthermore, political party affiliation cannot help voters decide among the candidates from their own party contesting the nomination: TV spots are an important source of information to support this decision.

A2. *Candidates must distinguish themselves from opponents.*

The idea that voting is a comparative act, in which the relative preferability of the contenders determines vote choice, leads to the second assumption of Functional Theory: Candidates must appear different from one another. Voters cannot make a choice; they have no reason to prefer one candidate over another, if the candidates look exactly the same on every comparison. Candidates need not differ on every possible point of comparison; everyone wants to reduce crime, decrease inflation, and improve the economy. However, if the candidates agreed on *every* issue (and projected all of the same character traits) there would be no basis for preferring one candidate over another. This means that it is essential for candidates in contested races to offer some distinctions between themselves and their opponents.

Candidates may attempt to differentiate themselves from opponents by discussing either policy (what they have done and/or will do if elected) or character (who they are). For example, in 2012, Obama's "Jobs" spot noted that "Our businesses have created almost 4.3 million new jobs over the last twenty-seven months," an example of a policy theme intended to improve perceptions of the president. In 2012, Romney's ad "Shame on You" said that Obama "attacked Hillary Clinton with vicious lies" during the 2008 Democratic primary. This statement illustrates a character theme designed to reduce his Democratic opponent's desirability. Both of these statements implicitly or explicitly draw a contrast between the candidates, providing voters a basis for choosing one as preferable to the other.

Theories of candidate behavior developed in political science have made similar observations. As indicated above, candidates will usually adopt some of the same issue positions. For example, Page (1978) explained that Downs's (1957)

> economic theory of democracy calls for a candidate's policy stands to echo the policy preferences of the public, and many spatial models—especially those of the public opinion variety—predict that the midpoint of public opinion on issues has an important influence upon the stands that a candidate takes. (p. 29; see, e.g., Enelow and Hinich, 1984)

Page offered evidence from the 1968 campaign that "Across a wide variety of issues, then, both Humphrey and Nixon took positions which corresponded fairly closely with what the average American favored" (p. 47). However, he also found that both Humphrey and Nixon *disagreed* with the mid-point of public opinion on 15 percent of the seventy-two issues he examined. Specifically, Democrat Humphrey took more liberal positions on some issues whereas Republican Nixon adopted more conservative stands on some issues. This result is, generally, what one would expect. Both candidates took similar issue positions on some issues, close to the majority of the public, but each candidate distinguished himself from the majority opinion on other issues, Humphrey (the Democrat) by moving to the left and Nixon (the Republican) to the right of the ideological spectrum. Page also suggested that in 1964 Goldwater may have been more of an ideologue who did not adapt to public opinion; this is not a winning strategy.

A3. *Political campaign messages allow candidates to distinguish themselves.*

Once a candidate decides which distinctions between him- or herself and opponents to stress to voters, those points of difference must be conveyed to voters. Citizens must be aware of these differences before such distinctions can influence their candidate preferences. Citizens cannot and should not depend solely on the news media to provide voters with information about the candidates' policy positions. News *may* inform voters, but it may not: research shows that the news concentrates most on the horse race (see, e.g., Benoit, Hemmer, and Stein, 2010; Benoit, Stein, and Hansen, 2005). Patterson and McClure (1976) reported that learning occurs from candidates' campaign messages:

> During the 1972 presidential campaign, people who were heavily exposed to political spots became more informed about the candidates' issue positions. . . . On every single issue emphasized in presidential commercials, persons with high exposure to television advertising showed a greater increase in knowledge than persons with low exposure. (pp. 116–117)

It is clear that election campaign messages, such as political TV spots, are an important source of political information.

Rather than discuss policy in great detail (impossible in any event in a thirty-second spot) candidates might take a simpler and possibly less risky approach when discussing issues is to focus on ends rather than means: "I favor a balanced budget [but I won't tell you whether I will increase taxes and/or reduce spending to achieve it]." A certain amount of strategic ambiguity may be useful to political candidates; however, Alverez (1998) found that too much ambiguity is undesirable. Still campaign messages help candidates establish the distinctiveness among contenders that gives voters a basis for choosing one candidate over another.

A4. *Candidates establish preferability through acclaiming, attacking, and defending.*

Of course, it is not sufficient for candidates to be distinctive in their messages, even on the issues that matter most to voters in that election year; a candidate must appear different from his or her opponents *in ways that most voters favor*. For example, a candidate who declared that "I am the only candidate who will raise taxes 60 percent for everyone" would surely stand apart from opponents, but not in a way that is likely to attract many votes. So, candidates must appear different *and better* than opponents; conversely, one can portray opponents as different *and worse*. Popkin (1994) observed that "Somehow, candidates manage to get a large proportion of the citizenry sorted into opposing camps, each of which is convinced that the positions and interests of the other side add up to a less desirable package of benefits" (p. 8). Three kinds of statements or functions of discourse are capable of helping a candidate appear *preferable* to opponents.

Acclaims

First, candidates may offer acclaims (Benoit, 1997), statements that stress a candidate's advantages or benefits. Such self-praise can address the candidate's character or policy record and/or stands. In 2012, for example, Obama declared that Romney "would be so out of touch with the average person in this country" (Obama, "The Question"), questioning the Republican nominee's character. Candidates can also acclaim their policy accomplishments. In 2012, Romney told voters that "We cut our spending. Our legislature was 85 percent Democrat and every one of the four years I was governor, we balanced the budget" ("Believe in Our Future"). It is clear that most voters would view this statement as acclaims, as a desirable accomplishment. So, one way to increase the likelihood that voters will see a candidate as preferable is for that candidate to produce campaign messages that acclaim, emphasizing the candidate's desirable qualities.

Attacks

Another way to increase one candidate's (net) favorability is to attack or criticize the opponent(s). Stressing an opponent's undesirable attributes or policy missteps should reduce that opponent's desirability, particularly for voters who value the attribute or policy discussed in the attack. Because voters make a comparative judgment about which candidate is preferable (Axiom 1), a successful attack increases the attacker's net favorability by reducing the desirability of an opponent. Obama's 2012 spot "Number One" criticized Romney:

> When Mitt Romney was governor, Massachusetts was number one. Number one in state debt. $18 billion dollars in debt . . . more debt per person than any other state in the country. At the same time, Massachusetts fell to forty-seventh in job creation. . . . One of the worst economic records in the country. First in debt. Forty-seventh in job creation.

This advertisement illustrates several attacks, focused on policy generally and past deeds or record in office in particular.

Of course, some candidates may be reluctant to attack opponents. Voters consistently report that they do not like mud-slinging (Merritt, 1984; Stewart, 1975) so some politicians may wish to avoid engaging in excessive character assassination. Candidates may refrain from attacking, attack less often, or even promise to eschew attacks because voters say they dislike mudslinging. However, attacks have the potential to reduce the preferability of an opponent, so candidates use this function in campaign their TV spots. Clearly, attacks are an option used strategically by political candidates with the potential to reduce the apparent preferably of opponents.

Complaints about the level of negativity in political campaigns are fairly common (see, e.g., Ansolabehere and Iyengar, 1995; Jamieson, 1992a; Pfau and Kenski, 1990). Kamber (1997), for example, notes that "previous eras saw severe personal attack on political candidates, but they also saw detailed and sometimes inspiring deliberation over the issues. Our present political discourse is nothing but spleen" (p. 4). Of course, vicious attacks are uncalled for and false attacks are detrimental to voters (Benoit, 2013d). Still, attacks can provide voters with useful information. Kamber (1997) explained that

> There is an argument to be made in defense of responsible negative advertisements. The voters need to know the whole story, and solely positive arguments do not provide it. A campaign is not going to willingly offer negative information about its own candidate, and yet that is essential information for the voters to make an informed decision. (p. 7)

So, accurate criticism of an opponent can be useful for voters who need to consider both the pros and the cons of the candidates when making a vote choice. False attacks, or attacks that are malicious in tone, are not justifiable (of course, false acclaims are also wrong). But legitimate criticism is a form of attack that can help voters make an informed choice. Geer (2006) argues that negativity in political campaigns "creates a competitive dynamic that should yield a richer information environment than if candidates just talked about their own plans for government" (p. 13).

We must realize that just because voters express distaste for attacks does not necessarily mean that attacking messages are never persuasive. Candidates use focus groups and public opinion polls to design messages—including attacking messages—and they obviously believe attacks can be persuasive. It seems clear that attacks are capable of reducing the desirability of the target of those attacks. However, some attacks may have a backlash effect and thus hurt both the sponsor (because voters dislike mud-slinging) as well as the target. This means the most important question when deciding whether to attack may be who is likely to suffer the most from an attack: the target of the attack or the attack's sponsor? Meta-analyses have established that both positive and negative ads can be persuasive (Allen and Burrell, 2002; Lau, Sigelman, and Rovner, 2007).

The topic of the attack may be one important factor in audience response. Johnson-Cartee and Copeland (1989) provide evidence that voters tend to consider policy attacks more acceptable than character attacks. Other studies (Pfau and Burgoon, 1989; Roddy and Garramone, 1988) indicate that policy attacks can be more persuasive than character attacks. Benoit (2003), analyzing multiple message forms (primary television spots, debates, and brochures; acceptance addresses; general television spots, debates, and brochures) over the last fifty years, found that winners are significantly more likely to attack more on policy, and less on character, than candidates who lose elections. Of course, this finding does not mean that policy attacks guarantee a win, or even that attacks on character can never be persuasive. It does suggest that it may be prudent to attack more on policy (and less on character) than one's opponent.

Defenses

The third function of campaign messages that is capable of affecting a candidate's apparent preferability is defense. If a candidate is attacked by an opponent—or perhaps it would be more realistic to say *when* one candidate is attacked by another—the recipient of the attack can choose to defend against (refute) that attack in a campaign message (see Bryant, 2004). Obama's spot "Blatant" defends against an attack from Romney: "Seen this? Mitt Romney claiming the President would end welfare reform's work requirements? The *New York Times* calls it 'blatantly false.' The *Washington Post* says, 'the Obama administration is not removing the bill's work requirements at all.'" This ad identifies a criticism and refutes it.

Research has investigated the circumstances under which political advertising is likely to attack (see, e.g., Elmelund-Praestekaer, 2010; Sullivan and Sapir, 2012). Several potential factors have been identified including incumbency (challengers tend to attack more), standing in public opinion polls (those behind usually attack more than leaders), being attacked by opponents tends to provoke attacks in response, competitiveness of race (attacking is positively related to competitiveness), and sponsor of advertisement (parties are usually more negative than candidates).

Defense can be important because a timely and appropriate defense may be able to prevent further damage from an attack and restore some or all of a candidate's damaged preferability. Defense, then, is the third potential function of campaign discourse. It attempts to restore, or prevent additional damage to, a candidate's perceived preferability. An interview with former presidential candidate Michael Dukakis indicated that he believed defense could be important, explaining that "he was glad President Clinton was responding quickly to attacks, something Mr. Dukakis said he failed to do in his 1988 campaign" (Clines, 1996, p. A12). Smith (1990) discussed two of these three functions when he explained that in politics "people pursue and defend jobs by publicly boasting and attacking others" (p. 107).

At times candidates may decide to forgo defenses when they are attacked. Some candidates may not wish to "dignify" an opponent's accusations with a response. This reluctance may also be related to the fact that defenses have three potential drawbacks. First, it is possible that presenting a response to an attack could make that candidate sound defensive, appearing reactive rather than proactive. Candidates want to project the image that they are in charge of events, not merely reacting to opponents. Second, it seems likely that a candidate is most likely to attack on topics that favor the attacker rather than the target of attack, which means that defending against an attack probably takes a candidate "off-message," devoting precious message time to issues that are probably better for one's opponent. Third, the only way to respond to a particular attack is to identify that criticism. Mentioning the attack, in preparation for refuting it, could inform or remind voters of the very weakness that the candidate is trying to combat. Defenses therefore have three potential drawbacks. Research has shown that candidates who are attacked more frequently in debates tend to defend more often than other candidates: Being the target of an attack provides both the opportunity and the motivation to defend (Benoit, 2007b).

Scholars have offered other lists of functions. For example, Gronbeck (1978) identified a number of instrumental and consummatory functions of presidential campaigning. Some of these sound like uses and gratifications for the audience. Of course, it is important to know how auditors make use of campaign discourse. However, those sorts of functions supplement, rather than compete with, this analysis of campaign functions because I explicitly privilege the viewpoint of the candidate's purposes rather than the voters' uses in this analysis. Certainly it is useful to consider the voters' perceptions, but Functional Theory is focused more on candidates.

Similarly, Devlin (1986; 1987a) discusses several functions of political ads. However, I believe that these three functions (acclaims, attacks, defenses) are more basic than his list. For example, one of the functions Devlin lists is raising money. Candidates tout their desirable features (acclaim) and/or criticize their opponents (attack) in order to convince donors to contribute. Another function identified by Devlin is reinforcing a candidate's supporters. Supporters are reinforced by stressing the good qualities of the candidate (acclaims; and, quite possibly, by attacking or stressing the negative qualities of the opponent). Thus, these three activities—attacking, acclaiming, and defending—are the *fundamental* functions of political advertising. Sabato (1981) made a similar point, albeit from the voters' point of view, when he observed that there are a limited number of ways to vote: "for or against either of the party nominees or not voting at all" (p. 324). Scholars who investigate televised political advertising often distinguish between positive and negative spots (see, e.g., Kaid and Johnston, 2001), which correspond to the functions of acclaims and attacks.

Trent and Friedenberg (2000) noted that televised political advertisements can accomplish three basic functions: extol the candidates' own virtues; condemn, attack, and question their opponents; and respond to attacks or innuendos. These three functions obviously correspond to acclaims, attacks, and defenses. Pfau and Kenski (1990) noted that television spots can be categorized in four types: positive, negative, comparative (positive and negative elements together), and response (defense). I explicitly privilege the candidate's purposes in this analysis, rather than voters' or reporters' purposes. So, several political scholars have recognized that political campaign messages acclaim and attack role of defensive or response advertisements. Only research from the Functional perspective investigates the frequency of defense in campaign messages.

Political candidates and their campaign advisors also recognize the fundamental principle that campaign discourse performs multiple functions. For example, H. R. Haldeman gave advice to President Richard M. Nixon on the 1972 reelection campaign: "Getting one of those 20 [percent] who is an undecided type to vote for you on the basis of your positive points is much less likely than getting them to vote against McGovern by scaring them to death about McGovern" (Popkin et al., 1976, p. 794n). Thus, Haldeman argued that the election hinged on the undecided voters and that Nixon could seek their votes by praising himself—acclaiming Nixon's "positive points"—or by attacking his opponent—"scaring them to death about McGovern." Similarly, Vincent Breglio, who was a part of Ronald Reagan's successful 1980 presidential campaign, acknowledged that "It has become vital in campaigns today that you not only present all the reasons why people ought to vote for you, but you also have an obligation to present the reasons why they should not vote for the opponent" (1987, p. 34). So, political campaign advisors, like political communication scholars, recognize that candidates can praise themselves and attack their opponents.

This is why the Functional approach analyzes political campaign discourse into utterances that *acclaim* the preferred candidate, *attack* the opponent, and *defend* the candidate from opponent's attacks. Although these three functions may not be equally common in discourse, they are three options that every candidate has available for use. These functions are very important because they provide voters a reason to vote for a candidate or against an opponent. A complete understanding of political campaign communication should consider all three functions.

One useful way to think about these three functions is as an informal form of cost-benefit analysis. Acclaims stress a candidate's benefits. Attacks reveal an opponent's costs. Defenses attempt to refute or minimize potential costs. A vote decision requires an understanding of the pros (acclaims) as well as the cons (attacks, defenses) of the contending candidates. This means that attacks serve a useful purpose—identifying costs—as long as they are neither false nor misleading. Political candidates can inform voters of an opponent's potential costs through attacks. Consistent with this analysis Kelley and Mirer (1974), using survey data from the 1952–1968 presidential elections, found that 82–87 percent of citizens voted for the candidate for whom they reported the largest number of reasons for liking that candidate and the smallest number of reasons for disliking that candidate (in other words, benefits and costs; this figure may be less than 100 percent because some pros or cons are more important to a particular voter than others).

It is important to acknowledge that characterizing vote choice as similar to cost-benefit analysis does not mean that I assume that every voter takes a rational approach to voting: gathering, weighing, and integrating as much information as possible to guarantee that they make the most rational decision possible. As Zaller (1992) correctly explained, "citizens vary in their habitual attention to politics and hence in their exposure to political information and argumentation in the media" (p. 1). Only political junkies avidly seek out huge amounts of information about the various candidates. As Popkin argued (1994; see also Downs, 1957), many voters use information shortcuts. They do not seek out information about the candidates or they wait until just before the election to do so. They base their voting decisions on the information they happen to encounter, including TV spots. This is why political candidates employ multiple media and repeat their basic campaign message: They want their message out there for whatever voters might be attending to a particular medium at a given point in time. TV spots are particularly important because they have the potential to reach all voters, even those who might not watch debates or read campaign news. Voters do not quantify bits of information or place the information they obtain about the candidates into mathematical formulas (i.e., benefits minus costs) to calculate their votes. Thus, although I believe that deciding how to vote is similar in principle to cost-benefit analysis, I do not claim that voters use numbers to quantify pros and cons or even that they systematically and consciously weigh the pros and cons of competing candidates. Acclaims tend to increase a candidate's perceived preferability, attacks tend to reduce an opponent's preferability, and defenses may restore lost preferability. All three functions work to make one candidate appear preferable to an opponent.

We must realize that the power of campaign messages has limitations. As noted above, many voters have little interest in political campaigns and are unlikely to watch debates or to read or watch political news. Some voters who do pay attention to candidate messages may not accept a candidate's statements at face value. Candidates may not always address the most prominent concerns of voters, and when that happens it surely would reduce the impact of the message. Different voters may interpret a message in different ways, and their reaction may not be what the candidate hoped (Reinemann and Maurer, 2005, reported that acclaims in German political leaders debates generated general support in the audience whereas attacks tended to polarize the audience). Furthermore, we should not assume that a single message is capable of making a voter choose the candidate touted in that message. Nevertheless, the messages to which are exposed during a campaign gradually shape their perceptions of the candidates' character and issue stands and, ultimately, a citizen enters a polling place and casts a vote based on those perceptions. Undecided and independent voters, as well as potential vote defectors, may be particularly susceptible to these messages.

Functional Theory argues that these three functions are likely to occur with different frequencies. Acclaims, if persuasive (if accepted by the audience) can increase a candidate's apparent preferability and have no drawbacks. This means that acclaims should be the most common campaign discourse function. In contrast, attacks, if persuasive, can increase a candidate's apparent net favorability by decreasing an opponent's preferability. However, many voters dislike mudslinging as noted above so the risk of backlash may encourage candidates to moderate their attacks. Accordingly, Functional Theory expects attacks to be less common than acclaims. Finally, defenses, if they are accepted by a voter, can help restore a candidate's lost preferability. As noted above, defenses have three drawbacks: They are likely to take a candidate off-message (because attacks are likely to concern the target candidate's weaknesses), they risk informing or reminding voters of a potential weakness (a candidate must identify an attack to refute it), and they may create the impression that the candidate is reactive (defensive) rather than proactive. Thus, Functional Theory makes two predictions about the functions of political campaign discourse:

H1. *Candidates will use acclaims more frequently than attacks and attacks more often than defenses.*

Studies have investigated this prediction with a variety of American presidential campaign messages. Research on American presidential primary and general debates (1952–2004) confirmed that the most common function was acclaims (62 percent); nominating convention Acceptance Addresses from 1952–2004 also emphasized acclaims (77 percent), as do primary and general election direct mail brochures from 1948–2004 (77 percent; Benoit, 2007a). As predicted, attacks were the second most common function in U.S. TV spots (34 percent), Acceptance Addresses (23 percent), and direct mail (23 percent; Benoit, 2007a). Defenses were the least common function in debates (5 percent), Acceptance Addresses (1 percent), and direct mail (0.3 percent; Benoit, 2007a). Subsequent chapters will offer data that test this prediction in different kinds of political TV spots (American presidential general, presidential primary, gubernatorial, senate, house, and local ads as well as election ads from other countries).

A5. *Campaign discourse occurs on two topics: policy and character.*

The fifth axiom of Functional Theory posits that political discourse can occur on two broad topics: *policy* (issues) and *character* (image). In other words, candidates try to persuade voters of their preferability on policy—what they do—and character—who they are. Pomper (1975), in fact, observed that many voters "change their partisan choice from one election to the next, and these changes are most closely related

to their positions on the issues and their assessment of the abilities of the candidates"
(p. 10). Functional theory defines policy and character in this way:

Policy utterances concern governmental action (past, current, or future) and problems
amenable to governmental action.

Character utterances address characteristics, traits, abilities, or attributes of the candidates.

Thus, these are the two broad topics on which candidates contend over their preferability (Functional Theory also subdivides policy and character utterances into finer
categories, as discussed later). Rountree (1995), for example, distinguishes between
actus (behavior, action) or *what we do* and *status* (nature) or *who we are* in political
campaign discourse.

Although Functional Theory dichotomizes the two potential topics of political
campaign discourse, it acknowledges that policy and character have a complex and
dynamic relationship (Benoit, Blaney, and Pier, 1998). First, it is possible that an
utterance which focuses explicitly on policy could have some influence perceptions
of the candidate's character. For example, this passage from Bill Clinton's 1996 Acceptance Address discusses his first term successes with the economy:

Four point four million Americans now living in a home of their own for the first
time; hundreds of thousands of women have started their own new businesses; more
minorities own businesses than ever before; record numbers of new small businesses
and exports. . . . We have the lowest combined rates of unemployment, inflation,
and home mortgages in twenty-eight years. . . . Ten million new jobs, over half of
them high-wage jobs, ten million workers getting the raise they deserve with the
minimum wage law.

Surely this is a policy utterance, for it discusses home ownership, business ownership,
exports, unemployment, inflation, mortgages, jobs, and the minimum wage. Of
course, these successes all work to implicitly reinforce Clinton's apparent leadership
ability, a character attribute, because they implicitly demonstrate that he possesses
the skills necessary to enact legislation (leadership ability is one aspect of character).
Similarly, a message that touted programs to help the poor or disadvantaged could
serve to create or reinforce an impression of that candidate's compassion (another
element of character).

On the other hand, this passage from one of Vice President George Bush's 1988
Republican primary television spots recounted his experience in the military, focusing on his experience and courage: "How does one man come so far? Maybe for
George Bush, it began when he became the youngest pilot in the Navy. Or perhaps
it began this day in 1944 when he earned the Distinguished Flying Cross for bravery
under fire." This passage clearly concerns Bush's character, the personal quality of
bravery, not what he will do if elected president. Nevertheless, voters might reason-
ably infer that this kind of person, a person with this kind of character, is likely to
support a strong military.

These two kinds of comments have distinctly different content. One passage (from Clinton) explicitly addresses policy and the other (from Bush) explicitly discusses character. These messages tell us more about Clinton's policies than Bush's policies; we can learn more from them about Bush's personal qualities than Clinton's. However, we should not be surprised if voters form impressions from these passages that are not explicitly addressed in the text (see Hacker, Zakahi, Giles, and McQuitty, 2000).

Furthermore, it appears that candidates sometimes attempt to shift the grounds of discussion from one topic to the other. For example, in the first Clinton/Dole debate of 1996, Jim Lehrer posed this question about Clinton's character: "Mr. President, what do you say to Senator Dole's point that this election is about keeping one's word?" Clinton's honesty (his character) was challenged, and he offered this answer:

> Let's look at that. When I ran for president, I said we'd cut the deficit in half in four years; we cut it by 60 percent. I said that our economic plan would produce eight million jobs, we have ten and a half million new jobs. We're number one in autos again, record numbers of new small businesses. I said we'd put, pass a crime bill that would put 100,000 police on the street, ban assault weapons, and deal with the problems that ought to be dealt with with capital punishment, including capital punishment for drug kingpins, and we did that.
>
> I said we would change the way welfare works, and even before the bill passed we'd moved nearly two million people from welfare to work, working with states and communities. I said we'd get tougher with child support and child support enforcement's up 50 percent. I said that I would work for tax relief for middle class Americans. The deficit was bigger than I thought it was going to be. I think they're better off, all of us are, that we got the interest rates down and the deficit down.

Clinton's response shifted the discussion away from the question of honesty or keeping one's word generally to keeping one's word on *campaign promises*, or policy accomplishments: jobs, autos, crime, welfare, middle-class tax cuts, interest rates, the deficit. He responded to an attack on character by shifting grounds and acclaiming his past successes on policy.

This process can also work in the other direction, moving from policy to character. For instance in the second debate of 2000, Vice President Gore attacked Governor Bush's record in Texas on the issue of health care.

> GORE: I'm sorry to tell you that, you know, there is a record here, and Texas ranks forty-ninth out of the fifty states in health care—in children with health care, forty-ninth for women with health care, and fiftieth for families with health care.
>
> LEHRER: Governor, did Vice President—are the vice president's figures correct about Texas?
>
> BUSH: *You can quote all the numbers you want, but I'm telling you, we care about our people in Texas*, we spend a lot of money to make sure people get health care in the state of Texas, and we're doing a better job than they are at the national level for reducing uninsured.
>
> LEHRER: Is he right? Are those numbers correct? Are his charges correct?

BUSH: *If he's trying to allege that I'm a hard-hearted person and I don't care about children, he's absolutely wrong.* We spend $4.7 billion a year in the state of Texas for uninsured people, and they get health care. (emphasis added)

Bush repeatedly tried to turn this policy question into an issue of character. Bush did talk some about spending in Texas on health care (policy), but there is a clear effort to shift this attack from policy to character: "we care about our people." Bush even responds to character attacks (that Bush is hard-hearted, that he doesn't care about children) that Gore never articulated: "If he's trying to allege that I'm a hard-hearted person and I don't care about children, he's absolutely wrong." Again, this is a clear effort to shift the topic from policy to character.

Functional Theory predicts that, particularly in presidential campaigns, policy will be a more frequent topic of campaign messages than character. We elect presidents to run our government, to implement policy. Although some voters believe that they elect positive role models—and surely we all hope our elected leaders are positive role models—the primary duty of our elected officials is to administer policy. Hofstetter (1976) explains that "issue preferences are key elements in the preferences of most, if not all, voters" (p. 77; see also Patterson and McClure, 1976). Furthermore, public opinion poll data from 1976 to 2000 reveals that the majority of voters believe that policy is more important than character in their vote for president (Benoit, 2003). Presidential candidates who discuss policy more, and character less, than their opponents are more likely to win elections (Benoit, 2003).

Character does matter, of course. We must trust candidates to work to achieve their campaign promises, and we must trust them to implement suitable policies in unexpected situations on which they did not take policy stands during the campaign. However, King (2002) summarized the results of several studies of the role of character in 51 elections held in 6 countries between 1960 and 2001:

> It is quite unusual for leaders' and candidates' personality and other personal traits to determine election outcomes. . . . [T]he almost universal belief that leaders' and candidates' personalities are almost invariably hugely important in determining the outcomes of elections is simply wrong. (p. 216)

Because of voter preferences, Functional Theory considers policy to be more important, in general, than character. Specifically, Functional Theory holds that candidates are likely to respond to these preferences so that policy will be discussed more frequently in presidential campaign messages than character. Of course character is discussed in campaign messages. These considerations lead to a second prediction:

H2. *Policy comments will be more frequent than character comments in presidential campaign discourse.*

Published research has investigated the topics of presidential campaign messages (Benoit, 2007a). In American presidential primary debates, policy was 78 percent of statements whereas character was 28 percent. Presidential primary brochures discussed policy more than character (62 percent to 38 percent). In nominating convention Acceptances, policy was discussed more often than character (55 percent to 45 percent). In general election debates, policy was a more frequent topic than character (75 percent to 25 percent). In direct mail advertising from the general election campaign, policy (76 percent) was addressed more frequently than character (24 percent). As with the first hypothesis, subsequent chapters will provide evidence on this prediction in a variety of political campaign advertisements.

A6. *A candidate must win a majority (or a plurality) of the votes cast in an election.*

The last axiom might appear to be so trivial that it is not worth mentioning. However, this proposition implies several key tenets of campaigning. First, candidates do not need to try to win every vote. This is extremely important because some policy positions are inherently divisive and will simultaneously attract some voters and repel others. That is, many issues dichotomize the electorate. For instance, in 2012 Barack Obama and Mitt Romney disagreed on such issues as how health care should be provided or federal tax policy. It is unrealistic to expect either candidate to win the votes of every citizen given the existence of divisive issues such as this one. Luckily, however, candidates need not receive all of the votes that are cast to win the election.

Second, it is important to realize that only those citizens who actually cast votes in the election matter to the outcome. This means that a candidate does not even have to win the votes of *most citizens*, but only of *most citizens who actually vote on election day*. Some candidates have explicitly attempted to encourage turnout, which seems to be consistent with the ideals of democracy. For example, in 1964 at least seventeen of Johnson's television spots included the statement "The stakes are too high for you to stay home." Thus, it should be possible to enhance a candidate's chances of winning by increasing the turnout of voters who favor that candidate (or, although this seems reprehensible, reducing the turn-out of voters who favor an opponent; see Ansolabehere and Iyengar, 1995).

Third, American presidential elections are peculiar because of the Electoral College and its rules. In a presidential election, a candidate only needs to persuade enough of those who are voting in enough states to win 270 electoral votes. This encourages candidates to maximize their resources by campaigning more vigorously in some states than others. The 2000 presidential election underlined the importance of the Electoral College vote. As voting returns came in on Tuesday night Florida was "given" to Gore, taken back, given to Bush, and then taken back again. Then the recounts in Florida made the nation wait for the winner to be determined as the outcome of the election hinged on whether Florida's twenty-five electoral votes belonged to Bush or Gore. The U.S. Supreme Court (in a five to four vote) decided to halt recounts in Florida, giving the Electoral College majority to Bush. Al Gore won the popular balloting by a margin of half a million votes, but because Bush won Florida by 537 votes, he won all of its Electoral College votes and the presidency (*New York Times*, 2001). Thus, a U.S. presidential candidate only needs to win a majority of votes in enough states to amass 270 electoral votes to win the presidency, and that influences the placement of campaign discourse.

These principles suggest six specific strategies candidates can use in an attempt to maximize the probability of winning the election. First, a candidate can attempt to *increase the election day turnout of voters who prefer that candidate*. If a citizen fails to vote, it does not matter which candidate that person prefers. This means that if the same number of people prefer the two leading candidates, but more of one candidate's supporters actually vote, that candidate will win the election (indeed, a candidate with *less* support than a rival coulc win if his or her supporters vote at a sufficiently higher rate than the other candidate's adherents).

Second, a candidate can *seek the support of undecided voters*. The number of independent voters has increased over time as the importance of political parties has diminished. Although there are some vote defectors, most Republicans will vote for the Republican nominee and most Democrats will vote for the Democratic nominee. Thus, a wise candidate will focus much of the general election campaign on the undecided voters. In 1996, for example, we heard a great deal about the so-called "soccer moms," swing voters who allegedly held the keys to the White House. Independents are less likely to vote than partisans; still, the difference between the number of Republicans and Democrats is so small, and the number of Independents is so large, that Independents are important even if a smaller percentage of Independents than partisans actually vote.

Third, a candidate can attempt to attract *potential vote-defectors from the other political party*. Candidates are unlikely to attract votes from those partisans who are strongly committed to the other political party, but some party members are willing to vote for the candidate of the other party (Nie, Verba, and Petrocik, 1999)—*if* they are given an adequate reason to do so in the candidates' campaign messages. This is a surprisingly large group, ranging from 14–27 percent (Nie, Verba, and Petrocik, 1999). Thus, political candidates can try to poach voters who have only soft support for their opponents.

Fourth, a candidate can attempt to *prevent members of his or her own party from defecting*. As just indicated, political candidates are not likely to lose the votes of strong partisans, but some party members may be open to persuasion from opponents. So, candidates can try to keep partisan supporters from defecting to the opposing party's candidate. We do not know how many partisans considered defecting but ultimately decided not to do so. It could be as many as the number who do defect, 14–27 percent.

Fifth, candidates may attempt to *discourage voter turnout from those who support another candidate*. This strategy runs counter to the ideals of democracy and I consider it to be reprehensible, so I would never recommend it to a candidate. However, it is a possible option, and Ansolabehere and Iyengar (1995) have argued that some negative political advertisements are intended to do so.

So, candidates should adopt positions on some issues in an attempt to build a winning coalition of voters. Adopting a desirable position on a particular issue (e.g., private school vouchers, tax cuts) could help the candidate achieve three goals: (1) attracting the votes of independent or third party voters, (2) discouraging one's own party members from defecting or voting for one's opponent, and (3) enticing some members of the opposing party to defect to you.

Forms of Policy and Character

Functional Theory offers more detail on the two topics of campaign messages, policy and character. Policy remarks can be divided into three subforms, past deeds, future plans, and general goals. *Past deeds* concern the record in office of an elected official (accomplishments or failures). Mention of, for example, jobs gained or lost concerns past deeds. The second form of policy utterance is *future plans*, or means to an end, specific proposals for policy action. A 15 percent across the board tax cut, such as proposed by Dole in 1996, exemplifies a future plan. The third form of policy utterance is *general goals*. Unlike future plans, goals refer to ends rather than means. Cutting taxes, without specifying which how much or which taxes to cut would illustrate a general goal. Acclaims and attacks can occur on each form of policy.

Character is divided into three subforms. *Personal qualities* are the personality traits of the candidate, such as honesty, compassion, strength, courage, friendliness. *Leadership ability* usually appears as experience in office, the ability to accomplish things as an elected official. Finally, *ideals* are similar to goals, but they are values or principles embraced by the candidates rather than policy outcomes. These three forms of character can be used to acclaim and attack. Appendix 2.1 illustrates acclaims and attacks for each form of policy and character.

Functional Theory offers predictions about the forms of policy and character (see also chapter 6 on Incumbency). Broad goals (e.g., creating jobs, keeping American secure, reducing the federal deficit) are easier to acclaim than to attack. Ideals, such as justice or equality, are also easier to acclaim than to attack. For this reason, Functional Theory predicts:

H3. *Candidates will use general goals more to acclaim than to attack.*

H4. *Candidates will use ideals more to acclaim than to attack.*

Past research on other campaign message forms (see Benoit, 2007a) confirms these predictions. In presidential primary debates, general goals are more often the basis of acclaims than attacks (91 percent to 9 percent) and ideals are more frequently about acclaims than attacks (87 percent, 13 percent). In direct mail advertising from the primary campaign, general goals were used more often in acclaims than attacks (96 percent to 4 percent); this is true of ideals as well (91 percent, 9 percent). In Acceptances, general goals more frequently employed more for acclaims (92 percent) than attacks (8 percent); ideals are used more often for acclaims than attacks (85 percent to 15 percent). The same relationship occurs in general debates (general goals: 85 percent acclaims and 15 percent attacks; ideals: 82 percent to 18 percent). Finally, general goals in direct mail advertising reveal the same relationship (88 percent acclaims to 12 percent attacks) as do ideals in brochures (81 percent to 19 percent).

Future plans are more specific than goals; they are means to an end (the end being a goal). It is more difficult to attack a goal, such as reducing the deficit, than means to achieve that end, such as raising taxes or reducing Social Security benefits. Accordingly, Functional Theory anticipates that

H5. *Candidates will attack more and acclaim less on future plans than general goals.*

Research on the functions of these two forms of policy confirms this prediction. Presidential debates (primary, general, and vice presidential) attack in 31 percent of themes on future plans but only 11 percent of themes on general goals (Benoit, 2014). When discussing future plans in acceptances, candidates attack 11 percent of the time compared with general goals, which are the basis for attacks in 21 percent of utterances (Benoit, 2007a). In presidential primary and general campaign brochures, 16 percent of statements on future plans are attacks whereas 9 percent of statements on general goals are attacks (Benoit and Stein, 2005).

Thus, Functional Theory views political campaign discourse as the means to an end—convincing voters to cast voters for a candidate—which is achieved through three functions: acclaiming, attacking, and defending to create the impression that you are the preferable candidate in the race. Functional Theory predicts that these functions are not equally likely to be used in campaign messages: Acclaims should be more common, defenses least common. These functions can address two topics, policy and character. Given the fact that more American voters consider policy more important than character, Functional Theory predicts that American presidential campaign discourse will address policy more often than character. Note that if more voters considered character more important than policy, Functional Theory would then predict that character utterances would outnumber policy comments. Functional Theory divides policy and character comments into more specific topics and predicts that acclaims will be more common than attacks when both general goals and ideals are discussed and attacks will be more common on future plans than general goals. These predictions are consistently confirmed through content analysis of presidential campaign discourse.

ADVANTAGES OF THE FUNCTIONAL APPROACH

Functional Theory enjoys several clear advantages over other approaches to studying political campaign discourse. This approach is consistent with other approaches to analyzing televised political advertisements, categorizing statements in spots as negative (attacking) or positive (acclaiming). However, it adds a third function, defense, which is overlooked in most approaches to understanding the nature of televised political spots. For example, a 1960 Nixon commercial started by acknowledging attacks on Nixon, who was running on the record of the Eisenhower/Nixon administration. The announcer then told viewers that "President Eisenhower answers the Kennedy-Johnson charges that America has accomplished nothing in the last eight years." Then viewers saw Eisenhower, who declared that "My friends, never have Americans achieved so much in so short a time," clearly denying the attack. Campaign discourse of this nature cannot be fully understood as negative—even though it rejects the opposition—or as positive—even though it refers to accomplishments. It begins by identifying an attack from an opponent ("the Kennedy–Johnson charges that America has accomplished nothing in the last eight years") and then explicitly rejects that attack: "never have Americans achieved so much in so short a time." Thus, one advantage of the Functional approach is that it extends analysis of campaign messages to include a third function, defenses. Defenses are not as common as acclaims or attacks in campaign messages, but they are distinctive utterances and they are capable of reducing perceived drawbacks (costs). Defenses are more common and arguably even more important in debates.

A second advantage of the Functional approach stems from its use of the *theme* (idea unit, argument, claim, assertion) as the coding unit instead of the entire spot. Most previous research on political spots classifies entire spots as positive or negative (a few studies add a third category, "comparative ad") or issue versus image. However, many television spots contain multiple utterances which may perform different functions, so each theme in an ad is categorized separately. Many political advertisements are mixed, containing both attacks and acclaims and/or policy and character, and that mix is not always 50/50. Benoit and Airne (2009), investigating nonpresidential TV spots from 2004, found that 42 percent of ads contained at least one acclaim and at least one attack; 75 percent of the ads in this sample addressed both policy and character. More importantly for the current project, it is important to unitize the candidates' statements in debates into themes (one could hardly code the "entire debate" as scholars code the "entire spot"). This provides a more precise measurement of these message's content (functions, topics) than coding entire ads.

Using the theme as the coding unit also facilitates comparisons of different campaign messages. For example, if those who content analyze television commercials using the entire spot as the coding unit were to analyze other messages, what would they use as the coding unit? An entire acceptance address? An entire debate? An entire candidate webpage? Using the theme as the coding unit facilitates comparison of different kinds of campaign messages by content analyzing all messages with the same coding unit.

This book relies on data produced by content analysis of political campaign messages. This method produces nominal or frequency data, which count the number of times certain kinds of content (e.g., acclaims, attacks, or defenses; policy or character), so many predictions will be tested with *chi-square*. This is a nonparametric statistic appropriate for investigating differences using frequency data. As the chapters will make clear, a large amount of data has been generated using Functional Theory. That is obviously desirable because it means that the conclusions drawn here are supported from many campaigns, many candidates, multiple message forms, multiple elective offices, and multiple countries. It also permits comparisons of the nature of various message forms. The *chi-square* statistic is sensitive to sample size (N); that is, this statistic is more likely to find significance with larger Ns. It is important to understand the difference between significance and effect size. The *significance test* tells us how likely a given result *would occur by chance*. The statement "$p < .05$" means that these results would occur just by chance fewer than 5 times out of 100. Similarly, "$p < .0001$" means that these results should occur by chance only once out of ten-thousand times. The *effect size*, in contrast, indicates the *magnitude of the relationship* between the independent and dependent variable. For example, these are two different questions:

> Do challengers attack more than incumbents than would be expected by chance?
> *How much more* do challengers attack than incumbents?

The former question is answered with a test of significant differences; the latter is answered with a measure of effect size. A possibility exists that a sample with a large N a result could be statistically significant (say, "significant" even at $p < .0001$) and yet not make much of a difference. Research using parametric statistics increasingly reports both the significance level and the effect size, like r, R^2, or eta^2. I will report comparable statistics for non-parametric data: Cramer's V and φ. This statistic, like Pearson's r, can vary from 0 (no relationship whatsoever) to 1 (a perfect relationship between two variables). Unlike r, however, V is always positive (and so it does not indicate direction of relationship; a positive r indicates a positive or direct relationship between variables; a negative r indicates an inverse or indirect relationship). This approach—reporting significance tests, consistency of effect, and effect size whenever possible—provides the best insight into the relationships investigated here. Two kinds of *chi-squares* are used. A *chi-square goodness of fit test* is used for predictions involving only one variable, such as "policy is more common than character." Because there is only one variable (topic) no effect size can be calculated for this test: only when two variables are tested, such as policy versus character (topic) for incumbents versus challengers (incumbency), can one estimate the size of the effect of one variable on another variable. A *chi-square test of cross-classification* tests predictions with two variables, such as "incumbents acclaim more, and attack less, than challengers," with two variables (incumbency, function).

CONTENT ANALYTIC APPROACH

There are four basic steps in the coding method used to generate the data discussed in this book. First, the messages must be unitized into themes, the coding unit in this method. A theme is the smallest unit of discourse capable of expressing a coherent idea (in this case, not just any idea, but acclaims, attacks, and defenses). Themes can vary in length from a phrase to a paragraph (several sentences). Second, themes are classified into function: acclaim, attack, or defense. Because defenses are rare in TV spots, they are not coded further. Third, acclaims and attacks are classified by topic: policy or character. Next, the proper sub-form of policy (past deeds, future plans, general goal) or character (personal quality, leadership ability, ideal) is identified.

First, the candidates' utterances must be unitized into themes. For example, a statement which said "I will reduce taxes, create new jobs, and keep our country safe from terrorism" would be unitized into three themes, one for each topic (taxes, jobs, terrorism), even though these are all contained in a single sentence. On the other hand, a statement which said "Jobs are the backbone of a strong economy. We cannot have economic recovery without jobs. That's why I will increase jobs" would be coded as one theme, jobs (the first two sentences explain why jobs are important, but do not actually establish the existence of a problem or offer a solution for jobs). Finally, a message which said "The present administration has lost over a million jobs. If elected, I will create new jobs" would be coded as two themes: the problem of lost jobs under the current administration; the candidate's solution: a goal of creating more jobs if elected.

Second, each theme's function is classified as an acclaim, an attack, or a defense. A few themes do not function as acclaims, attacks, or defenses (themes which do not enact these functions are not coded). Coders must decide whether a theme performs one of these functions, and, if so, identify which one.

Acclaims are themes that portray the candidate (or the candidate's political party) in a favorable light.

Obama's ad "Wonderful" in 2012 declared that "He believes smaller class sizes and great teachers are a key to a stronger economy and a stronger middle class." A stronger economy and middle class would be seen as desirable by voters.

Attacks are themes that portray the opposing candidate (or that candidate's political party) in an unfavorable light.

In the spot from 2012 "Who Will Do More," Romney criticized Obama, claiming that the President "Obama took GM and Chrysler into bankruptcy, and sold Chrysler to Italians who are going to build Jeeps in China." American firms going bankrupt, particularly those as large and as important as GM and Chrysler, would be perceived as undesirable.

Acclaims can be identified in two ways. First, acclaims are positive: Virtually all statements made by a candidate about himself or herself are positive; almost all statements about an opponent are negative. Occasionally, a candidate may say something like, "My honorable opponent," but those statements are throw-away lines designed to show the speaker is a reasonable person, not to genuinely praise an opponent. Second, acclaims are about the candidate supported by the spot, whereas attacks are about the opponent. These two statements jointly differentiate acclaims from attacks.

Defenses are themes that explicitly respond to a prior attack on the candidate (or a political party).

Obama ran an ad that defended against Romney's attack ("Collapse"): "After Romney's false claim of Jeep outsourcing to China, Chrysler itself has refuted Romney's lie." To count as a defense, a statement must acknowledge or allude to a criticism and then attempt to refute it. In this example, Obama points to "Romney's false claim of Jeep outsourcing to China" before refuting that criticism.

Third, themes which were classified as acclaims or attacks are then coded by topic (because defenses are so rare, topic of defense is not identified).

Policy: Utterances that concern governmental action (past, current, or future) and problems amenable to governmental action.

In 2012, Romney aired a spot called "Secretary of Business": "Under Obama, millions of people can't find work. And more families on welfare and a record number of Americans on food stamps." Unemployment and poverty are examples of policy topics.

Character: Utterances that address characteristics, traits, abilities, or attributes of the candidates (or their parties).

In the ad "Seen," Obama criticized Romney's character, saying that he was "Trying to mislead us." Honesty is a clear example of a character trait.

The next step in the content analytic method is to classify each policy or character utterance according to the forms of policy and character. Policy utterances can address past deeds, future plans, or general goals. Past deeds are, of course, actions taken in the past (a candidate's record in office), whereas future plans are proposed actions (means) and general goals are ends. Character utterances can address personal qualities (e.g., courage, compassion, honesty), leadership ability (e.g., experience, vision), or ideals (i.e., values, principles). As noted earlier, appendix 2.1 provides examples of acclaims and attacks on each form of policy and character. As campaign messages are coded, other relevant information is also recorded, such as the candidates' political party, incumbency status, campaign phase (primary or general), office sought, and country.

The data generated using the Functional Approach have strong reliability on each variable (functions, topics, forms of policy, forms of character); reliability is reported in each study. I compared data on presidential TV spots reported here with data from similar studies by Kaid and Johnston (1991, 2001), West (1997), and Geer (2006). Kaid and Johnson's data on negative ads correlated highly with the data reported here (r [$n = 10$] = .95, $p < .0001$) as do Geer's data (r [$n = 12$] = .87, $p <$

.0001). West's data, based on a flawed sample (limited to "prominent" ads), do not correlate with the data reported here (*r* [*n* = 10] = .24, *ns*). The sample employed in this book includes 7256 political advertisements: 1465 presidential primary ads, 1313 presidential general spots, 66 presidential third party advertisements, 3467 nonpresidential commercials, and 945 ads from other countries.

I also present data on Issue Ownership Theory and Functional Federalism Theory in chapter 9. These data are generated using computer content analysis. Benoit and McHale (2003) used grounded theory—the method of constant comparison (Glaser and Strauss, 1967)—to develop a typology of traits discussed by political candidates. Texts discussing personal qualities from American presidential television spots were used to develop this typology. These procedures produced four clusters or dimensions of personal qualities: Morality (decency, integrity, responsibility, fairness), Empathy (fights for the people, compassionate, understanding), Sincerity (honesty, trust, promises, openness, consistency), and Drive (strength, hard work, determination, courage). Each term had multiple synonyms in the search list. Examples of each dimension can be found in Benoit and McHale (2003). In each of the four clusters these qualities were used to praise the candidate who sponsored the commercial (e.g., honest) and their opposites were used to attack the opponent (e.g., dishonest). After developing this typology, Benoit and McHale (2003) used the categories (and associated word lists) in computer content analysis to investigate the use of personal qualities in American primary and general election TV spots. Benoit and McHale (2004) extended this work to American congressional TV spots. The program Concordance used the word lists to count the number of times each word was used in each group of TV spots.

ANALYTICAL CHAPTERS

The next section of the book (part II) presents my analysis of presidential advertising campaigns, grouped four campaigns per chapter (chapters 3–6). Presidential primary (chapter 7) ads and general election ads from third party candidates (chapter 8) are also addressed. The third section (part III) offers of political advertising and two theories from political science, Issue Ownership and Functional Federalism (chapter 9) and U.S. nonpresidential, and non-U.S. political advertising (chapter 10). When giving examples, I "cite" excerpts from ads by giving the candidate, year, and title of the spot (not all spots have clear titles, so I created some titles). Material placed inside square brackets ("[," "]") are descriptions of visual images (including words displayed on the screen) or sounds in the commercial. In these chapters, I discuss the functions (attacks, acclaims, and defense), the topic (policy versus character), forms of policy utterances (past deeds, future plans, general goals) and forms of character comments (personal qualities, leadership ability, ideals). To illustrate the results of my analysis, I also provide excerpts from spots, without specific citations. In part IV, chapter 11 discusses several contrasts in political advertising, chapter 12 discusses the development of American presidential election advertising, and chapter 13 addresses conclusions and implications of the study.

APPENDIX 2.1: EXAMPLES OF ACCLAIMING AND ATTACKING ON EACH FORM OF POLICY AND CHARACTER

Policy

Past Deeds: Acclaim
   Reagan (1984): Today, inflation is down, interest rates are down. We've created six and a half million new jobs. Americans are working again, and so is America.

Past Deeds: Attack
   Eisenhower (1952): Man: General, the Democrats are telling me I never had it so good.
   Eisenhower: Can that be true when America is billions in debt, when prices have doubled, when taxes break our backs, and we are still fighting in Korea?

Future Plans: Acclaim
   Ford (1976): Under my proposal to increase the personal exemption, you would get an additional exemption of $1,250. Now that would make a sizeable increase in your weekly take-home pay.

Future Plans: Attack
   Johnson (1964): The other candidate wants to go on testing more atomic bombs. If he's elected, they might start testing all over again.

General Goals: Acclaim
   Reagan (1980): We must act to put Americans back to work. We must balance the budget. We must slow the growth of government. We must cut tax rates.

General Goals: Attack
   Forbes (1996 Primary): The politicians can keep on raising your taxes and wasting your money.

Character

Personal Qualities: Acclaim
   Humphrey (1968): Humphrey is without question a man that I feel everyone in this country can trust.

Personal Qualities: Attack
   Dukakis (1988): The other side has pursued a campaign of distortion and distraction, of fear and of smear.

Leadership Ability: Acclaim

Nixon (1960): Above everything else, the American people want leaders who will keep the peace without surrender for America and the world. Henry Cabot Lodge and I have had the opportunity of serving with President Eisenhower in this cause for the last seven and a half years. We both know Mr. Krushchev. We have sat opposite the conference table with him.

Leadership Ability: Attack

Kennedy (1960): [Republicans want you to believe Mr. Nixon has experience in the White House.] A reporter recently asked President Eisenhower for an example of a major idea of Nixon's that Eisenhower had adopted. [Eisenhower]: If you give me a week, I might think of one. I don't remember.

Ideals: Acclaim

Humphrey (1968): [Woman] Humphrey is a man who has a very strong liberal background.

Ideals: Attack

Johnson (1964): Senator Goldwater said on Oct. 12, 1960, in Jacksonville, FL, the child has no right to an education. In most cases the child can get along just as well without it.

II

PRESIDENTIAL CAMPAIGNS

3

In the Beginning: 1952, 1956
The Democrats Ascend: 1960, 1964

The campaigns of 1952 and 1956 are unique for at least two reasons. First, and most importantly, these are the earliest presidential campaigns to employ television spots (Senator William Benton of Connecticut ran the first political TV spot in 1950; Wisconsin Public Television, 2001). This form of message was novel: Especially in 1952, the candidates could not look to the trials and errors of previous presidential races as guides. Television was a relatively new medium and people were understandably fascinated by it; the campaigns wanted to try to harness this new tool for their own purposes. Of course, this is not to say there were no reservations about the use of television. Jamieson (1996) reports that the Republicans were willing to devote over ten times as much as the Democrats to broadcast their advertisements in this campaign, $800,000 to $77,000.

Second, these are the only campaigns to feature the same presidential candidates: Republican Dwight D. Eisenhower and Democrat Adlai E. Stevenson. Of course, several other candidates ran in two elections: Jimmy Carter, Ronald Reagan, George Bush (who also ran for vice president twice with Reagan), Bill Clinton, and Barack Obama. Richard Nixon ran three times for president: losing to Kennedy in 1960, defeating Humphrey in 1968 and McGovern in 1972 (and successfully campaigning twice for vice president with Eisenhower). However, the only difference in the tickets in the 1950s was Stevenson's running mates: John Sparkman in 1952 and Estes Kefauver in 1956. After two terms of Republican control, Kennedy (1960) and Johnson (1964) won the White House. This chapter examines the first four presidential campaigns to employ TV spots.

IN THE BEGINNING: 1952, 1956

One aspect of the 1952 campaign that is especially noteworthy is Eisenhower's series of twenty-second spots entitled "Eisenhower Answers America." Thus, the very first presidential campaign with television spots produced a series of spots with a common theme. These began with their title and a still photo of Eisenhower. Then citizens asked questions which were answered, of course, by Eisenhower. Forty of these spots were made and at least twenty-nine different commercials in this format survive today (Griese, 1975). These questions ranged from inflation and taxes ("food prices, clothing prices, income taxes, won't they ever go down?"), to governmental waste ("Recently, just one government bureau actually lost $400 million. And not even the FBI can find it"), to inadequate benefits ("I can't live on my social security. Nobody can"), to corruption in Washington ("What's wrong down in Washington? Graft, scandal?"), to military preparedness ("We won't spend hundreds of billions and still not have enough tanks and planes for Korea"). Here are two examples of this series of spots:

MAN: General, the Democrats are telling me I never had it so good.

EISENHOWER: Can that be true when America is billions in debt, when prices have doubled, when taxes break out backs, and we are still fighting in Korea? It's tragic and it's time for a change. ("Never Had it So Good")

WOMAN: You know what things cost today. High prices are just driving me crazy.

EISENHOWER: Yes, my Mamie gets after me about the high cost of living. It's another reason why I say, it's time for a change. Time to get back to an honest dollar and an honest dollar's work. ("Honest Dollar")

Notice that the concept of "Eisenhower Answers America" subtly suggests two points: first, that Americans have many important questions about the current (Democratic) administration, and, second, that Eisenhower has the answers. Commercials using citizens and answers to questions became staples of the political television commercial. Furthermore, the idea that American needs a change in leadership is one that would serve many challengers well (although Stevenson never served as president, his party held the White House in 1952, so he is the candidate of the incumbent party). Eisenhower also developed "The Man from Abilene," a biographical spot, in the 1952 campaign.

One-third of Stevenson's spots in 1952 were songs, and two were mini-soap operas (which included songs at the end). In the following advertisement, a woman sang a song.

Here, Stevenson attempts to point out the risks of putting a man from the military (General Eisenhower) into the White House. It also touts (vaguely) his leadership experience as governor of Illinois. Two of Stevenson's ads ("Ike and Bob" 1 and 2) used cartoons and suggested that Eisenhower would be controlled by Republican Robert Taft:

> Ike. Bob. Ike. Bob. [slowly, in soft voices like lovers, with two hearts labeled Ike and Bob]
> We must lower taxes Bob.
> Yes Ike, we must lower taxes.
> But we have to spend more for defense, Bob.
> You see Ike, we agree perfectly.
> Bob. Ike. Bob. Ike.
>
> ANNOUNCER: Will Bob give Ike the additional money for defense after Ike cuts taxes? Stay tuned for a musical interlude.

Although they occasionally occur in subsequent campaigns, the concepts of songs and mini-soap operas ultimately proved far less popular than the concepts pioneered by Eisenhower in his 1952 spots.

As mentioned above, in 1952 one of Eisenhower's spots was partly biographical and called "The Man from Abilene." In the 1956 rematch, Stevenson produced three longer "Man from Libertyville" spots. These were "informal chats" designed to help us get to know the candidate, his family, and his running mate Estes Kefauver. He also attacked his opponent, as this passage from a 1956 spot illustrates:

> Eisenhower said that there would be tax relief. And there has been, to some degree, but it was for the benefit of the well-to-do and for the big corporations. The Republicans gave the lion's share of it to them. Out of every dollar of tax cut savings, ninety-one cents went to the higher income families and to the big corporations. And for the rest of Americans, eighty percent of all American families, got only nine cents out of each tax cut dollar. Now for older people, for you people who live on pensions, on fixed incomes, for the younger people just getting started, this is a serious matter. ("Man from Libertyville 2")

This advertisement attacks Eisenhower for giving most of the tax cut he promised to the rich. Several of Stevenson's spots in his second run for the presidency focused on the broken promise argument at work in this advertisement. To further illustrate this kind of spot, consider "How's That Again General?"

> ANNOUNCER: How's that again, General? During the 1952 campaign, General Eisenhower promised a great crusade:
>
> EISENHOWER: Too many politicians have sold their ideals of honesty down the Potomac. We must bring integrity and thrift back to Washington.
>
> ANNCR: How's that again, General?

EISENHOWER: Too many politicians have sold their ideals of honesty down the Potomac. We must bring back integrity and thrift back to Washington.

KEFAUVER: This is Estes Kefauver. Let's see what happened to that promise. Wesley Roberts, a Republican National Chairman, sold Kansas a building it already owned for eleven thousand dollars. He got a silver tree from Mr. Eisenhower. Hal Talbott pressured defense plants to employ a firm which paid him a hundred and thirty thousand dollars while he was Air Force Secretary. He received the General's warm wishes and an official welcome. And there are many others, like Strobel, the Public Buildings Administrator; Mansure, the General Services Administrator. ("How's That Again, General?")

The argument of broken campaign promises, and the tactic of employing the opponent's own words in the indictment, have proved quite durable over time. Eisenhower had health problems, including a heart attack, in 1955 and Stevenson also produced spots suggesting that voters should be nervous about the prospect of President Nixon. However, Jamieson (1996) reports that these commercials never aired.

In their second clash Eisenhower eschewed twenty-second ads (this sample includes only one twenty-second advertisement from 1956), but used several five-minute spots. These featured ordinary citizens, "people on the street," to praise the candidate and his first-term record.

MAN: I want to see President Eisenhower reelected. He's brought honesty and integrity to the White House, and peace and prosperity to the country. That's good enough for me.

WOMAN: Eisenhower strikes me as a fundamentally peaceful man. And I think he knows enough about war that he would keep us out of it. ("People in the Street")

Tributes from ordinary citizens have become another common device in political advertising.

Thus, these candidates inaugurated presidential television advertising. They developed several different formats for political spots that subsequently functioned as models for subsequent campaigns. Each of these candidates had two opportunities to defeat the other and secure the White House. But what about the content of the advertisements?

Functions of Presidential TV Spots 1952–1956

These campaigns stressed acclaiming: 65 percent of their utterances were instances of self-praise (although in 1952 Eisenhower attacked more than he acclaimed). For example, a 1952 Stevenson ad explained that "The farmer, the businessman, the veteran, and the working man, to each in turn he has said that he will represent not their interests alone, but the interests of all of us. That's why I am excited about Governor Stevenson. He will be a President for all the people." This utterance praises Stevenson for caring about all Americans rather than just for some special interest groups. Eisenhower declared in 1952 that "I stand for expanded social security and more real benefits. Believe me sir: If I am President, I'll give you older folks action, not just sympathy." Although this passage ends with a swipe at Democrats for providing sympathy rather than action, the main point is that Eisenhower promises to improve social security for older Americans. Thus, both candidates repeatedly acclaimed in their advertisements.

Both candidates also relied on attacks in their television spots: 35 percent of their remarks were negative. For instance, in 1952 Eisenhower posed questions that functioned to attack the Democratic status quo: "Today across the nation, Americans everywhere are burdened with a multitude of problems. What to do about skyrocketing prices? What to do about backbreaking taxes? What to do about the staggering national debt? And, close to our hearts, when will we have an end to war in Korea?" Stevenson also attacked his opponent. Several of his 1952 advertisements featured songs. Here, he questioned whether Eisenhower or Robert Taft would really be in charge if Eisenhower won the election: "Rueben, Rueben, I've been thinking 'bout the Gen'ral and his mob. If you're voting for the Gen'ral, you really are electing Bob." Neither candidate used defense in any of the television spots examined here.

Topics of Presidential TV Spots 1952–1956

In these two contests the candidates devoted 59 percent of their utterances to policy matters, discussing character in 41 percent of their comments. For example, in 1956 Eisenhower acclaimed his past deeds accomplished in his first term, explaining to voters that:

> You will hear your Secretary of Treasury, George Humphrey, tell how his department has checked the galloping inflation, cut taxes, balanced the budget, and reduced the debt. You will hear your Secretary of Defense, Charles E. Wilson, tell how we have saved billions of dollars on the Armed Forces, reduced our manpower requirements, and still provided a more secure defense. You will hear your Secretary of Labor, James Mitchell, tell how employment, wages, and income have reached the highest levels in history. You will hear your Attorney General, the Secretary of our new Department of Health, Education, and Welfare, and other Cabinet officers tell what we have done to combat monopoly, to extend Social Security for seventy million Americans, and other accomplishments of this Republican administration.

However, Eisenhower addressed his goals for the future as well: "We in the Republican party pledge ourselves to continue our program of peace, security, and prosperity, that has made our party the party of the future."

These candidates discussed character as well in their television spots. This Stevenson spot from 1952 discusses his leadership ability, referring to his experience as governor of Illinois. Notice that he criticizes Eisenhower's lack of governmental experience at the same time: "I sure think that this is no time for an amateur in the White House. We need a man who knows civilian government. I switched to Stevenson." Eisenhower combines an attack on the establishment with praise of his personal qualities in this passage from 1952: "Too many politicians have sold their ideals of honesty down the Potomac. We must bring back integrity and thrift back to Washington. This we are determined to do." So, Eisenhower and Stevenson offered character as well as policy appeals in these campaign advertisements.

Forms of Policy and Character in Presidential TV Spots 1952–1956

The form of policy utterance which was used most often in the 1950s was past deeds. Overall, 66 percent of Eisenhower's and Stevenson's policy utterances employed past deeds. An Eisenhower spot from 1956 observed that "Eisenhower promised he'd get us veteran servicemen out of the war there and he did." In 1956, Stevenson lamented Eisenhower's first-term performance: "Small business profits are down 52 percent. . . . Farm income is down 25 percent. . . . Your schools like this one need a third of a million more classrooms." Past deeds were used to acclaim and attack in these campaigns.

Future plans were virtually non-existent in these campaigns (a single instance by Stevenson in 1952). However, general goals accounted for one-third of their policy comments. In 1952, Eisenhower promised that "We will put the lid on government spending." In the second campaign, Stevenson revealed his goal of achieving peace: "I'm Adlai Stevenson, and this is what I believe—that there is only one sound formula for peace: a sturdy defense, cooperation with our friends, and intelligent action to win the hearts and minds of the uncommitted peoples." Goals were a fairly common topic in these commercials.

When Eisenhower and Stevenson discussed character, they discussed personal qualities (46 percent) the most, followed by leadership ability (31 percent) and ideals (22 percent). In 1952, one of Stevenson's advertisements noted that he has the courage to stand up for his beliefs. In 1956, one of Eisenhower's commercials praised his leadership ability: "That's why we all depend on Ike so much. He can stand up to Krushchev and those fellows. He's a big man who's used to handling big problems." A 1952 Stevenson spot reported on the Democratic candidate's ideals: "In the South, he has made a strong statement for civil liberties and full equality." Character was a substantial component of these television ads.

Conclusion: The Beginning

Although both candidates invented types of spots that would be used in subsequent campaigns, Eisenhower's use of spots was better than Stevenson's. He adapted his use of acclaims and attacks appropriately, using more attacks and fewer acclaims as a challenger than he did as an incumbent. Stevenson's use of these two functions was roughly the same in both campaigns. Eisenhower also had more important innovations: a series of thematically related spots, use of endorsements by ordinary citizens, biographical spots, and question and answer formats. Both candidates used songs and cartoons. In the second campaign, Stevenson used reluctant testimony to argue that Eisenhower had failed to fulfill his campaign promise. Finally, especially in the "Eisenhower Answers America" series, Eisenhower addressed a variety of topics, making it likely that his spots touched on topics important to most voters (while still maintaining a campaign theme). It should come as no surprise that Eisenhower won both campaigns.

THE DEMOCRATS ASCEND: 1960, 1964

In 1960, Republican Vice President Richard M. Nixon ran against Democratic Senator John F. Kennedy. Nixon ran heavily on the administration's record, arguing that he was partly responsible for its successes and had the experience, as vice president, to continue that record. Nixon pledged to campaign in all fifty states, a commitment he fulfilled only with difficulty (a symbolic gesture that flies in the face of the strategy of devoting time, energy, and money in the states that are most likely to tip the balance in the candidate's favor). This campaign also featured the first general election presidential debates.

Nixon's television spots addressed a relatively limited number of themes. The topic of national defense—including peace and the Communist threat—is illustrated in advertisements like this one in 1960:

> ANNOUNCER: Mr. Nixon, what is the truth about our defenses? How strong should they be?
>
> NIXON: Well, they must be strong enough to keep us out of war, powerful enough to make the Communists in the Soviet Union and Red China understand that America will not tolerate being pushed around, that we can if necessary retaliate with such speed and devastation to make the risk too great for the Communists to start a war any place in the world. We have this kind of strength now, and we are getting stronger every day. We must never let the Communists think we are weak. This is both foolish and dangerous. And so I say, let's not tear America down. Let us speak up for America.
>
> ANNOUNCER: Vote for Nixon and Lodge November 8. They understand what peace demands. ("Defense Truth")

This topic alone accounted for almost half of the Nixon commercials in this sample.

This spot also illustrates a series of at least seven advertisements that imitate Eisenhower's "Eisenhower Answers America" commercials of 1952. Here, an announcer asks a question, prefaced by "Mr. Nixon, what is the truth about. . . ?" As in Eisenhower's spots, this format enacts the theme that Nixon is the one with answers. In fact, he did not simply have answers, but he had "the truth." These ads may also have, like Eisenhower's spots, created the impression that citizens had questions that needed answering. In Eisenhower's advertisements (produced when the Republicans were challenging the Democratic White House), this impression helped him challenge the party in control. In Nixon's spots, this factor might have inadvertently undermined confidence in the Eisenhower/Nixon administration.

A second theme concerned the qualifications of the candidates, Vice President Nixon and Ambassador Henry Cabot Lodge, for office.

> ANNOUNCER: Yes, our nation needs Nixon. Experience counts.
>
> MYLER: I'm Mrs. Robert Myler Jr., and I think Nixon and Lodge are the best-trained to win the cold war and to keep the peace. I also like Nixon because he's a native Californian and knows our problems. ("Experience Counts")

This spot echoes, in brief form, Eisenhower's 1956 commercials of ordinary citizens endorsing his candidacy.

Nixon also discussed jobs and the economy quite frequently. He acclaimed the strength of the economy in spots like this one:

> ANNOUNCER: Mr. Nixon, what is the truth? Is America lagging behind in economic growth?
>
> NIXON: Certainly not. The fact is that Americans are earning more, investing more, saving more, living better than ever before. More Americans than ever before are bringing home the weekly paycheck. Sixty-eight million people are employed today. Now this is growth. The kind that ensures our strength at home, and it exceeds the economic growth in Russia today. Ours is a growth based on paying our bills, too. Not a system of reckless borrowing that will burden our children tomorrow. This is the kind of economic growth we must continue to have, in order to continue to help us keep the peace. ("Truth Economy")

Thus, Nixon acclaimed the economic record of the incumbent (Republican) administration in which he served as vice president.

Kennedy addressed far more topics in his 1960 commercials than Nixon discussed. His television spots addressed such topics as education, leadership, defense and Communism, civil rights, social welfare (including Medicare and Social Security), jobs and the economy, the environment, and urban affairs. This spot illustrates his treatment of several issues:

> KENNEDY: I believe if we're moving ahead here, we'll move ahead around the world. We are opposing those in this election who wish to stand still. Those who in their legislative careers, and the Republican party, have stood still. Those who opposed all that we've tried to do during the past years to strengthen our country and strengthen our economy, and protect our farmers, and protect small businessmen, build homes, provide better educational facilities for our children. Provide medical care for our older citizens under social security. This is the unfinished business of our generation. And I come now to ask your help in this campaign. And I can assure you that if we are successful, we will

give leadership to this country through the Democratic party, and we'll start America moving again. ("Moving Ahead")

He discusses strengthening the economy, protecting farmers and small businesses, providing housing, education, and medical care for the aged. Similarly, the next advertisement discusses several topics related to urban affairs:

KENNEDY: Hello, my name is John Kennedy. I live in one of the oldest cities in the United States, and I believe that these problems that our cities face really one of the most important if undiscussed problems that now face our great country. Most of our people live in cities. Many of those cities are old. The housing is old. The schools are crowded. The teachers are inadequately compensated. The streets are narrow and can't stand the great transportation mass which we now have in the center of our cities at the rush hour. If our cities are going to maintain their vitality, they're going to remain a good place to live, if our property taxes are going to remain in reason, then we're going to have to go to work: the community, the state, the national government. I believe we should create a department of Urban Affairs for housing, transportation, and all the rest and begin to move our cities forward again. ("Urban Affairs")

He pointed to many problems that need work: housing, schools, transportation, and property taxes. In these ads he doesn't discuss specific plans to solve them, but he does lay out an ambitious agenda (while suggesting that the present administration has not done much to help these problem areas).

The Kennedy campaign also produced a memorable song, with still photos and cartoon signs:

Kennedy, Kennedy, Kennedy, Kennedy, Kennedy, Kennedy, Kennedy, Ken-Ken,
    Kennedy for me. Kennedy, Kennedy, Kennedy.
Do you want a man for president who's seasoned through and through?
But not so doggoned seasoned that he won't try something new.
A man who's old enough to know and young enough to do.
It's up to you, it's up to you, it's simply up to you.
Do you like a man who answers straight, a man who's always fair.
We'll measure him against the others and when you compare.
You'll cast your vote for Kennedy and the change that's overdue.
So it's up to you, it's up to you, it's simply up to you.
Kennedy, Kennedy, Kennedy, Kennedy, Kennedy, Kennedy, Kennedy for me.
    Kennedy, Kennedy, Kennedy, Kennedy, Kennedy, Kennedy, Kennedy, Kennedy,
    Kennedy. ("Jingle")

Thus, Kennedy's spots addressed a much wider range of topics than did Nixon's advertisements.

Vice President Lyndon B. Johnson took office after Kennedy was assassinated in 1963, and as a sitting president (albeit one elected as vice president) he was the Democratic nominee in 1964. Senator Hubert Humphrey was selected as the vice-presidential nominee. Johnson was challenged by Senator Barry M. Goldwater and his running mate, Representative William Miller. The Gulf of Tonkin Resolution was passed in August of 1964, initiating the Vietnam conflict. The Democrats believed Nixon was wrong to have agreed to debate when he was ahead in 1960, and did not want to make the same mistake in 1964 (Democrats in the Senate prevented suspension of the equal time television rule, effectively prohibiting debates; Splaine, 1995).

Several of Johnson's spots worked from the idea that Goldwater was a warmonger. The "Daisy" spot is the most famous of these ads:

GIRL [small girl picking petals from a daisy]: One, two, three, four, five, seven, six, six, eight, nine, nine.

TECHNICIAN: Ten, nine, eight, seven, six, five, four, three, two, one, zero. [zoom to girl's eye, revealing mushroom cloud. Sound of blast.]

JOHNSON: These are the stakes: to make a world in which all God's children can live, or go into the dark. We must either love each other or we must die.

ANNOUNCER: Vote for President Johnson on November 3. The stakes are too high for you to stay home. ("Daisy")

This spot employed very powerful images to evoke its message: an innocent little child with a flower and the mushroom cloud of an atomic bomb. Johnson provided an equally powerful contrast in his words: Love one another or die. Another such advertisement concerned Goldwater's support for nuclear weapons tests. One commercial argued that the red "hot line" telephone must be in responsible hands. These concerns were fueled in part by fears about Russia, Communist China, and the cold war.

The Johnson campaign attempted to portray Goldwater as an extremist on other issues besides defense. This spot argues that he would threaten social security:

ANNOUNCER [Social Security card on table]: On at least seven different occasions, Barry Goldwater has said that he would drastically change the present Social Security system. In the *Chattanooga Tennessee Times* [newspaper put on card], in a "Face the Nation" interview [film can on newspaper], in the *New York Times Magazine* [put on top], in a "Continental Classroom" television interview [television reel on top], in the *New York Journal American* [paper on top], in a speech he made only last January in Concord, New Hampshire [speech manuscript on top], and in the *Congressional Record* [journal on top]. Even his running mate William Miller [hands tear Social Security card in two] admits that Barry Goldwater's voluntary plan would wreck your Social Security.

JOHNSON: Too many have worked too long, and too hard, to see this threatened now by policies which threaten to undo all that we have done together over all these years [whole Social Security card].

ANNOUNCER: For over thirty years, President Johnson has worked to strengthen Social Security. Vote for him on November 3. The stakes are too high for you to stay home. ("Social Security")

Many people were concerned about having enough money to survive in retirement, and this ad suggested that Goldwater could be a threat to domestic as well as foreign policy. Another creative Johnson spot suggested that Goldwater, who was a senator from Arizona, would not be equally concerned about the fate of the entire country.

> [sounds of sawing and water lapping] In a *Saturday Evening Post* article dated August 31, 1963, Barry Goldwater said: "Sometimes I think this country would be better off if we could just saw off the eastern seaboard and let it float out to sea" [saw cuts through wooden map; eastern seaboard falls into the water and floats away]. Can a man who makes statements like this be expected to serve all the people justly and fairly? Vote for President Johnson on November 3. The stakes are too high for you to stay home. ("Eastern Seaboard")

Clearly, voters want a president who will represent the entire country, not just one geographical region. Another spot reinforced this premise, suggesting that Goldwater opposed spending federal funds on dams unless they were built in his home state of Arizona.

The Johnson campaign also addressed character issues. This commercial mentions several issues to make the argument that the Republican candidate is inconsistent:

> When somebody tells you he's for Barry Goldwater, you ask him which Barry Goldwater he's for [Goldwater faces on both sides of screen; pans from side to side]. Is he for the one who said, we must make the fullest possible use of the United Nations, or is he for the one who said the United States no longer has a place in the United Nations? Is he for the Barry who said, I've never advocated the use of nuclear weapons anywhere in the world, or is he for the one who said I'd drop a low yield atomic bomb on the Chinese supply lines in North Vietnam? Is he for the Barry who said, I seek the support of no extremist, or is he for the one who said extremism in the defense of liberty is no vice? And how is a Republican supposed to indicate on his ballot which Barry he's voting for? There's only one Lyndon Johnson. Vote for him on November 3. The stakes are too high for you to stay home. ("Which Barry Goldwater?")

This spot is interesting in that it mentions policy topics (the UN, the use of nuclear weapons) but argues for a character claim, that he is inconsistent (and possibly untrustworthy). It also manages to revisit the charges of extremism. Voters who decide on character will want their president to be consistent, and voters who decide on policy want to be able to accurately predict what their president will do after the election.

These Democratic attacks (and perhaps his remark in his acceptance address as well) forced Goldwater to defend in several of his spots. Here is one of his defenses against the accusation that he is rash:

> ANNOUNCER: Mr. Goldwater, what's this about your being called imprudent and impulsive?

GOLDWATER: Well, you know, it seems to me that the really impulsive and imprudent president is the one who is so indecisive that he has no policy at all, with the result
that potential aggressors are tempted to move because they think that we lack the will to
defend freedom. Now there was nothing impulsive or imprudent about Dwight Eisenhower when he moved with firmness and clear purpose in Lebanon and the Formosa
Straits. Compare these Eisenhower policies with the appalling actions of this administration—in Laos and the Bay of Pigs, in Berlin and the Congo. We need a clear and
resolute policy, one which is based on peace through strength. Only when we have such
a policy will we reclaim our rightful role as the leader of the free world.

ANNOUNCER: In your heart, you know he's right. Vote for Barry Goldwater.
("Impulsive")

This advertisement is designed to deny the accusations and to reassure voters that
Goldwater was not a warmonger. It also attacked the Kennedy/Johnson administra-
tion for foreign policy failures like the Bay of Pigs fiasco. Another spot used Ronald
Reagan to dispute attacks on Goldwater.

Goldwater revisited a favorite Republican approach in 1964, question and answer.
Several of his spots began with the statement: "The people ask Barry Goldwater."
This was followed by a question from a citizen, and then Goldwater's response.

ANNOUNCER: The people ask Barry Goldwater.

WOMAN: I have a question for Mr. Goldwater. I'm Cynthia Port. We keep hearing
about hot wars, cold wars, and brushfire wars. I have an older brother and many of my
former classmates who are now serving in the armed forces. I'd like to know what Mr.
Goldwater will do to keep us out of war.

GOLDWATER: Well, let me assure you here and now, and I've said this in every
corner of the land throughout this campaign and I'll continue to say it, that a Gold-
water-Miller administration will mean once more the proven policy of peace through
strength that was the hallmark of the Eisenhower years. The Eisenhower approach to
foreign affairs is our approach. It served the cause of freedom and avoided war during
the last Republican Administration. It will do so again. We are the party of preparedness and the party of peace.

ANNOUNCER: In your heart you know he's right. ("Out of War")

He also made several other spots that did not begin with the phrase "The people
ask Barry Goldwater," but which did start with a question posed by a citizen and a
response from the candidate (a similar idea to the Nixon "What is the truth about"
ads). As with Eisenhower's "Eisenhower Answers America" series of commercials,
these spots suggested that the candidate with answers was Goldwater. However,
unlike Eisenhower's more effective spots, many of Goldwater's questions did not
concern problems of the current administration. Some were defenses (what will he
do about Social Security?) and others were simply springboards for Goldwater to
explain his viewpoint.

Functions of Presidential TV Spots 1960–1964

These four candidates devoted 70 percent of their comments in television spots to acclaims. For example, Nixon boasted that "the record shows there's been more progress in civil rights in the past eight years than in the preceding eighty years, because this administration has insisted on making progress. And I want to continue and speed up that progress." In 1964, a Johnson spot declared that "America is stronger and more prosperous than ever before—and we're at peace. Vote for President Johnson on November 3."

About a quarter (26 percent) of the utterances in these spots were attacks. One of Kennedy's attacking ads noted that "Every Republicans politician wants you to believe that he [Nixon] has actually been making decisions in the White House—but listen to the man who knows best." This was followed by video from an Eisenhower press conference, in which he was asked for "an example of a major idea of his [Nixon's] that you had adopted." Eisenhower paused and answered, "If you give me a week, I might think of one. I don't remember." Eisenhower's answer was shown twice to underline the attack on Nixon's credentials. A spot by Goldwater showed video of anti-American protests around the world. Goldwater then asked, "Is this what President Johnson means when he says we are 'much beloved'? Well, I don't like to see our flag torn down and trampled anywhere in the world. . . . I don't like to see American citizens pushed around, and there's no good reason for letting it happen. All this results from weak, vacillating leadership." Thus, these candidates relied heavily on acclaims and attacks.

Defenses, which did not appear in the 1950s spots, were used for the first time in television advertisements in 1960 and 1964. However, they were far less common than acclaims and attacks, accounting for 4 percent of the utterances (and only used by Republicans in these campaigns). For instance, one Nixon spot in 1960 began by announcing that "President Eisenhower answers the Kennedy-Johnson charges that America has accomplished nothing in the last eight years." Then, Eisenhower reported that "I am proud of you, proud of what you have done. And proud of what has been done by America. And let no one diminish your pride and confidence in yourselves or belittle these accomplishments. My friends, never have Americans achieved so much in so short a time." Although rambling and vague, this spot is clearly meant as a defense. Similarly, Goldwater noted in one of his spots that "Our opponents are referring to us as war-mongers" and Eisenhower replied, "Well, Barry, in my mind, this is actual tommyrot," explicitly denying the accusation. Thus, these spots made use of defense.

Topics of Presidential TV Spots 1960–1964

These campaigns had a slight tendency to prefer character (52 percent) over policy (48 percent). Goldwater attacked his opponent's leadership ability in 1964: "Our country has lacked leadership that treats public office as a public trust" ("Public

Trust"). A Johnson spot, in contrast, praised his leadership with a spot about the "hot line" telephone linking Washington with Moscow: "This particular phone only rings in a serious crisis. Leave it in the hands of a man who has proven himself responsible. Vote for President Johnson on November 3" ("Hot Line"). Thus, character served as a ground for both acclaims and attacks in these advertisements.

Policy was also used frequently in these commercials. A spot for Kennedy acclaimed his goals in 1960:

> The Democratic party, and our standard-bearer, Senator John F. Kennedy, is determined to see to it that agricultural income goes up. We believe that our food abundance is a blessing and not a problem. We believe in putting food to work at home and abroad to help humanity. We believe in the family farm as the best system of agriculture and we seek an economic program for agriculture that will protect it. ("Agriculture")

Nixon acclaimed the Eisenhower/Nixon administration's record on civil rights: "The last eight years have seen more progress toward equal rights and equal opportunity for all Americans than the previous twenty years. We must continue that progress" ("Civil Rights"). He ends with a statement of goals on this issue. A Johnson spot featured a little girl eating an ice cream cone discussing the nuclear test-ban treaty, attacking Goldwater's past deeds and future plans:

> They got together and signed a nuclear test ban treaty and then the radioactive poison started to go away. But now, there's a man who wants to be President of the United States, and he doesn't like this treaty. He fought against it. He even voted against it. He wants to go on testing more bombs. His name is Barry Goldwater. And if he's elected, they might start testing all over again. ("Ice Cream")

Testing of nuclear weapons is clearly a policy topic. An announcer in a Goldwater spot explained that "Here is Barry Goldwater, who calls him [Johnson] to account for this Administration's colossal bungling on Cuba and Castro." Then Goldwater declared "The same bearded dictator is still ninety miles off, thumbing his nose at us. And the Bay of Pigs has left us not a monument to freedom, but a dark blot on our national pride." Thus, policy was used in both acclaims and attacks in these spots.

Forms of Policy and Character in Presidential TV Spots 1960–1964

These spots tended to emphasize past deeds (45 percent) and general goals (45 percent) when they discussed policy, and leadership ability (41 percent) and personal qualities (37 percent) when they addressed character. In 1964, for example, a Johnson spot acclaimed his accomplishments while attacking Goldwater's past deeds: "President Johnson has signed over a dozen laws for the improvement of education. Laws about education for handicapped children, people displaced by automation, medical schools, graduate schools, training programs, and others. Senator Goldwater voted against all of them" ("Educaton"). In response to a question about how to "keep the Communists from taking over in Africa," Nixon acclaimed his goals: "Well, I believe we can if we keep on working through the United Nations" ("UN"). These excerpts illustrate their use of the two most common forms of policy utterances. Future plans were infrequently discussed in these spots.

In the realm of character, Adlai Stevenson praised Kennedy's leadership ability: "The great majority of the world's nations wait eagerly for America to assume again the leadership for freedom and for peace. I believe Senator Kennedy offers us the vigorous, principled direction which will answer Krushchev's bluster" ("Foreign Policy"). There is also an implied attack on the current lack of leadership. A Goldwater commercial in 1964 stressed his personal qualities: "Put a man of honesty, integrity, and strength in the White House. Vote for Barry Goldwater" ("Integrity"). Although ideals were used in some themes, they were relatively uncommon in these campaigns.

Conclusion: The Democrats Ascend

In 1960, Kennedy defeated Nixon. The Republican candidate would have to wait eight years before ascending to the presidency. Although Eisenhower did appear on Nixon's behalf in a few of his advertisements, Eisenhower's lack of enthusiastic support (as showcased prominently in the Kennedy "Ike's Press Conference" spots) surely hurt Nixon's campaign. There are of course numerous factors at work in this campaign (Nixon's ill-considered pledge to campaign in all fifty states; Kennedy's strong performance in the presidential debates), but Kennedy's advertising campaign was well conceived. He addressed more issues than did the Republican nominee. Nixon, on the other hand, appeared to be somewhat on the defensive. Nixon's "What is the Truth . . ." spots were not nearly as effective as Eisenhower's "Eisenhower Answers America" advertisements.

Johnson won the next election, defeating Goldwater. Among other themes, the Democrat President secured election on his own in part by playing on many voters' fears that Goldwater would be too militarily aggressive. The "Daisy" spot, although only once aired in a paid broadcast (but shown repeatedly on the news), neatly encapsulated these concerns. Johnson's television spots were generally well developed. As mentioned earlier, some of Goldwater's own statements may have worked against him here. Goldwater's spots attacked Johnson, but not as effectively as Eisenhower had attacked the incumbent Democratic administration in 1952. Goldwater was also on the defensive in many of his commercials (even if he wasn't always explicitly responding to charges, he spent much time attempting to explain away voters' fears). His "The People Ask Barry Goldwater" advertisements again fall short of the standard established in "Eisenhower Answers America." Thus, Johnson's spots were more effectively developed than Goldwater's advertisements.

4

Nixon's Return: 1968, 1972
After Watergate: 1976, 1980

In 1968, President Johnson had decided not to seek another term in office. His vice president, Hubert Humphrey, was selected as the Democratic nominee. Senator Edmund Muskie was chosen to be his running mate. Richard Nixon, who had lost the presidential campaign to Kennedy in 1960 and the 1962 gubernatorial campaign to Edmund Brown, was nominated to lead the Republican Party. Governor Spiro Agnew was selected as his running mate. Governor George Wallace and General Curtis LeMay ran on the American Independent Party ticket, winning some electoral votes (see Splaine, 1995). The Vietnam War was very controversial and Martin Luther King was assassinated in October of 1968, indicating the importance of civil rights unrest. Nixon won both in 1968 and in 1972. However, his vice president, Spiro Agnew, resigned as part of a plea deal for accusations concerning his tenure as governor of Maryland. Nixon appointed Representative Gerald Ford as vice president and, when Nixon resigned in the wake of Watergate, Ford became president even though he had not been elected as president or vice president. Jimmy Carter wrested the presidency away from Ford in 1976 but lost to Ronald Reagan in 1980. This chapter examines presidential advertising from these four elections.

NIXON'S RETURN: 1968, 1972

Nixon's spots attacked the status quo, arguing that the Johnson/Humphrey administration had been inept, and that Nixon would improve matters. Several of these spots discussed foreign affairs:

> Never has so much military, economic, and diplomatic power been used as ineffectively as in Vietnam. And if after all of this time and all of this sacrifice and all of this support

there is still no end in sight, then I say the time has come for the American people to turn to new leadership not tied to the policies and mistakes of the past. I pledge to you: We will have an honorable end to the war in Vietnam. ("Vietnam")

Other spots lamented the state of domestic affairs and pledged improvements at home if we elect Nixon to be president:

> In recent years crime in this country has grown nine times as fast as the population. At the current rate, the crimes of violence in America will double by 1972. We cannot accept that kind of future. We owe it to the decent and law-abiding citizens of America to take the offensive against the criminal forces that threaten their peace and security, and to rebuild respect for law across this country. I pledge to you that the wave of crime is not going to be the wave of the future in America. ("Crime")

These spots functioned both to attack the past deeds of the incumbent party and to acclaim the general goals of Nixon's alternative approach.

Humphrey used some of his spots in the 1968 presidential contest to highlight his past accomplishments:

> When he fought for civil rights twenty years ago, a lot of people said he was ahead of his time. He was. He was ahead of his time when he outlined health insurance for the aged, sixteen years before Medicare. He was ahead of his time when he urged a nuclear test ban treaty ten years before it was signed. He was ahead of his time when he proposed job training for unemployed young people, seven years before the job corps. He was ahead of his time when he defined food for peace five years before the program saw life. And he was ahead of his time when he dreamed up the Peace Corps, four years before Congress adopted it. Hubert Humphrey has been ahead of his time for the last twenty years, that's why he's the man we need for the future. Don't just vote for the right ideas, vote for the man who thought of them. With Hubert Humphrey, it's not just talk. He gets it done. ("Ahead of his Time")

The argument that he has been ahead of his time flows smoothly into the claim that he would be good for the future. He is portrayed here as a man of action, not just of words. His advertisements also employed quotations from ordinary citizens to acclaim Humphrey's leadership ability:

> ANNOUNCER: These are critical times. Who do you want to be the next President?
>
> MAN: As things stand right now, I definitely feel Mr. Humphrey would be the best, best possible candidate for the Presidency.
>
> MAN: This is a man who has had a very strong liberal background.
>
> WOMAN: He's not only a man of new ideas, he's a man who's ahead of the times.
>
> MAN: I think he's a man who's ready for the job. He can handle it because he's very familiar with the problems involved, the issues.

MAN: He was very active and very much acquainted with the problems of the cities many years ago when we talked about civil rights and the poor people.

MAN: Vice President Humphrey is without question a man that I feel that everyone in this country can trust.

MAN: I think Mr. Humphrey is a leader. He's one who can unite all the people behind him. He's just the best man for the job right now.

ANNOUNCER: People believe in Humphrey. The country needs him. ("Critical Times")

This commercial briefly mentions policy (civil rights), but it focuses primarily on Humphrey's character.

Humphrey also attacked his opponents in his television advertisements. Notice how this spot intersperses acclaims of Humphrey with attacks on Nixon as a voter muses on the question of what Nixon has done for America:

ANNOUNCER: What has Richard Nixon ever done for you?

MAN: What has Richard Nixon ever done for me? Ah, Medicare. No, that was Humphrey's idea. Nixon, Nixon, oh the bomb, the bomb. No, that was Humphrey's idea to stop testing the nuclear bomb. Nixon. Well, what has Richard Nixon ever done for me? Ah, let's see. Working people, I'm a worker. Nixon ever do anything—No, Humphrey and the Democrats gave us Social Security. But Nixon. Nothing in education. Nothing in housing. Hasn't done anything there either.

MAN: That's funny. There must have been something Nixon's done. ("What Has Nixon Done?")

This spot manages to praise Humphrey and his party while attacking his Republican opponent's record. Nixon's running mate, Spiro Agnew, was also the target of attacks in this campaign:

[heart monitor screen] "Never before in our lives have we been so confronted with this reality [Edmund Muskie, Spiro Agnew]. Who is your choice to be a heartbeat away from the presidency?" ("Heartbeat")

These examples give a general idea of the nature of the advertising in the 1968 campaign.

In 1972, Nixon and Agnew were nominated by the Republican Party to run for a second term in office. The Democrats selected Senator George McGovern to run for president and Senator Thomas Eagleton for vice president. When it was revealed that Eagleton had been treated for depression, McGovern initially supported him but later replaced him with Sargent Shriver (causing concern about both McGovern's loyalty and his indecisiveness). The Vietnamese War continued. President Nixon had visited both Communist China and Russia in his first term. The Watergate break-in at the Democratic campaign headquarters occurred in June of 1972.

In his campaign for a second term in the office of the president, Nixon acclaimed his first term accomplishments.

[slow pans over still photos; "America" playing softly in background]: He has brought home over 500,000 men from the war, and less than 40,000 remain. None engaged in ground combat. He has overhauled the draft laws and made them fair for everyone, black and white, rich and poor. He certified an amendment giving 18-year-olds the right to vote. He has created an economy that is growing faster than at any time in years. The rate of inflation has been cut in half. He created the first governmental agency we have ever had to deal solely with the problems of our environment. He is using the vast resources of government to find a cure for cancer and sickle cell anemia. He's gone to China to talk peace with Mao Tse Tung. He's gone to the Soviet Union to talk peace with Leonid Breshnev. For four years President Nixon has responded to the needs of the people. That's why we need President Nixon, now more than ever. ("Record")

Notice that both domestic and foreign affairs are used to support the argument that Nixon has been successful in his first four years as president. The implication, of course, is that a second term in office would extend his praiseworthy record with clear benefits for voters.

Some of Nixon's 1972 television spots attacked his opponent in the presidential race, Senator George McGovern:

In 1967, Senator George McGovern [photo of McGovern] said he was not an advocate of unilateral withdrawal of our troops from Vietnam. Now of course he is [photo flips from facing left to right]. Last year the Senator suggested regulating marijuana along the same lines as alcohol, which means legalizing it. Now he's against legalizing it and says he always has been [photo flips back]. Last January Senator McGovern suggested a welfare plan that would give a thousand dollar bill to every man, woman, and child in the country [photo flips]. Now he says maybe the thousand dollar figure isn't right [photo flips back]. Last year he proposed to tax inheritances over $500,000 at 100 percent [photo flips]. This year he suggests 77 percent [photo flips]. In Florida he was pro-busing [photo flips]. In Oregon he said he would support the anti-busing bill now in Congress [photo flips]. Last year, this year. The question is, what about next year [photo flips around and around rapidly]? ("McGovern Turnaround")

This theme of inconsistency appeared in other Nixon advertisements that year as well. Notice that like Johnson's attack on Goldwater in 1964, this spot uses policy (Vietnam, legalizing marijuana, welfare, busing) to argue for inconsistency (and possible lack of trustworthiness).

Some of Nixon's spots attacked McGovern's policy proposals. This spot criticized McGovern's plans for our national defense:

The McGovern defense plan. He would cut the marines by a third [hand sweeps some toy soldiers off table], the Air Force by a third [more toy soldiers swept off table]. He would cut Navy personnel by one-fourth [more toy soldiers swept off]. He would cut interception planes by one-half [hand removes toy planes], the Navy fleet by one-half [hand removes ships], and carriers from sixteen to six [hand removes carriers]. Senator Hubert Humphrey had this to say about the McGovern proposal: "It isn't just cutting into the fat. It isn't just cutting into manpower. It is cutting into the very security of this country" [jumble of toys]. President Nixon doesn't believe we should play games with our national security. He believes in a strong America to negotiate for peace from strength. ("McGovern Defense Plan")

This spot used reluctant testimony (from fellow Democrat Hubert Humphrey) and its use of toys to vividly illustrate the effects of McGovern's proposals was innovative. Other McGovern spots used the opinions of ordinary citizens to attack Nixon:

ANNOUNCER: Most people have deep feelings about President Nixon.

WOMAN: He has put a ceiling on wages and done nothing about controlling prices.

MAN: The one thing I knew his last four years was that he knew in some way he would have to please me come this election. And what frightens me is that if he gets in again he doesn't have to worry about pleasing me anymore.

WOMAN: He was caught in the act of spying and stealing. They used to go to jail for these things. He is the president and should set an example.

WOMAN: There always seems to be some big deal going on with the Nixon people, some wheat deal or something.

WOMAN: When I think of the White House, I think of it as a syndicate, a crime outfit, as opposed to, you know, a government.

WOMAN: All I know is that the prices keep going up and he is president.

MAN: I think he's smart. I think he's sly. He wants to be the president of the United States so badly he will do anything.

ANNOUNCER: That's exactly why this is brought to you by the McGovern for President Committee. ("Deep Feelings")

This spot mixes policy (e.g., wages and prices) with character (he is a liar and a thief).

Functions of Presidential TV Spots 1968–1972

Presidential television spots from 1968 and 1972 tended to emphasize acclaims (65 percent), although McGovern attacked more than he acclaimed in 1972. For example, in 1968 Humphrey praised his general goals: "What this country needs are more decent neighborhoods, more educated people, better homes" ("Needs"). His opponent Nixon praised his own ideals: "Dissent is a necessary ingredient of change. But in a system of government that provides for peaceful change there is no cause that justifies resort to violence. There is no cause that justifies rule by mob instead of by reason" ("Dissent"). Given the riots at the 1968 Democratic National Convention in Chicago, there is an implied criticism of the opposing party as well. In 1972, McGovern identified his goals on drug abuse: "We've got to have a program that's better than the one we have now to deal with drugs if we're gonna get on top of the crime problem" ("Drugs"). That same year a spot for Nixon acclaimed his past deeds: "Since taking office, President Nixon has brought over 500,000 men from the war and completely ended our involvement in ground combat" ("Accomplishment"). These excerpts illustrate how these candidates praised themselves in their television advertisements.

Attacks were also fairly common in these commercials, accounting for 35 percent of the utterances. For example, in 1968 Nixon discussed the need for a new initiative for fighting crime, combining attacks on the Democratic administration with his ideas for solving these problems:

> I pledge to you that our new Attorney General will be directed by the President of the United States to launch a war against organized crime in this country. I pledge to you that the new Attorney General will be an active belligerent against the loan sharks and the numbers racketeers that rob the urban poor in our cities. I pledge to you that the new Attorney General will open a new front against the filth peddlers and the narcotics peddlers who are corrupting the lives of the children of this country. ("Attorney General")

This commercial both attacks the incumbents for the increase in crime and promises to take action to avert a future crime wave if Nixon is elected. A McGovern spot in 1972 attacked the failures of the first Nixon term:

> Since Mr. Nixon became President, the cost of whole wheat bread has gone from 31 cents to 45 cents. Since Mr. Nixon became President, the cost of hamburger has gone from 58 cents to 89 cents. Since Mr. Nixon became President, the cost of frozen fish has gone from 69 cents to $1.29. Since Mr. Nixon became President, the cost of living has gone up 19 percent—and your wages have been frozen. ("Prices")

The pain of inflation is even worse when wages are stagnant. In the campaign for his second term in office, a Nixon spot questioned McGovern's consistency [a photo of McGovern flipped back and forth during the spot]:

> In 1964, Senator McGovern voted in favor of the Gulf of Tonkin Resolution which supported escalation of the war in Vietnam. Now he says he is against the war and always has been. In 1965, McGovern said we should wage war rather than surrender South Vietnam to Communism. Three years later he said it would not be fatal to the United States to have a Communist government in South Vietnam. In 1967, he was against unilateral troop withdrawal. Now of course he favors unilateral withdrawal. Throughout the year he has proposed unconditional amnesty for draft dodgers. But his running mate claims he proposed no such thing. For the war, against the war. For amnesty, against amnesty. The question is, where will he stand next year? ("McGovern Turnaround")

Inconsistency is hardly considered a virtue. This spot clearly suggests that McGovern's inconsistency means we don't know what he would do if elected president.

There is also a hint that he is pandering to his audience rather than operating from firm principles.

Defense was relatively uncommon at 1 percent of the utterances in these spots, and Nixon (who defended in 6 percent of his utterances in his 1960 loss) did not defend in either campaign. When it was suggested in 1968 that Humphrey was not sufficiently independent, he replied: "I've been reading that Hubert Humphrey ought to be his own man. That's exactly what I am. . . . Hubert Humphrey as Vice President is a member of a team. Hubert Humphrey as President is captain of a team. There's a lot of difference" ("Team Captain"). In 1972, McGovern dismissed an attack from Nixon: "Richard Nixon goes around talking as if I'm some kind of a radical because I believe in guaranteed jobs for people he's throwing out of work" ("Guaranteed Jobs"). Note that this is coupled with an attack on Nixon on joblessness. Thus, the candidates in 1968 and 1972 employed acclaiming, attacking, and a little defending in their television commercials.

Topics of Presidential TV Spots 1968–1972

These candidates showed a preference for policy (56 percent) over character (44 percent) in their television spots (only Humphrey in 1968 had more character than policy utterances). For instance, in 1968 Nixon argued that "In recent years crime in this country has grown nine times as fast as the population. At the current rate, the crimes of violence in America will be doubled by 1972" ("Crime"). A Humphrey advertisement acclaimed his accomplishments as a senator: "Let's keep score. The 1964 Civil Rights Act. Medicare. The Job Corps. Project Head Start. Get behind the man behind them all: Hubert H. Humphrey for President" ("Score"). A Nixon commercial in 1972 featured Democrat John Connally attacking the future plans of the Democratic nominee:

> Senator McGovern has made proposals to cut an unprecedented thirty-two billion dollars' worth of men and weapons out of the United States' defense budget. The McGovern defense budget is the most dangerous document ever seriously put forth by a presidential candidate in this century. It would end the United States' military leadership in the world; it would make us inferior in conventional and strategic weapons to the Soviets. The total United States Armed Forces level would be cut to a point lower than at the time of Pearl Harbor. Dean Rusk, Secretary of State in the administrations of John F. Kennedy and Lyndon Johnson, has termed the McGovern defense, and I quote him, "insane." ("National Defense")

McGovern attacked Nixon's economic record in 1972: "Well, I don't know how you can pay twice as much for a tractor, and taxes that are twice as high and interest rates that are at 7–8 percent a year and then make it with corn at a dollar a bushel" ("Agriculture"). Thus, policy was a common topic in these commercials.

These ads also took up character issues. A Nixon spot in 1968 touted his leadership ability: "Well I think Richard M. Nixon probably is more qualified in world affairs than anybody I know." The 1968 Humphrey "Weathervane" ad depicted Nixon as a weathervane spinning in the wind, stressing his inconsistency and strongly hinting that he pandered without principles: "Ever notice what happens to Nixon when the political winds blow? Last year he said, I oppose a federal open housing law. This year he said, I support the 1968 Civil Rights Bill with open housing. Again this year he said, I just supported it to get it out of sight. Which way will he blow next?" Again, inconsistency is not a praiseworthy attribute. In 1972, a Nixon spot proclaimed that "He's a very positive man. He's a leader," acclaiming his personal qualities and leadership ability. That same year a McGovern spot questioned Nixon's integrity in this commercial: "One of the reasons I'm disturbed about the President's $10 million secret election fund is that it indicates that there's something there that he's afraid to disclose. What are they hiding? I'm perfectly willing to publish the name of every dollar contributed to my campaign. And I don't see what the President is covering up. But it's that kind of thing that puts a kind of a damper on the moral tone of the whole nation" ("Secret Donations"). McGovern also acclaims his own integrity ("I'm perfectly willing to publish the name of every dollar contributed to my campaign") in this spot. Thus, character was the basis of both acclaims and attacks in these campaigns.

Forms of Policy and Character in Presidential TV Spots 1968–1972

Policy utterances most often appeared in these advertisements as past deeds (56 percent), with general goals (33 percent) and future plans (11 percent) also appearing (only Nixon in 1968 deviated from this pattern, devoting 52 percent of his policy remarks to goals and 44 percent to deeds). For example, a 1968 Nixon ad reported that "Crimes of violence in the United States have almost doubled in recent years. Today a violent crime is committed every sixty seconds. A robbery every two and a half minutes. A mugging every six minutes. A murder every forty-three minutes" ("Violent Crime"). The implication is that the current (Democratic) administration has failed to adequately deal with crime. A Humphrey commercial that same year attacked third-party candidate George Wallace's past deeds: "Mr. Wallace talks about law and order, but under the Wallace administration, Alabama had the highest murder rate in the country" ("Crime in Alabama"). In 1972, this McGovern advertisement sympathized with the problems faced by farmers under the Nixon administration: "Well, I don't know how you can pay twice as much for a tractor, and taxes that are twice as high and interest rates that are at seven to eight percent a year and then make it with corn at a dollar a bushel" ("Farmers"). Thus, utterances concerning the candidates' past deeds were quite common in these campaigns.

To illustrate their use of general goals, consider this 1968 spot talking about Nixon: "I believe that he will back up the efforts of our state and local law enforcement officers through block grants and other means. I think he would appoint to the court judges who are as interested in protecting the law abiding citizen as the criminal. And I believe that he would see that federal laws are vigorously enforced and wage an active campaign against organized crime" ("Law Enforcement"). Utterances on future plans were less common, but still occurred. This 1972 Nixon spot contrasted the two candidate's proposals:

> Seems to me that this election is a lot more than a simple choice between two men or two parties. It's a choice between Senator McGovern's plan to walk out of Vietnam now, or the President's plan to make sure of the release of our prisoners first. It's a choice between the Senator's radical tax and welfare schemes or continuing the economic growth of the past four years. It's a choice between the Senator's plan to cut our military budget to the point that we would become a second class power, or keeping this country as strong as it needs to be. ("Choice")

This ad juxtaposed the two candidates' positions on ending the war in Vietnam, tax and welfare, and the defense budget. These candidates all discussed policy in their television spots.

Character utterances most often occurred as discussions of personal qualities (49 percent). For instance, in 1968 Senator Fong declared that Nixon could be trusted to follow through with his promises: "I know Richard Nixon: when he says he's going to do a thing, he will do it" ("Follow Through"). This Humphrey commercial used an ordinary person to acclaim the Democratic candidate's integrity: "I believe Mr. Humphrey and I can trust him" ("Trust Him"). In 1972, this Nixon advertisement impugned McGovern's character: "Since the beginning of this thing with McGovern he's been saying one thing and then turning around a week or two or three weeks later and doing something entirely different" ("Inconsistent"). Leadership abilities were also common topics of spots (32 percent; Nixon used this form of character utterance the most in 1968, and just as often as personal qualities in 1972). For instance, in this spot from 1968, Nixon's qualifications for leadership are touted: "Dick Nixon has that kind of resolution, knowledgeability, and purpose which is urgently needed in dealing with the foreign policy of our country today" ("Qualified"). Ideals were the subject of 19 percent of the utterances in these campaigns. In 1972, McGovern articulated the principle of fairness in taxation: "Now if you had a president who was working in the other direction on behalf of ordinary taxpayers rather than these big corporations, we could have a tax system that's fair" ("Fairness"). These passages illustrate how these campaigns addressed character issues.

Conclusion: Nixon's Return

Nixon won both of these campaigns. He did seem to shift the proportions of the three functions in his advertising for these campaigns. He curtailed his use of acclaims somewhat from 1960 (1960: 85 percent; 1968: 71 percent; 1972: 78 percent), increased his attacks noticeably (1960: 9 percent; 1968: 29 percent; 1972: 22 percent) and eschewed defenses altogether (1960: 6 percent; 1968: none; 1972: none). There was also a shift away from character to policy (character dropped from 64 percent in 1960 to 46 percent in 1968 and 38 percent in 1972; policy increased from 36 percent in 1960 to 54 percent in 1968 and 62 percent in 1972). Although he discussed foreign policy, his second and third campaigns addressed a wider range of topics than in 1960, when he had focused so heavily on Communism.

AFTER WATERGATE: 1976–1980

Vice President Spiro Agnew resigned during Nixon's second term in October 1973 after pleading no contest to charges of tax evasion. President Nixon appointed Representative Gerald Ford in Agnew's stead. However, in the wake of Watergate, Nixon himself resigned in August of the following year, making Gerald Ford a president who had not been elected as either president or vice president. The Vietnam War was over by 1976, no longer an albatross around the neck of the incumbent party, but Ford's decision to pardon Nixon was widely unpopular. Robert Dole was selected as Ford's running mate. Jimmy Carter, governor of Georgia, was chosen to be the Democratic nominee. Senator Walter Mondale was selected as Carter's vice presidential candidate.

In 1976 President Ford attempted to campaign on his first-term record (as did Nixon in 1972), but unfortunately for Ford the economy wasn't doing very well. His spots, accordingly, sandbagged: "He came to the office of the president in troubled times" said one, and another made the excuse that "Two years ago we were mired in the worst economic crisis since the depression." The point here is not that these statements weren't true, but that they sounded defensive to voters. These excuses made it sound more like Ford was apologizing for his record rather than boasting of it. Here is one advertisement that emphasized his record:

> He came to the office of the president in troubled times. He began an open administration. Now, quietly and firmly, he is leading us out of the worst recession in years. Rather than loose promises, he has made the hard decisions. Rather than frantic spending he has had the courage to say no. The worst is over. Over two million more Americans are working than at the bottom of the recession. Inflation is cut almost in half. President Ford is your president. Keep him. ("Accomplishment")

Creating two million additional jobs is an important accomplishment, but phrases like "The worst is over" pale in comparison with Nixon's acclaims of his first-term accomplishments, as illustrated above. Ford also acclaimed his foreign policy accomplishments:

> In just two years, he has strengthened the ties with our allies in Europe, Japan, and Israel [series of relevant still photos]. He has negotiated firmly and fairly with our adversaries, while making sure our military strength is second to none. He has directed the peace efforts in the Middle East, and Africa. And today, there is not a single American soldier fighting anywhere in the world. Let's keep President Ford in charge. ("Foreign Policy")

Thus, Ford's campaign attempted to convince voters that his record as president, both in domestic and foreign policy areas, justified keeping him in office.

Another recurrent theme in this campaign was that Ford was a nice person: "He's just a downright decent, honest person, seems to me," and "I trust the man, I think he's an honest man and that's the kind of guy that I want representing me" ("Decent"). He also used testimony from ordinary citizens to acclaim himself and then to attack Carter:

> MAN: The thing that I like the most about Mr. Ford is that he's steady. He's not erratic; we can count on him to do what's in the best interests of the country.
>
> MAN: I think he offers solidarity.
>
> WOMAN: I think he's a strong person. I think he stands up for what he thinks is right.
>
> MAN: I think Ford's been very stable.
>
> WOMAN: He takes things very gradual, and very carefully. And I don't think he's gonna make any big mistakes. I'm afraid that Carter is too ambiguous.
>
> MAN: Carter is not quite sure which direction he goes. He changes his mind on his stand every other day or so.
>
> MAN: He contradicts himself from one day to another.
>
> MAN: Well, he's changed his opinions from one day to the next.
>
> WOMAN: He's much too wishy-washy.
>
> MAN: He's very, very wishy-washy.
>
> MAN: He seems to be a little wishy-washy.
>
> MAN: If he'd stand up and say what he was for he'd be a little easier to understand and maybe to believe.
>
> WOMAN: All the things we've read about Jimmy Carter I think are true: that he is fuzzy on a lot of the issues. I like President Ford, a man who will tell you just exactly where he does stand. ("Man in the Street 3")

This spot managed to acclaim Ford's character as stable while attacking Jimmy Carter on the same grounds.

Ford also attacked Carter's record as the governor of Georgia. This spot played off Carter's acclaims of his record (discussed below) and his campaign slogan.

> What Jimmy Carter did as governor, he'll do as president. His ads say that he will do the same as president that he did as governor of Georgia. Then you should know that during his one term as governor, government spending increased by 58 percent. Government employees went up 25 percent. And the state of Georgia went 100 percent deeper into debt. Don't let Jimmy Carter give us more big government. Keep President Ford. ("Carter Record")

This ad argues from his past failures to likely future problems if elected president.

As Mondale had attempted to do in 1972, but with more success, Carter attacked the record of the Ford administration in its first-term of office:

> The Republican television commercials assure us the economy is healthy, inflation's controlled, our leadership is great. But when I look around, I see: every trip to the supermarket a shock, cities collapsing, suburbs scared, policemen cut, welfare skyrocketing. That's reality. The Republicans won't face up to it, but we can change it. ("Reality")

Thus, Carter focused on Ford's dismal record as president in his political advertisements.

In 1980, Carter and Mondale were nominated by the Democratic Party to seek a second term in office. However, the economy was still not in very good shape. Ronald Reagan, former governor of California (and former actor), was nominated by the Republican Party to challenge Carter, and George Bush was chosen as his running mate. Illinois Representative John Anderson ran as an Independent candidate.

Not surprisingly, Reagan's advertisements in 1980 attacked Carter's first-term record in office:

> [Just for the Record, in red]: For the last three and a years, every American has been staggered by the economic record of the Carter administration [bar graphs; each goes up in red as announcer mentions it]. Food prices up over 35 percent. Auto prices up over 31 percent. Home prices up over 46 percent. Clothing up over 20 percent. Transportation up over 50 percent [bar goes off screen]. The new Carter economics will give us more of the same. That adds up to less for everyone. The Carter record speaks for itself. The time is now for Reagan. ("Everything Up")

This spot not only attacks Carter's past failures, but it also predicts future problems if he is re-elected ("more of the same"). Although the incumbents' records in office were not the only topics covered in these campaigns, they were very prominent topics in these commercials.

Carter's nomination had been contested in the primaries by fellow Democrat Senator Edward Kennedy. Reagan, the Republican challenger, made use of this in the general campaign by revisiting Kennedy's primary jibes:

> ANNOUNCER: Senator Kennedy speaks out on foreign policy [March 1980].
>
> KENNEDY: I call this administration's foreign policy the surprise foreign policy, Soviet troops go into Cuba, and the administration is surprised. Soviet troops go into Afghanistan, and this administration is surprised.
>
> ANNOUNCER: A reminder, from Democrats for Reagan. ("Kennedy Foreign Policy")

Reagan's advertisements also used Carter's statements against him. In 1976, Carter had attacked the Ford administration for economic difficulties. This Reagan spot from 1980 allowed Gerald Ford the chance to attack the man who had ejected him from the White House four years earlier:

FORD: When I left the White House inflation was 4.8 percent. This year under Carter its reached 18 percent. Can any president do anything about inflation? We did. The president must be a leader. Jimmy Carter has had five different economic programs and we still have 13 percent inflation and sky-high interest rates. We need strong leadership. We need Ron Reagan, our next president.

ANNOUNCER: The time is now for strong leadership: Reagan for President. ("Ford/Inflation")

This spot suggests both that Carter has no consistent policy ("five different economic programs") and no effective policy ("still have 13 percent inflation") to help the economy.

Reagan's advertising campaign also used acclaiming. Several spots praised Reagan's record as governor of California:

This is a man whose time has come. A strong leader with a proven record. In 1966, answering the call of his party, Ronald Reagan was elected governor of California—next to president, the biggest job in the nation. What the new governor inherited was a state of crisis. California was faced with a $194 million deficit, and was spending a million dollars a day more than it was taking in. The state was on the brink of bankruptcy. Governor Reagan became the greatest tax reformer in the state's history. When Governor Reagan left office, the $194 million deficit had been transformed into a $550 million surplus. The *San Francisco Chronicle* said, Governor Reagan has saved the state from bankruptcy. The time is now for strong leadership. ("Record")

This commercial argues that being the governor of California is very difficult but that Reagan had faced these challenges effectively.

Carter sounded apologetic about the economy during his term as president in his acclaims during the 1980 campaign, ironically reminiscent of Ford's sandbagging advertisements from four years earlier:

CARTER: There's a limit to how much I want the government to stick its nose into people's private affairs, including your family's.

ANNOUNCER: The president of the United States, in Mrs. Reed's backyard.

CARTER: Back in March, we had absolutely uncontrollable inflation and interest rates—they were both approaching 20 percent—and we put in some very mild credit restraints. And people like you, all over the nation, in a spirit of cooperation and patriotism, just clamped down on credit and charges, and the results of our very mild restraints were ten times more effective than we had ever dreamed. And it really tightened up credit a little too much. This began to put people out of work. So we had to take those credit restraints off. They served their purpose, and the inflation rate had dropped sharply.

ANNOUNCER: President Carter: for the future. ("Femalation")

This format (appearing in Mrs. Reed's backyard) presumably is intended to give Carter a "common touch," showing him out communing with ordinary citizens.

As with Ford's campaign from four years earlier, these excuse-laden acclaims pale in comparison to Nixon's accomplishment spots of 1972.

Carter's campaign adopted another tactic from the Ford campaign in 1976: He used testimony from citizens of Reagan's home state, California.

MAN: His problem as governor was the same as he has now, mainly that he always shot from the hip [Sacramento].

MAN: He once stated that if you've, ah, seen one redwood tree you've seen them all [San Francisco].

MAN: Statement about if we're gonna have a bloodbath on campus let's get it over with [Sacramento].

MAN: Some of the recent goofs that he's pulled with regard to China [Los Angeles].

MAN: When you're dealing with governments like Russia [Los Angeles].

ANNOUNCER: A lot of Californians feel pretty good about Ronald Reagan, but others feel a sense of continuing concern.

MAN: I think it makes a lot of people uneasy, and it certainly makes me uneasy [San Francisco].

MAN: I think he's the kind of guy who shoots from the hip [San Francisco].

WOMAN: He did shoot from the hip [Sacramento].

MAN: He shoots from the hip [Fresno].

MAN: As a governor it really didn't make that much difference because the state of California doesn't have a foreign policy, and the state of California isn't gonna be going to war with a foreign nation. And it was just amusing. But as president, ah, you know, it's scary [Sacramento].

MAN: Oh, my decision is made, I'm going to stick with President Carter [Los Angeles]. ("Shoots from the Hip")

These statements by ordinary citizens from Reagan's home state (and remember he campaigned on his record as governor) questioned his character generally and his leadership ability in particular.

Another Carter advertisement attempted to counter Reagan's ad which used Kennedy's primary campaign attacks against Carter with an endorsement from Kennedy:

During the Democratic Convention, I spoke about my deep belief in the ideals of the Democratic Party. And that's why I'm asking you now to make sure your vote will count in 1980. I am convinced that President Carter represents the only real chance to prevent a Reagan victory and preserve our hope for an America of progress and fairness. There is a clear choice in this election, and that is why I am working for the re-election of President Carter. ("Kennedy")

It is unclear how successful this spot was at controlling damage with this "retraction," but the Carter campaign tried. These examples give an indication of the advertising campaigns in these two election years.

Functions of Presidential TV Spots 1976–1980

These campaigns, collectively (64 percent) and individually, stressed acclaims. For example, in 1976 a Ford commercial acclaimed the president's accomplishments: "In just two years, he has strengthened the ties with our allies in Europe, Japan, and Israel. He has negotiated firmly and fairly with our adversaries, while making sure our military strength is second to none. He has directed the peace efforts in the Middle East, and Africa. And today, there is not a single American soldier fighting anywhere in the world. Let's keep President Ford in charge" ("In Charge"). This spot discusses Ford's foreign policy accomplishments in particular. In this advertisement from the 1976 campaign, Carter praised his record as governor of Georgia: "We had three hundred agencies and departments in the state government. We abolished two hundred-seventy-eight of them and set up a very simple economical structure of government. . . . With a new budgeting technique called zero-based budgeting, we eliminated all the old obsolescent programs, put into effect long-range goals and planning and cut administrative costs more than 50 percent" ("Budgeting"). Carter boasts that he eliminated 278 government agencies, instituted long range planning, and cut administrative costs by over half. These excerpts all illustrate how these campaign spots acclaimed.

These spots also contained numerous attacks (35 percent). In one Ford spot, he attacked Carter's future plans: "A middle-income taxpayer earns today around $14,800. Mr. Carter wants to raise taxes on that group in order to pay for these new programs he's proposing. I don't think the $15,000 a year taxpayer ought to get any more tax increases" ("Taxes"). Carter attacked Ford's economic record and his leadership ability in this advertisement from 1976: "Well, 7.9 percent unemployment is what you arrive at when incompetent leaders follow outdated, unjust, wasteful, economic policies" ("Outdated"). This line came back to haunt Carter four years later when Reagan used it to attack Carter: "Jimmy Carter came to Washington promising to do something about unemployment, to give people who were out of work a chance to restore their hopes and dreams. 7.8 percent unemployment is what you arrive at when incompetent leaders follow outdated, insensitive, unjust, wasteful economic policies. Jimmy Carter did do something about unemployment—two million more people became unemployed this year alone" ("Outdated Again"). These passages illustrate how the spots in these campaigns used attacks.

Defenses occurred in 1976 and 1980, but they were quite rare (1 percent). Ford tended to rely on defeasibility, suggesting that circumstances beyond his control hampered his efforts at revitalizing the economy. For example, one spot noted that

"Two years ago, we were mired in the worst economic crisis since the great depression" ("Mired"). Another spot noted that "He came to the office of the president in troubled times" ("Troubled Times"), so presumably we shouldn't blame him if things aren't going so well. Four years later, Carter used the same basic approach: "The progress toward a comprehensive peace for the Middle East is very slow and very tedious, but we've got a lot of hatred still in the Mideast" ("Mideast"). So, defenses were used occasionally in these advertisements.

Topics of Presidential TV Spots 1976–1980

These spots were split almost evenly between policy (51 percent) and character (49 percent). One candidate (Reagan) stressed policy (67 percent), Carter's utterances in 1976 were almost exactly divided between policy and character, and both Ford (57 percent) and Carter (58 percent) emphasized character in 1980.

Policy comments were very common in these advertisements. For instance, in 1976 Ford boasted that "We have ended the war in Vietnam and we have peace. We have turned the economy around, and we have reduced the rate of inflation significantly, by better than 50 percent" ("Economy"). That same year Carter found problems in the status quo:

> I'll tell you what I've seen. Workers with two jobs to make up for the disappearing income. Homes run down, property taxes skyrocketing. Hospitals closing and welfare lines growing. Enormous waste, unbelievable mismanagement of our tax money. And hard work and our savings thrown away by a far-away, unconcerned bureaucracy. ("Bureaucracy")

Reduced income, housing, tax, health care, welfare, and governmental waste are clear policy topics. In 1980, Reagan acclaimed three specific policy goals: "If we make a deep cut in everyone's tax rates, we'll have lower prices, an increase in production, and a lot more peace of mind" ("Peace of Mind"). Carter touted his accomplishments in the area of energy policy in 1980: "The energy laws are now on the books. Four years ago the oil companies dominated the Congress, and now we've changed that and the consumers of oil have an equal voice at least" ("Energy"). These statements are indicative of the kinds of policy acclaims present in these campaigns.

Character utterances were also frequent topics in these campaigns. Ford argued in 1976 that "We have restored integrity and candor and forthrightness in the White House." A Carter spot in his first presidential campaign acclaimed his character:

> In the beginning, Jimmy Carter's campaign was a lonely one. But through the months, more and more people recognized him as a new leader; a man who will change the way this country is run. A competent man, who can make our government open and efficient. But above all, an understanding man, who can make ours a government of the people once again. ("Of the People")

This spot touts his leadership ability (competence) as well as personal qualities (understanding). Four years later a Carter commercial featured attacks by ordinary citizens from California (who presumably knew best) on Reagan's character. Here are several excerpts from this ad:

> MAN: His problem as governor was the same as he has now, mainly that he has always shot from the hip.
>
> MAN: Some of the recent goofs that he's pulled with regard to China.
>
> WOMAN: He's talking too much and he doesn't know what he's saying.
>
> MAN: He talks like nobody else is listening.
>
> WOMAN: The more he opens his mouth up, I think he's putting himself in a real deep hole. ("Talking")

These candid observations do not enhance Reagan's desirability. Thus, character was a recurrent theme in these commercials.

Forms of Policy and Character in Presidential TV Spots 1976–1980

Consistently the most common form of policy comment was past deeds (63 percent overall, and the most common form for each candidate and campaign). Ford in 1976 attacked Carter's record as governor of Georgia: "His ads say that he will do the same as president that he did as governor of Georgia. Then you should know that during his one term as governor, government spending increased by 58 percent. Government employees went up 25 percent. And the state of Georgia went 100 percent deeper into debt" ("Georgia"). Carter touted his accomplishments in foreign affairs: "I hope that when I finish my terms in office, that when the history books are written, that one of the most important things there will be that I helped to bring a comprehensive peace to the Middle East" ("Peace in the Mideast"). Thus, past deeds were the most common form of policy arguments.

These candidates also argued from general goals (23 percent) and future plans (15 percent). For example, in 1976, Ford explained "we can have additional tax cuts, and we can have a balanced budget by 1978" ("Budget"). Reagan offered these future plans for dealing with inflation: "I'll place an immediate freeze on federal hiring, I'll call in the best minds in America to tell us where waste can be cut. I'll eliminate completely any program that serves the bureaucrats and not the needs of the people" ("Cut Waste"). These excerpts illustrate the other forms of policy utterances used by these candidates.

Character utterances were divided almost equally between leadership ability (43 percent) and personal qualities (42 percent). In 1976 a Ford spot combined both of these appeals: "I believe that President Ford is a strong, honest, and decent man." ("Decent"). However, a Carter spot attacked Ford's leadership: "If you agree that it's time we stopped paying for the lack of leadership in our country, do something about it. Vote for Jimmy Carter" ("Leader"). Of course, the idea that the United States had been devoid of leadership while Ford was president is a serious accusation. Ideals also occurred occasionally (15 percent). For example, in 1980, Carter explained that "I would like to . . . enhance the quality of life of people in other nations and promote freedom and human rights and democratic principles as well" ("Human Rights"). Thus, these spots primarily emphasized both personal qualities and leadership ability when they discussed character.

Conclusion: After Watergate

Carter defeated President Ford in 1976 but then lost to Reagan in 1980. One could argue that the economy was largely responsible for both of these outcomes—and it played a major role in these campaigns and in the elections. Voters must be convinced both that the economy is the most important issue and that the economy favored Carter in 1976 and Reagan in 1980. Carter attacked the economy under Ford while acclaiming his record as governor of California. Ironically, Reagan used the same approach in his bid to oust Carter, attacking the economy under Carter and acclaiming his record as governor of California. As we have seen, Carter's commercials in 1976 and Reagan's advertisements in 1980 effectively exploited the opportunities presented by economic conditions in these campaigns.

5

Republicans in Control: 1984, 1988
The End of the Millennium: 1992, 1996

Reagan and Bush were nominated by the Republican Party to run again in 1984. Walter Mondale, who had served as Vice President with Jimmy Carter (and who lost the bid for re-election in 1980), was nominated as the Democratic candidate for president in 1984. The Democrats selected Congresswoman Geraldine Ferraro as the first woman nominee for Vice President from either of the two major parties. After Reagan's second term, Vice President Bush won the Republican nomination and, with Senator Dan Quayle as running mate, Bush defeated Massachusetts governor Michael Dukakis. Bush ran for re-election in 1992 but was upended by Arkansas Governor Bill Clinton and Senator Al Gore.

REPUBLICANS IN CONTROL: 1984, 1988

President Reagan ran on his first term record in the 1984 campaign. One theme played out in several spots was that it was "Morning in America"—Reagan's accomplishments were revitalizing and renewing the economy and restoring hope to the United States:

> It's morning again in America. Today more men and women will go to work than ever before in our country's history. With interest rates and inflation down, more people are buying new homes, and our new families can have confidence in the future. America today is prouder, and stronger, and better. Why would we want to return to where we were less than four short years ago? ("Morning in America")

He also repeatedly associated Mondale with his former running mate, Jimmy Carter, and reminded voters of the woes of 1976. Besides comparing the Reagan record to the Carter record of four years earlier, Reagan also contrasted his approach with that of Mondale:

REAGAN: The American people have a very clear choice this year about their economic future. And it's a very simple choice between our opponents' old policies and our new policies. When you hear their prescription for the economy—higher taxes, bigger government, sure to follow high inflation—it makes you wonder if they remember how things used to be. There's a better life ahead, but only if we look ahead. ("Economic Choice")

Higher taxes, larger government, and inflation are undesirable consequences associated with a Mondale presidency.

This spot from Reagan's re-election campaign discussed the importance of being prepared for potential communist aggression using an interesting metaphor.

There's a bear in the woods. For some people, the bear is easy to see. Others don't see it at all. Some people say the bear is tame. Others say it is vicious and dangerous. Since no one can be sure who is right, isn't it smart to be as strong as the bear? If there is a bear. ("The Bear")

This clever use of metaphor is a very low key use of the communist threat to appeal to voters. Thus, these spots give some idea of Reagan's television advertising in the 1984 election.

Democratic candidate Mondale outlined some of his ideals and goals in this 1984 television spot:

MONDALE: The government of the United States is not up for sale; it belongs to the people of this country and we want it back.

ANNOUNCER: Fritz Mondale, underdog, fighting for what he believes. Tough questions, straight answers. Protecting social security and Medicare. Cleaning up toxic waste. Tax reform, closing loopholes. This is the debate. This is the fight. It must be fought; it will be won. ("Domestic")

Character issues ("straight answers") and policy (social security, Medicare, the environment, taxation) are both used here to acclaim Mondale. Other Mondale spots were much more straightforward attacks on the Republican candidate and on his policies:

In this building [Treasury], Mr. Reagan's people are borrowing the money that's putting each of us $18,000 into debt: deficit spending. And who walks away with the money? 90,000 profitable corporations that pay no taxes [people leaving and getting into limos]. Defense contractors on bloated budgets. Foreign interests who make money on our debt. What the deficit really means is that you're paying for their free ride [limos driving away]. But in November you can stop it: Mondale/Ferraro, they're fighting for your future. ("Limo")

This commercial relates the growing federal deficit directly to tax-payers: Reagan's spending is putting every voter $18,000 into debt. To add insult to injury, others (corporations, defense contractors, foreign interests) are benefitting at our expense.

In 1988, Vice President George Bush was chosen as the Republican nominee. His running mate was Senator Dan Quayle. Michael Dukakis, Governor of Massachusetts, was the Democratic nominee. Senator Lloyd Bentsen was selected to be the Democratic Vice Presidential nominee.

Running on his record succeeded for Reagan in 1984, and Bush took some credit for the Reagan/Bush administration's record when he ran in 1988:

> Over the past six years, 18 million jobs were created. Interest rates were cut in half. Today, inflation is down, taxes are down, and the economy is stronger. So, while some might try to tell you we're on the wrong road, or have gone as far as we can go, I believe that today America is better off than we were eight years ago, and by building on the gains we've made we'll all be better off in four years, than we are today. ("Bush Positive Economy")

He discusses employment, interest rates, and inflation. Bush argues that we are better off now than in 1980 (when Reagan/Bush ascended to the presidency) and that we will be better off in the future if we elect Bush in 1988.

The Bush campaign attacked his Democratic opponent, Michael Dukakis, on several grounds. This spot criticizes his record and policy stands on crime:

> A Crime Quiz: [Crime Quiz, Bush on left, Dukakis on right]. Which candidate for President gave weekend passes to first degree murders who were not even eligible for parole? Michael Dukakis [his picture zooms to fill screen, then zooms back out]. Who vetoed mandatory jail sentences for drug dealers? Michael Dukakis [his picture zooms to fill screen, then zooms back out]. Who opposes capital punishment in all cases and even vetoed the death penalty for cop killers? Michael Dukakis [his picture zooms to fill screen, then zooms back out]. Which candidate for President can you really count on to be tough on crime? George Bush [Bush's photo zooms to fill screen]: Experienced Leadership for America's Future. ("Crime Quiz")

Weekend furloughs, mandatory sentences, capital punishment are all aspects of Dukakis' record on crime.

Dukakis acclaimed his accomplishments as Governor of Massachussets in a series of ads on his leadership:

> Leadership. It's taking charge, taking responsibility. Michael Dukakis balanced ten budgets in a row and still cut taxes five times. Leadership: Its making life better. He increased working people's income at twice the national rate. And pioneered the first universal health care program in the country. And that's why America's governors, both Democrat and Republican, voted Michael Dukakis the most effective governor in the nation. Michael Dukakis for President. Let's take charge of America's future. ("Leadership 1")

This spot, and others like it in his campaign, used his record of accomplishments as Governor to argue that he was an effective leader and would be a good President.

Dukakis also attacked Bush's policies in several areas. This commercial targets his record on education:

> ANNOUNCER: For seven and a half years, George Bush supported cutbacks in American education [BUSH 1981, 1982, 1982, 1983, 1984, 1985, 1986, 1987; the word EDUCATION on blackboard is erased bit by bit]. He sat by while college loans for working families were cut. And now suddenly, George Bush says he'll be the education President. Michael Dukakis won't just give us slogans. He's committed to a new national college loan program to make sure that any American kid can afford to go to college. Michael Dukakis for President: A real commitment to education: the best America is yet to come. ("Education")

This message argues that Bush has not supported education, even though he claims to be the "Education President." This manages to criticize his policy and character.

Dukakis also made several spots that responded to Bush's attacks on Dukakis. This illustrates his response to Bush's "The Harbor" spot:

> George Bush is complaining about Boston Harbor. But Bush's administration cut funds to clean up Boston Harbor. Bush's administration cut funds to clean up California's coast from San Diego Harbor to San Francisco Bay. Bush opposed a crackdown on corporations releasing toxic waste. Bush even favored a veto of the Clean Water Act—not once, but twice. The non-partisan League of Conservation Voters has endorsed Mike Dukakis. So when you hear George Bush talk about the environment, remember what he did to the environment. ("Bush's False Advertising 1")

This spot counter-attacks Bush's environmental record while rebutting his attacks on Dukakis. These examples convey a flavor for the 1988 advertising campaigns.

Functions of Presidential TV Spots 1984–1988

Acclaims were the most common form of utterance, both collectively (64 percent) and individually. For example, Reagan boasted in 1984 that "During the past year, thousands of families have moved into new homes that once seemed out of reach. People are buying new cars they once thought they couldn't afford. Workers are returning to factories that just four years ago were closed. And America is back, with a sense of pride people thought we'd never feel again" ("America Is Back"). That same year a Mondale commercial praised Dukakis's qualifications on national defense: "An Army veteran, a solid leader, Mondale's defense plan calls for real growth in military spending, combat readiness, and active pursuit of a mutual verifiable freeze on nuclear arms. It's a plan for peace that deals from strength" ("Peace Through Strength").

Attacks comprised 36 percent of the utterances. For instance, in 1984, a Reagan spot attacked Mondale based on his record as Carter's Vice President:

Under Carter/Mondale, the price of Connie McCole's groceries went from $272 a month, to almost $400. Under Carter/Mondale, the cost of a mortgage for Warren Bothis increased by nearly $500. And the weakest economy in recent history helped Edward Blair lose his job. Now Mr. Mondale says he wants to help Connie, Warren, and Edward again. If this is help, how much help can they afford to have? ("Afford")

This Mondale advertisement attacked Reagan's deficit spending: "The four budgets Ronald Reagan sent to Congress, his budgets, his signature, his deficits: Five and six billion dollars. He has never submitted a balanced budget to Congress. He has never submitted a budget that came close" ("Never Came Close"). In 1988, a Bush spot showed video of a man (who by the end of the commercial could be identified as Dukakis) riding in a tank:

> Michael Dukakis has opposed virtually every new defense system we developed. He opposed new aircraft carriers. He opposed anti-satellite weapons. He opposed four missile systems, including Pershing II missile deployment. Dukakis opposed the Stealth bomber and a ground emergency warning system against nuclear attack. He even criticized our rescue mission to Grenada and our strike on Libya. And now he wants to be our commander-in-chief. America can't afford that risk. ("Tank Ride")

Dukakis did look rather goofy riding around on the tank in this video footage, and this does not sound like a policy for a strong national defense. Thus, these campaign commercials employed numerous attacks on both the candidates and their policies.

Defense was quite rare, accounting for a mere 0.5 percent of the utterances in these spots. A Dukakis spot in 1988 ("Counterpunch") began with a television displaying the Bush "Tank Ride" spot. Dukakis turned off the television and declared: "I'm fed up with it. Never seen anything like it in twenty-five years of public life. George Bush's negative tv ads. Distorting my record, full of lies, and he knows it. I'm on the record for the very weapons systems his ads say I'm against." Although launching a counter-attack on Bush for this negative and distorted campaign, this statement clearly denies the accusations in the attack. This is a clear illustration of defense in presidential television spots.

Topics of Presidential TV Spots 1984–1988

Policy was the dominant topic in these campaigns, constituting 65 percent of the remarks in these advertisements. For example, in 1984 Reagan attacked his opponents' policies in this commercial: "The American people have a very clear choice this year about their economic future. And it's a very simple choice between our opponents' old policies and our new policies. When you hear their prescription for the economy—higher taxes, bigger government, sure to follow high inflation—it makes you wonder if they remember how things used to be" ("Simple Choice"). This excerpt ends with a thinly-veiled reference to the economy problems under Carter and Mondale. This spot from Mondale mentioned his general policy goals: "Protecting social security and Medicare. Cleaning up toxic waste. Tax reform, closing loopholes. This is the debate. This is the fight. It must be fought; it will be won" ("The Fight"). In 1988, this Bush advertisement touted his accomplishments: "Appointed CIA Chief, revitalized the agency during its toughest time, rebuilt our intelligence capability. Headed regulatory reform, cut government red tape saving billions, and sent new life-saving drugs to the marked place" ("Service"). In this commercial, Dukakis attacked Bush's policies: "This administration has cut and slashed programs for children, for nutrition, for the kinds of things that can help these youngsters live better lives. Has cut federal aid to education, has cut Pell Grants and loans to close the door to college opportunity to youngsters all over this country" ("Slashed"). Thus, these spots frequently discussed the policies of the candidates.

Character was also a common topic for discussion, accounting for 35 percent of the utterances in these campaigns. In 1984, for example, this Reagan spot used ordinary citizens to attack Mondale:

MAN: Well, I think Fritz Mondale is probably a good man, but I don't think he's a good leader.

MAN: I don't believe that he has the quality of leadership.

WOMAN: He lacks charisma and he lacks leadership.

MAN: Walter Mondale is wishy-washy.

WOMAN: I see no strength in Mondale. ("Wishy-Washy")

This commercial attacked Mondale's leadership ability. This spot for the Democratic candidate contrasted the two contenders on leadership: "Presidential leadership should be exerted to gain control of the federal budget. Mr. Mondale, the challenger, is showing leadership. President Reagan is ducking it" ("Ducking"). Thus, character played a role in these campaigns.

Forms of Policy and Character in Presidential TV Spots 1984–1988

Policy comments were dominated by discussion of past deeds (61 percent). This 1984 Reagan spot, for example, focused on Reagan's first term accomplishments:

It's morning again in America. Today more men and women will go to work than ever before in our country's history. With interest rates at about half the record highs of 1980, nearly two thousand families today will buy new homes, more than at any time in the past four years. This afternoon six thousand five hundred young men and women will be married. And with inflation at less than half of what it was just four years ago, they can look forward with confidence to the future. It's morning again in America, and under the leadership of President Reagan, our country is prouder, and stronger, and better. ("Prouder, Stronger, Better")

Although most of this passage concerns Reagan's past deeds, notice that the last sentence included praise of Reagan as a leader. In the same campaign, Mondale asked:

"Who's going to pay for your deficits? In your first term you cut aid to seniors, the unemployed, students, and the disabled. Where are your cuts this time, Mr. Reagan? You gave tax breaks to the rich and to profitable corporations, then signed one of the biggest tax increases in history" ("Pay"). Dukakis managed to attack Reagan's past deeds (giving tax breaks to rich while increasing taxes on the rest of the people) and his lack of a plan to reduce the federal budget deficit. Thus, these campaign commercials frequently focused on policy matters.

Character remarks most commonly concerned leadership ability (50 percent) and personal qualities were the second most frequent form of character utterance (37 percent). For example, in 1984 this Reagan ad praised his leadership ability when a citizen observed: "There's a lot of things need to be done to this country and I think Ronald Reagan's the man to do it" ("Country"). Perhaps he meant "done for" rather than "done to," but this statement acclaims Reagan's ability nevertheless. A spot supporting Mondale also discussed his leadership ability on the nuclear arms freeze issue: "A steady hand. A savvy negotiator, he will direct not delegate the most awesome issue of our time" ("Steady"). To illustrate how personal qualities were used in these campaigns, consider this passage from a Dukakis spot in 1988: "The other side has pursued a campaign of distortion and distraction, of fear and of smear" ("Fear and Smear"). These are hardly the noble qualities one ought to associate with a president. Ideals were the least common form of character utterance in these campaigns (13 percent). For instance, in 1984, this Reagan spot acclaimed his ideals: "It was a dream that built a nation. The freedom to work in the job of your choice, to reap the rewards of your labor, to leave a richer life for your children and their children beyond. Today the dream lives again." Thus, these excerpts illustrate how these campaigns addressed character in their spots.

Conclusion: Republicans in Control

Reagan and Bush had beaten the Carter/Mondale ticket in 1980, and they were able to defeat the Mondale/Ferraro team in 1984. The economy was a recurrent theme in these campaigns. Arguably, the economy favored Reagan over Carter. However, in 1984, unlike 1976 and 1980, the economy seemed to be improving. Reagan clearly (and effectively) exploited the economy in his advertisements. Bush defeated Dukakis in this Republican's first run for the Presidency. He was able to raise questions about Dukakis, especially on the topics of crime, defense, and the environment. Dukakis tried to answer them in his advertising, but it was too little, too late.

THE END OF THE MILLENNIUM: 1992, 1996

George Bush was nominated in 1992 to lead his party to a fourth consecutive term in the White House, with Dan Quayle running as his vice president again (although Pat Buchanan unsuccessfully challenged Bush's re-nomination). Bill Clinton, governor of Arkansas, along with Senator Al Gore, were the challengers in 1992. Millionaire businessman H. Ross Perot created the Reform Party and ran for president as a third-party candidate. His strong showing led the Commission on Presidential Debates to invite him to participate in the 1992 debates.

By the time of the 1992 campaign, Bush had won a great victory in Operation Desert Storm. He worked hard to use this foreign policy and military success into a second term in office. This advertisement exemplifies his approach:

> BUSH: Just two hours ago, allied air forces began an attack on military [nighttime missile video; The Persian Gulf Crisis—1991].
>
> NEWS ANNOUNCER: President Bush said today that he reassured Mr. Yeltsin the US would stand by democracy.
>
> NEWS ANNOUNCER: If revolutionaries and terrorists are armed with nuclear and chemical weapons it may pose new challenges to the president.
>
> ANNOUNCER: In a world where we're just one unknown dictator away from the next major crisis, who do you most trust to be sitting in this chair? ("Persian Gulf Crisis")

This commercial makes explicit the claim that his past record is good evidence about how he will probably respond to future crises. Clinton, as a governor, had little foreign policy experience.

However, Bush also attacked his Democratic opponent repeatedly in this campaign. This spot questioned Clinton's character, arguing that he was inconsistent:

> ANNOUNCER [split screen, two candidates with grey dots over faces]: The presidential candidate on the left stood for military action in the Persian Gulf, while the candidate on the right agreed with those who opposed it. He says [candidate on the left] he wouldn't rule out term limits. While he says [candidate on the right] he's personally opposed to term limits. This candidate [on the left] was called up for military service, while this one [on the right] claims he wasn't. One of these [two candidates again] candidates is Bill Clinton [left dot removed to reveal Clinton]. Unfortunately, so is the other [right dot removed to reveal a second Clinton].
>
> CLINTON: There is a simple explanation for why this happened. ("Grey Dots")

The clip from Clinton at the end adds an additional touch of humor to this condemnation—the simple explanation, of course, is that he has no consistent position. The Bush campaign devoted several commercials to attacking Clinton's record as governor of Arkansas:

> In his twelve years as governor, Bill Clinton has doubled his state's debt, doubled government spending, and signed the largest tax increase in his state's history. Yet his state remains the forty-fifth worst in which to work, the forty-fifth worst for children. It has the worst environmental policy. And the FBI says Arkansas has America's biggest increase in the rate of serious crime. And now Bill Clinton says he wants to do for America what he's done for Arkansas. America can't take that risk. ("Arkansas Record")

This spot's tag-line (and its general premise) echoes one that Bush used successfully in 1988 against Governor Michael Dukakis: "Michael Dukakis says he wants to do for America what he's done for Massachusetts. America can't afford that risk."

Part of Clinton's advertising campaign in his first presidential contest attacked Bush's record, and the Reagan-Bush record as well:

> We've been under trickle-down economics for twelve years. Just keep taxes low on the wealthy and see what happens. Well, I'll tell you what's happened. Most Americans are working harder for less money. Unemployment is up. Health care costs are exploding. We are not doing what it takes to compete and win. I've worked hard on a different plan. Let's give incentives to invest in new jobs. Let's spend more on education and training. Let's provide basic health care to all Americans. Putting our people first, rebuilding this economy. Making us competitive. If we do those things, we'll compete and win. And we'll bring this country back. ("Rebuild America")

This spot then moves smoothly from attacks on Bush into a list of Clinton's proposals for improving America.

Clinton attacked Bush's domestic record in his campaign. He used some of Bush's statements against him in this spot:

ANNOUNCER: 1988:

BUSH: "Thirty million jobs in the next eight years."

ANNOUNCER: 1990: America's jobless rate hits three year high.

BUSH: "I'm not prepared to say we're in recession."

ANNOUNCER: March 1992: Jobless rate hits six year high.

BUSH: "The economy is strengthening."

ANNOUNCER: George Bush vetoes unemployment compensation.

BUSH: "The economy continues to grow."

ANNOUNCER: July 1992: Unemployment rate is the highest in eight years. If George Bush doesn't understand the problem, how can he solve it? We can't afford four more years. ("Curtains")

Not only does this advertisement attack Bush's first-term record, but it also portrays him as out of touch with reality. This spot reminded voters of Bush's famous promise of "No new taxes" during 1988 campaign:

BUSH: "Read my lips."

ANNOUNCER: Remember?

BUSH: "You will be better off four years from now than you are today."

ANNOUNCER: Well, it's four years later. How're ya doin'? ("Remember")

This spot broadens the indictment from his broken promise to the state of the economy, reminding viewers that Bush also promised that they would be better off after his first-term. These advertisements give a general idea of the nature of these advertising campaigns.

In 1996, Bill Clinton and Al Gore were selected by the Democratic Party to seek a second term in the White House. Bob Dole, along with Jack Kemp, were the Republican challengers. Ross Perot represented the Reform Party in both campaigns, but was more of a presence in 1992 than in 1996.

Bob Dole ran hard on his proposed 15 percent tax cut in 1996 and on the character issue as well. This ad acclaims his proposed tax cut and other policy proposals from the Republican candidate:

> The stakes this election? Keeping more of what you earn. That's what Bob Dole's tax cut plan is all about. The Dole plan starts with a 15 percent tax cut for working Americans. That's $1,600 more for the typical family. A $500 per child tax credit. Education and job training incentives. Replacing the IRS with a fairer and simpler tax system. And a Balanced Budget Amendment to stop wasteful spending. The Dole plan. Helping you keep more of what you earn. ("The Stakes")

In addition to a specific child tax credit and passing the Balanced Budget Amendment, Dole outlines a general policy proposal (reforming the IRS) here. The next ad criticized him for tax increases and tried to pin the label of tax and spend liberal onto the Democratic candidate:

> ANNOUNCER: The truth about Clinton on taxes? Remember?
>
> CLINTON: "I will not raise taxes on the middle class."
>
> ANNOUNCER: But he gave the middle class the largest tax increase in history [CNN "Moneyweek," 8/7/96]. Higher taxes on your salary [Clinton's FY '94 budget, OBRA '93]. Gasoline [Clinton's FY'94 budget, OBRA '93]. Social Security [Clinton's FY'94 budget]. Clinton even tried higher taxes on heating your home [Clinton's FY'94 budget]. 255 proposed tax and fee increases in all [255 tax and fee increases [Clinton's FY'94–'97 budgets]. Clinton says . . .
>
> CLINTON: Sept. 23, 1996: "But I don't think that qualifies me as a closet liberal."
>
> ANNOUNCER: Sorry Mr. Clinton. Actions do speak louder than words. The real Bill Clinton: A real spend and tax liberal. ("Sorry—Taxes")

Notice also that this spot begins by promising to reveal "The Truth on Clinton on Taxes," suggesting that Clinton was not being honest about his tax record.

The Dole campaign also used defense. This spot responds to Clinton's accusation that Dole and Gingrich had tried to cut Medicare:

> ANNOUNCER: How many times have you seen this?
>
> CLINTON: "Last year Dole/Gingrich tried to cut Medicare $270 billion" [Red DC over ad "Wrong"].

ANNOUNCER: It's wrong . . . and the AARP, the largest and most respected senior citizen group, agrees. AARP Letter: Both sides have proposals "which would slow the rate of growth." They said we need ". . . an end to the political finger-pointing." They agree with Bob Dole we need a bipartisan agreement to fix Medicare, not false political ads that scare seniors. So next time you see a Clinton ad, don't let him fool you. ("Fool")

This controversy centered around the question of whether reducing project growth (of Medicare) is a cut or not (although neither side made this point clear). Clearly, in this spot, Clinton is trying to misrepresent Dole's proposal. These spots give an indication of the 1996 Dole general election campaign.

In 1996, Clinton relied on domestic successes (as well as a number of relatively small policy initiatives, like college tax credits) in his second campaign. For example, this spot (Although incredibly concise), touts Clinton's first-term accomplishments: "Ten million new jobs. Family income up one thousand six hundred dollars. Signed welfare reform—requiring work, time limits. Taxes cut for fifteen million families. Balancing the budget. America's moving forward with an economic plan that works" ("Accomplishments"). Several of Clinton's spots used footage from Senator Dole. This one uses Dole's own words and deeds to indict his views on Medicare and on education:

DOLE: "I will be the president who preserves and strengthens and protects Medicare. I was there, fighting the fight, voting against Medicare, one of twelve, because we knew it wouldn't work."

ANNOUNCER: Last year, Dole/Gingrich tried to cut Medicare $270 billion.

DOLE: "Give children a chance in life, give them an education. We're going to eliminate the Department of Education. We don't need it in the first place. I didn't vote for it in 1979."

ANNOUNCER: Dole tried to slash college scholarships.

DOLE: "Voting against Medicare."

ANNOUNCER: Wrong in the past.

DOLE: "We're going to eliminate the Department of Education."

ANNOUNCER: Wrong for our future. ("Preserve")

Notice also the attempt to use guilt by association. Several of Clinton's spots referred to "Dole/Gingrich" as if they were a single entity (Gingrich's approval ratings were low at the time).

Functions of Presidential TV Spots 1992–1996

In these campaigns, acclaims and attacks occurred at roughly the same level. However, the two Republicans, Bush and Dole, attacked more than they acclaimed. For example, in 1992 Bush attacked Clinton's character with these ordinary citizens:

MAN: Bill Clinton's not telling anything honestly to the American people.

WOMAN: I don't think he tells the truth. I think he evades a lot of questions.

WOMAN: I don't think he's honorable. I don't think he's trustworthy.

MAN: One minute he said he didn't, the next he said he did. ("Evades")

Clearly we want a president who is truthful and trustworthy, or his campaign promises are worthless. In that same campaign Clinton attacked Bush's character in this commercial:

[Irangate, Arms for hostages, the Savings and Loan Bailout, Willie Horton, the Education president, the Environmental president, "I'll do what I have to to be re-elected," "You'll be better off in four years," "It is not a recession," "Read my lips" Four more years?].

Announcer: George Bush is right: It is a question of character. ("Character")

This spot reminded voters of ten episodes or statements that shed an unfavorable light on the Republican candidate, and attempted to turn Bush's assault on Clinton's character back onto Bush. In 1996, Dole attacked Clinton on the issue of the increase in teenage drug abuse in this advertisement:

The stakes of this election? Our children. Under Clinton, cocaine and heroin use among teenagers has doubled. Why? Because Bill Clinton isn't protecting our children from drugs. He cut the drug czar's office 83 percent, cut 227 Drug Enforcement agents, and cut $200 million to stop drugs at our borders. Clinton's liberal drug policies have failed. Our children deserve better. ("The Stakes")

During the same campaign Clinton attacked Dole's (and Gingrich's) recent actions in Congress: "Newt Gingrich. Bob Dole. Dole-Gingrich. Against Family Leave. Against a woman's right to choose. Dole. Gingrich. Cutting Vaccines for Children. Against Brady Bill and assault weapons ban. Against higher minimum wage. Cutting college scholarships" ("Against"). Thus, attacks were common components of these advertising campaigns.

Acclaims were also quite common in the 1990s. In his first presidential campaign, Clinton acclaimed his policy successes as governor of Arkansas. "Twelve years battling the odds in one of our nation's poorest states. Arkansas now leads the nation in job growth. Incomes are rising at twice the national rate. Seventeen thousand people moved from welfare to work. That's progress, and that's what we need now" ("Progress"). This advertisement discusses accomplishments on jobs, income, and welfare. Bush acclaimed his foreign policy accomplishments: "Today, for the first time in half a century, America is not at war" ("Century"). In 1996, Dole explained his vision for America:

Before you vote, I want you to know the America I see. I see an America with a government that works for us, not the other way around. Where parents can choose safe schools for their kids. Where the family is strengthened and honored, not battered, by the government. Where we wage a real war on drugs and our leaders set the right example. An America where you keep more of what you earn, because it's your money. If you agree with this America, I'd really appreciate your vote. ("Your Money")

These ideals and goals are given as reasons to vote for Dole.

Defenses were uncommon, accounting for 1 percent of these utterances. Bush used no defense in his advertising. Responding to accusations about his lax drug policies, this Clinton spot rejected Dole's attack:

Dole's attack ad—wrong again. President Clinton expanded the death penalty for drug kingpins. Nearly forty percent more border agents to stop drugs. Record number of drug felons in federal prisons. President Clinton expanded school anti-drug programs. Dole and Gingrich tried to cut them. Voted against 100,000 police. Bob Dole even voted against creating the drug czar. President Clinton appointed a four-star general drug czar—and is leading the fight to protect our children. ("Wrong")

In denying Dole's charges, Clinton recounts (acclaims) his actions in his first-term in office on drug abuse.

Topics of Presidential TV Spots 1992–1996

These spots focused more on policy (70 percent) than on character (30 percent). The only exception was Bush, who devoted 62 percent of his television spot utterances in 1992 to character. In this spot from 1992, Bush discusses Clinton's tax policy:

Bill Clinton says he'll only tax the rich to pay for his campaign promises. But here's what Clinton economics could mean to you: $1,088 more in taxes [John Cannes, steam fitter], $2,072 more in taxes [Lori Huntoon scientist]. One hundred leading economists say his plan means higher taxes and bigger deficits. $2,072 more in taxes [Wyman Winston, Housing Lender, $2072 more in taxes]. ("Steamfitter")

This argument uses concrete examples as well as experts (economists) to support the criticism of Clinton's proposals. In 1992, Clinton acclaimed his plan for reducing the nation's welfare rolls:

I have a plan to end welfare as we know it, to break the cycle of welfare dependency. We'll provide education, job training, and child care, but then those who are able must go to work—either in the private sector or in public service. I know it can work: In my state we've moved 17,000 people from welfare rolls to payrolls. It's time to make welfare what it should be: a second chance, not a way of life. ("Welfare to Work")

Note that Clinton also draws on his accomplishments as governor to reinforce this proposal. In 1996, Dole contrasted his approach to government with Clinton's: "Which plan puts more money in the pockets of seniors? Under Bill Clinton's plan, our huge federal government will grow another 20 percent, costing us plenty. The Dole plan: our government still grows, but only 14 percent to protect Medicare and Social Security. See, that's how the Dole plan will cut your taxes 15 percent and repeal Bill Clinton's big tax on Social Security. The Dole plan: more money in the pockets of seniors" ("Plan"). Thus, Dole argues that his proposals will increase the disposable income of senior citizens, compared with Clinton. Thus, all of these candidates addressed policy issues in their television spots.

The topic of character was also addressed in these campaigns. Clinton acclaimed his character when he explained in 1992 that after he met President Kennedy in 1963, "That's when I decided that I could really do public service 'cause I cared so much about people" ("Cares"). In 1996, this Clinton spot managed to attack the Republicans for their criticism of the president while acclaiming Clinton's character: "I hear people question the president's character and integrity. It's just politics. When it came to protecting children, the president had the courage to make a difference" ("Courage"). Thus, candidates in these campaigns discussed character as well as policy.

Forms of Policy and Character in Presidential TV Spots 1992–1996

These candidates relied heavily on past deeds (56 percent) when discussion policy (Bush, who discussed past deeds in only 21 percent of his ad remarks, is the exception). For example, in 1992 this spot for Bush charged that "Arkansas is at the bottom of the list. Why does he keep bragging about Arkansas?" ("Bottom"). Clinton, of course, had a different view of his record in Arkansas:

> For twelve years he's battled the odds in one of America's poorest states and made steady progress. Arkansas is now first in the nation in job growth. Even Bush's Secretary of Labor just called job growth in Arkansas enormous. He moved 17,000 people from welfare to work. And he's kept taxes low: Arkansas has the second lowest tax burden in the country. ("Battled")

Keying into Clinton's pledge to end welfare "as we know it," this Dole spot attacked Clinton's record here: "But he vetoed welfare reform not once, but twice. He vetoed work requirements for the able-bodied. He vetoed putting time limits on welfare. And Clinton still supports giving welfare benefits to illegal immigrants. The Clinton rhetoric hasn't matched the Clinton record" ("Rhetoric"). This message faults Clinton's record on four aspects of welfare reform. Thus, these spots frequently discussed past deeds when they addressed policy matters.

Future plans (24 percent) and general goals (20 percent) occurred at roughly the same rate. In 1992, Bush touted his Agenda for American Renewal. One component was his plan for job training: "It provides job training, so workers have the new skills to compete" ("Compete"). Clinton attacked Bush's tax cut proposal: "Now George Bush wants to give a $108,000 tax break to millionaires. $108,000. Guess who's going to pay?" ("Guess"). These utterances illustrate acclaims and attacks on future plans.

The candidates also discussed general goals. In 1996, Dole attacked Clinton for his (failed) health care reform initiative, characterizing his goal as "Government run health care." Clinton acclaimed his goals in 1996: "This country's future [Balance the budget for a growing economy] will be even brighter than its brilliant past" ("Brighter"). Thus, these spots addressed goals as well as specific plans for the future.

All candidates chose to stress personal qualities (77 percent) when discussing character. A Bush commercial in 1992 attacked Clinton's honesty: "He said he was never drafted. Then he admitted he was drafted. Then he said he forgot being drafted. He said he was never deferred from the draft. Then, he said he was. He said he never received special treatment. But he did receive special treatment. The question then was avoiding the draft. Now for Bill Clinton, it's a question of avoiding the truth" ("Question"). The question of Clinton and the draft is used to attack his personal qualities (honesty). However, integrity was an issue for the Democrats as well as the Republicans. In 1992, this advertisement for Clinton impugned Bush's trustworthiness:

> George Bush. The *Observer* says new information about Mr. Bush's role in the Iran arms for hostages deal and the breaking of his read my lips no tax pledge raise doubts about his trustworthiness. The *Current* says he has been shifty on key issues. The *Oregonian*, We refocused on Bush's flip flops on abortion and taxes, his secret arming of the brutal Iraqi regime: Frankly, we no longer trust him. The *Philadelphia Daily News*: Bush is without a principle or a clue. It does come down to who you trust. That's why it comes down to Bill Clinton for president. ("Trust")

In the 1996 campaign, this Dole ad (featuring Elizabeth Dole in part) spoke of his recovery from his war injury to acclaim Dole's personal qualities: "He persevered. He never gave up. He fought his way back from total paralysis" ("Elizabeth"). A citizen spoke of Clinton action on crime legislation, functioning both to defend his character and to acclaim his courage: "President Clinton forced Congress to pass his tough crime bill—life in prison for dangerous repeat offenders, an expanded death penalty. I hear people question the president's character and integrity. It's just politics. When it came to protecting children—the president had the courage to make a difference" ("Courage"). These passages illustrate how these campaigns used personal qualities as a topic for character appeals.

Ideals was the second most common topic (16 percent) and leadership was relatively uncommon (6 percent). In 1996, this spot (broadcast in Spanish) praised Clinton's ideals: "Clinton wants us to be prepared for the future. . . . He wants us to have more opportunities, to improve our quality of life" ("Opportunties"). In this spot from 1992, Clinton questions Bush's leadership ability:

> ANNOUNCER: George Bush says you can trust him in a crisis. But we're in a crisis, an economic crisis, and we haven't been able to trust George Bush.
>
> BUSH: "It is not recession. It does not fit the definition of recession."

ANNOUNCER: George Bush has ignored the facts, blamed others, failed to take action.

BUSH: "Far better than doing something bad to this economy is doing nothing at all."

ANNOUNCER: If George Bush can't be trusted to use the powers of the Presidency to get our economy moving, it's time for a president who will. ("Trust")

Ignoring the facts, blaming others, and failing to take needed actions are not the hallmarks of a skilled leader. Thus, these commercials used several forms of character and policy utterances.

Conclusion: The End of the Millennium

Clinton won the election of 1992 and was re-elected in 1996. Although Kennedy won in 1960 and Johnson in 1964, the 1990s saw the first time a Democrat had won two terms in the White House in recent memory (Republicans had done so in 1952 and 1956, 1968, and 1972, and 1980 and 1984). The economy surely played a role in both of his victories (an economy that was perceived by many to be doing poorly in 1992 undermined Bush's incumbency; an economy that most people thought was doing well bolstered Clinton's incumbency in 1996). However, Clinton's advertisements effectively exploited both situations by attacking Bush's record in 1992, when Clinton was the challenger, and by acclaiming Clinton's first-term accomplishments in 1996, when he was the incumbent. Bush was not able to persuasively defend (or acclaim) his domestic record, and Dole was not able to adequately attack Clinton's first-term record or character in 1996.

6

George W. Bush in the Oval Office: 2000, 2004
Barack Obama, African-American President: 2008, 2012

In the year 2000, Bill Clinton was completing his second term as president and accordingly was not eligible to run for re-election. His vice president, Al Gore, was nominated as the Democratic Party attempted to retain control of the White House. Joe Lieberman (Senator from Connecticut) was Gore's running mate. Texas governor George W. Bush (son of our forty-first president, George H. W. Bush) emerged as the Republican Party's nominee. Dick Cheney, who had served as a member of the House of Representatives and as Secretary of State, was chosen as Bush's running mate. Governor Bush won the electoral college after the results of voting in Florida were contested; the Supreme Court eventually halted vote-counting. Ultimately, it was determined that Gore won the popular vote (Miller Center, 2013) but, because of his electoral college victory, Bush became president.

Bush and Cheney ran for re-election in 2004, challenged by Senators John Kerry (Massachusetts) and John Edwards (North Carolina), running as presidential and vice presidential candidates, respectively. The war in Iraq was an extremely hot topic in the election, which Bush won.

In 2008, George W. Bush was term-limited and Vice President Dick Cheney decided not to run for president. This set up the first election since 1952 in which neither the sitting president nor the vice president contended for the Oval Office. John McCain secured the Republican nomination and selected Governor Sarah Palin as his running mate (this is only the second time a woman had been nominated as vice president, and the first time in the Republican Party). Barack Obama won the Democratic nomination and chose Senator Joe Biden to be the vice presidential nominee. Obama won; he faced Mitt Romney and Paul Ryan in 2012, when Obama won again.

GEORGE W. BUSH IN THE OVAL OFFICE: 2000, 2004

As in 2000, the advertising campaign was limited to a short list of battleground states (and some buys on national cable): In 2004 "Hundreds of ads—from an astounding fifty separate sponsors on the Democratic side and another 19 on the Republican side—have aired 675,000 times on cable and in top markets" (Anderson, 2004, p. 19). The spending was astronomical, $580 million from all these sources, almost three times as much as the $200 million spent in the 2000 presidential campaign (Anderson, 2004). The general advertising campaign in 2004 began earlier than ever. President Bush broadcast his first general campaign ad on March 4, 2004, after it became clear that Senator John Kerry would be the Democratic nominee. Kerry responded about a week later. Never before had both presumptive nominees started their general ad campaigns in early March. The phenomenon of "shadowing" emerged in 2004, in which ads attacking a candidate were produced quickly and aired locally during that candidate's visit to a state or city. Furthermore, advances in computer video editing and satellite delivery of ads facilitated the advertising bombardment. On the morning of September 22 the Bush campaign unveiled an ad attacking John Kerry ("Windsurfing"). Within several hours the Kerry campaign had created and started running a spot in response ("Juvenile").

In the 2000 presidential campaign, Governor Bush linked candidate Gore with second-term president Bill Clinton:

> ANNCR: Is the status quo in America's schools good enough? Under Al Gore and Bill Clinton, national reading scores stagnated. America's high school students place almost dead last in international math tests. The achievement gap between poor and non-poor students remains wide. Gore and Clinton had eight years, but they've failed. As President, George W. Bush will challenge the status quo with a crusade to improve education. He'll fight for reforms hailed as the most fundamental in a generation: demand high standards and accountability for students and teachers, restore local control of schools, increase funding but change the system so successful schools are rewarded and failing ones must improve. He'll turn Head Start into a reading program and close the achievement gap that hurts those on the edges of poverty. His goal? Teach every child to read because there are no second rate children, no second rate dreams. Governor George W. Bush: A Fresh Start for Education. ("Challenge the SQ")

This spot on education began with criticism of the Clinton-Gore record and then moved to Bush's ideas on education. Another Bush ad talked about Social Security and Medicare:

> BUSH: We will strengthen Social Security and Medicare for the greatest generation and for generations to come. I believe great decisions are made with care, made with conviction. We will make prescription drugs available and affordable for every senior who needs them. You earned your benefits. You made your plans. And president George W. Bush will keep the promise of Social Security. No changes. No reductions. No way. ("No Changes, No Reductions")

This commercial acclaims his policy proposals. Bush also talked about character in his ads. In "Trust," he explained

> I believe we need to encourage personal responsibility so people are accountable for their actions. And I believe in government that is responsible to the people. That's the difference in philosophy between my opponent and me. He trusts government. I trust you. I trust you to invest some of your own Social Security money for higher returns. I trust local people to run their own schools. In return for federal money, I will insist on performance. And if schools continue to fail, we'll give parents different options. I trust you with some of the budget surplus. I believe one fourth of the surplus should go back to the people who pay the bills. My opponent proposes targeted tax cuts only for those he calls the right people. And that means half of all income tax payers get nothing at all. We should help people live their lives but not run them. Because when we trust individuals, when we respect local control of schools, when we empower communities, together we can ignite America's spirit and renew our purpose.

Bush attacked Gore's character in "Nonsense."

> ANNCR: Remember when Al Gore said his mother-in-law's prescription cost more than his dog's [headline: Aides Concede Gore Made Up Story]? His own aides said the story was made up. Now Al Gore is bending the truth again. The press calls Gore's Social Security attacks "nonsense" [*Wall Street Journal*, 10/24/00, nonsense]. Governor Bush sets aside $2.4 trillion to strengthen Social Security and pay all benefits.

> GORE [video from debate]: There has never been a time in this campaign when I have said something that I know to be untrue. There's never been a time when I've said something untrue.

> ANNCR: Really?

This ad used evidence from a newspaper to support this attack on Gore. Initially the Democrat's character was criticized (for making up a story about his mother-in-law's prescription) but then the ad rejected an attack on Bush's Social Security policy.

Vice President Gore used a biographical ad early in the general election:

> ANNCR: 1969. America in turmoil. Al Gore graduates college. His father, a U.S. senator, opposes the Vietnam War. Al Gore has his doubts but enlists in the Army. When he comes home from Vietnam, the last thing he thinks he'll ever do is enter politics. He starts a family with Tipper, becomes an investigative reporter. Then Al Gore decided that to change what was wrong in America, he had to fight for what was right. He ran for Congress, held some of the first hearings on cleaning up toxic waste, made the environment his cause, broke with his own party to support the Gulf War, fought to reform welfare with work requirements and time limits. His fight now is to ensure that prosperity enriches all our families—not just the few, strengthen Social Security, take on big drug companies to guarantee prescription drugs for seniors, hold schools accountable for results, tax cuts for working families and the middle class. Al Gore—married thirty years, father of four, fighting for us. ("1969")

This spot slid into a discussion of policy before it ended, talking about the environment, the War in the Gulf, families, school, and taxes.

This television spot from Gore criticizes Bush's tax cut proposal and then acclaims
Gore on the national debt, Social Security, Medicare, and college tuition.

> ANNCR: The facts on George W. Bush's $1.6 trillion tax cut promise: Almost half goes
> to the richest 1 percent. What trickles down? An average of 62 cents a day for most tax-
> payers. Bush gives almost half to the richest 1 percent, leaving 62 cents to trickle down
> to us. [*Wall Street Journal*, 10/5/00; Citizens for Tax Justice, 8/00]
>
> Al Gore builds on a foundation of fiscal discipline. Pay down the nation's debt. Pro-
> tect Social Security and Medicare. A $10,000 a year tax deduction for college tuition.
> Because the middle class has earned more than trickle down. ("Down")

Gore offered both defenses against attacks from Bush on prescription drugs and then
attacks his Republican opponent:

> ANNCR: Newspapers say George Bush's prescription drug ad misrepresents the facts.
> [*Washington Post* 9/15/00]
>
> In fact, Al Gore's plan covers all seniors through Medicare, not an HMO. Under
> Gore, seniors choose their own doctor, and doctors decide what drugs to prescribe.
> George Bush forces seniors to go to HMOs and insurance companies for prescription
> drugs. They have no choice. [*Boston Globe*, 9/13/00, *Time* 9/18/00]
>
> And Bush leaves millions of middle-class seniors with no coverage. [*The Economist*,
> 9/9/00]
>
> Al Gore—the only prescription plan that gives all seniors coverage and choice.
> ("Cover")

This spot also uses newspapers and journals for evidence to support these arguments.
    Bush in 2004 touted his optimism and economic record and then questioned
Kerry's attitude:

> BUSH: I'm optimistic about America because I believe in the people of America.
>
> ANNCR: After recession, 9-11 and war, now our economy has been growing for ten
> straight months. The largest tax relief in history. 1.4 million jobs added since August. In-
> flation, interest and mortgage rates low. Record homeownership. John Kerry's response?
> He's talking about the Great Depression. [America's job recovery is the worst since the
> Great Depression . . . John Kerry for President Press Release 05/07/04] One thing's sure
> . . . pessimism never created a job. ("Pessimism")

The President also acclaimed his record on education and then questioned his opponent's consistency:

> ANNCR: Better education is about accountability. For years, low standards and poor
> accountability plagued our schools. Then President Bush signed the most sweeping
> education reforms in thirty-five years. John Kerry praised the president's reforms. Even
> voted for them. But now, under pressure from education unions, Kerry has changed his

mind. Kerry's new plan: less accountability to parents. John Kerry: Playing politics with education. ("Better Education")

The president also questioned his opponent's priorities:

ANNCR: When it comes to issues that affect our families, are John Kerry's priorities the same as yours? Kerry voted against parental notification for teenage abortions. [S. 323, CQ Vote #131, 7/16/91, Kerry Voted Nay] Kerry even voted to allow schools to hand out the morning-after pill without parents' knowledge. [H.R. 4577, CQ Vote #169: 6/30/00, Kerry Voted Yea] He voted to take control away from parents by taking away their right to know. John Kerry has his priorities. The question is, are they yours? ("Priorities")

Senator Kerry stuck his foot in his mouth when he said he voted for $87 billion to support the war before he voted against it. The Bush campaign used Kerry's own words to attack the Democrat:

KERRY: It was the right decision to disarm Saddam Hussein, and when the president made the decision I supported him. I don't believe the president took us to war as he should have. The winning of the war was brilliant. It's the wrong war, in the wrong place, at the wrong time. I have always said we may yet even find weapons of mass destruction. I actually did vote for the $87 billion before I voted against it. [How can John Kerry protect us . . . when he doesn't even know where he stands?] ("Stand")

The Bush re-election campaign discussed policy as well as character.

The Democratic candidate talked about his policy in his television spots:

KERRY: I'm John Kerry, and I approved this message. I've proposed a new economic plan for America. It begins by putting an end to tax incentives that are encouraging American companies to ship jobs overseas. It invests in new technologies like alternative fuel sources that'll be a job engine in the future. And it focuses on educating our children. [Protect American Jobs; Invest In New Technologies; Invest In Education] You can read the whole plan yourself at JohnKerry.com. Jobs aren't just statistics. They're the lifeline for America's families. ("Lifeline")

The economy, energy, and education are all discussed in this ad. In "Workers" Kerry attacked the incumbent administration on jobs:

KERRY: I've met workers who have been out of work for two years. I've met steelworkers and mineworkers and autoworkers who are now laid-off workers. And some of them have told me what it's like to have to unbolt their own equipment, pack it up, put it in a crate and send it to another country. Some have even told me what it's like to train their own replacement. That's wrong, and when I am president, we're going to change that.

Kerry's campaign ads also discussed character. This ad acclaimed his character:

Born in an Army hospital in Colorado. A husband and father. A hunter. Hockey player. Tough prosecutor. Advocate for kids. A man of faith. A combat veteran who earned three Purple Hearts, risking his life to save others. Praised by former chairmen of the Joint Chiefs of Staff under Presidents Reagan and Clinton. Stronger at home. Respected in the world. John Kerry for President. ("Born in Colorado")

Kerry's running mate also praised the Democratic challenger:

EDWARDS: Here's some things about John Kerry you may not know: He volunteered for Vietnam, earned three purple hearts and risked his own life to save others. A family man, a person of strong faith. Our agenda is your agenda: jobs, health care, a safer America, the things that matter in people's lives. Strength of character, toughness, good values—the John Kerry I know will fight for you.

These ads illustrate the commercials deployed in this campaign.

Functions of Presidential Television Spots 2000–2004

These television spots featured numerous acclaims; only Bush in 2004 had more attacks than acclaims in his spots. For example, the spot "Bean Counter" by Gore in 2000 said that "we need a patients' bill of rights to take the medical decisions away from the HMOs and insurance companies and give them back to the doctors and nurses." This utterance acclaimed the candidate's future plan to improve the treatment of patients by giving them the right to control their medical care. This idea would surely appeal to many voters. Similarly, Bush declared in 2000 that "We will strengthen Social Security and Medicare for the greatest generation and for generations to come" ("No Changes, No Reductions"). This is a goal that many voters would embrace. These excerpts show how acclaims were used in these campaign messages.

However, these advertisements also frequently attacked the opposition (41 percent). For example, the Democrats argued that during the 2000 election "In Texas he [Bush] appointed a chemical company lobbyist to enforce environmental laws. He made key air pollution rules voluntary—even for plants near schools. Schools now use smog meters to see if it's safe to play outside. Texas now ranks last among all states in air quality" ("Smog"). The argument here is that his record in Texas has serious environmental problems. Bush's record on the environment is clearly a policy topic. Similarly, the Republicans ran an ad in 2000 which claimed that "America's having a recession—an education recession that's hurting our children. Out students rank last in the world in math and physics and most fourth graders in our cities can't read. The Clinton–Gore education recession: It's failing our kids" ("Education Recession"). The current administration (of which Gore is a part) was blamed for problems in our educational system, so voters should not continue the Clinton–Gore policies by electing Gore to be the next President. Thus, attacks were common in these television spots.

Defense was quite rare in these commercials (1 percent). The Democrats, for example, had charged that Bush threatened Social Security, promising the same money to young workers and retirees. However, in this Republican spot ("Solvent") we are told that Gore's "attacks on George Bush's Social Security plan" are "exaggerations.

The truth: Nonpartisan analysis confirms George Bush's plan sets aside $2.4 trillion to strengthen Social Security." This advertisement functions to deny the Democratic attacks on Bush's Social Security proposal. Defense was used in the general television spots of 2000, but it was uncommon.

Topics of Presidential Television Spots 2000–2004

These presidential spots from the focused more on policy than on character: All four candidates stressed policy more than character. For instance, Bush's 2000 ad "Expect More" talked about education: "We need to raise standards in our schools. We need more accountability and more discipline." These reforms clearly address policy. Gore ("Ball") employed a retired Social Security Commissioner to critique Bush's Social Security plan during the 2000 campaign:

> I've looked at Governor Bush's plan. He takes one trillion dollars out of Social Security for savings accounts. But Social Security is counting on that money to pay benefits. His plan simply doesn't add up and would undermine Social Security.

A discussion of Social Security reforms concerns policy rather than character. Thus, these passages show how the candidates discussed policy in their general television spots.

Character themes were also found in these messages (39 percent). Republican ads routinely questioned Gore's credibility. For example, two Republican ads ("Newspapers," "Solvent") in 2000 began by asking, "Why does Al Gore say one thing when the truth is another?" Clearly this question was intended to impugn his honesty. This Democratic ad ("Penny") from 2000 discusses Bush's Social Security proposal. However, it begins and ends by questioning his character:

> George W. Bush is back in New Hampshire. Will he come clean on Social Security? In this year's election John McCain said Bush's plan has not one penny for Social Security. Now Bush is promising young workers one trillion dollars from Social Security for them to invest. Yet the same money is needed to pay current benefits. If Bush gives it away, it could cut benefits for Seniors. Think about it. Bush is promising younger workers and Seniors the same money. That's anything but straight talk.

First, it was alleged that Bush needs to "come clean." Then, the ad used John McCain and his slogan ("The Straight Talk Express") to attack fellow-Republican Bush (this ad includes both with policy and character themes). These excerpts illustrate how these spots discussed character. The second spot also shows how a campaign message can slide from policy (Social Security) to character (honesty).

Forms of Policy and of Character in Presidential Television Spots 2000–2004

Overall, the policy remarks tended to distributed among the three forms of policy in roughly equal amounts in these two campaigns: past deeds 39 percent, future plans 26 percent, and general goals 35 percent. For instance, in the 2000 Bush ad, "Challenge the Status Quo," voters were asked:

> Is the status quo in America's schools good enough? Under Al Gore and Bill Clinton, national reading scores stagnated. America's high school students place almost dead last in international math tests. The achievement gap between poor and non-poor students remains wide. Gore and Clinton had eight years, but they've failed.

This ad addresses Gore's failures in education over the eight years he was vice president (past deeds). Gore also focused on the record for the last eight years in this spot from 2000: "You know, for the last eight years, we've had the strongest economy in all of American history" ("Prosperity"). Past deeds, or record in office, were used in these commercials.

Some policy remarks had to do with campaign promises in the form of future plans. For example, a Democratic ad ("Promise") in 2000 attacked Bush for his proposed legislation on Social Security:

> He's promising to take a trillion dollars out of Social Security so younger workers can invest in private accounts. Sounds good. The problem is: Bush has promised the same money to pay seniors their current benefits. The Wall Street Journal shows he can't keep both promises. Which promise is he going to break? George W. Bush: his promises threaten Social Security.

This spot claimed that Bush's proposal, to let younger workers to invest part of their Social Security funds in the stock market, would put Social Security at risk. This excerpt from a Republican commercial addressed Bush's tax cut proposal during the 2000 election: "Under Bush, every taxpayer gets a tax cut and no family pays more than a third of income to Washington." Thus, when candidates discuss policy, one option is to talk about their policy proposals or future plans (means to achieve policy ends).

The third option when discussing policy is to discuss ends rather than means, or general goals. For instance, Gore talked about health care in this advertisement from 2000 ("Prosperity II"): "In a time when our health is everything, we've got to have more access to affordable health care." No reference was made to a particular proposal for achieving this goal, so this illustrates a general goal. Similarly, in the 2000 Republican ad "Save Michigan Jobs," Lee Iacocca argued that "Al Gore's extreme ideas about cars could cost a lot of Michigan families their jobs. Mr. Gore writes: 'We need to raise gas taxes, and the gasoline engine is a threat to our future and we should scrap it.'" This concerned Gore's general goal of eliminating gasoline powered cars. Thus, candidates dispute over policy ends as well as means in their political TV spots.

When these spots from the 2000 and 2004 general campaigns discussed character, they focused much more heavily on personal qualities (63 percent) than on leadership ability (17 percent) or ideals (20 percent). The Republican ad "Agenda" from 2000 complained that Gore had allowed zinc mining on his land. However, the conclusion drawn was one of character: "Even on the environment, Al Gore says one thing but does another." This utterance clearly questions Gore's integrity. In this spot from Gore, he told voters something about his character: "And I believe the next president has to have a passion in his heart to fight for the people who most need a champion" ("Keep the Faith"). Thus, these ads discussed the candidates' personal qualities.

A second form of character utterance discussed a candidate's leadership ability or experience in office. Phyllis Hunter explained in a Bush spot from 2000 that "we have George leading the way. People ask me why have I followed him so intently in education and reading. I followed him because he's been a leader" ("Hunter"). A TV spot for Gore in the same campaign began with policy, arguing that Governor Bush gave a tax break to "Big Oil," opposed health care for children, failed to raise the minimum wage, allowed polluters to regulate themselves, and is now promising the same trillion dollars to younger workers and retirees. The spot concluded by asking, "Is he ready to lead America?" ("Ready to Lead"). The implication, of course, was that Bush was not ready to lead our country. These excerpts illustrate how leadership ability was used in these ads.

The third form of character utterance, "ideals," discusses the values or principles held by the candidates. The Democratic commercial "Protect" discussed the need for protection for crime victims. It articulated the principle that "The people who are hurt by crime need to be heard." Bush's ad explained his philosophy of educational control: "I trust local people to run their own schools" ("Trust"). These passages show how ideals were used in these television spots from 2000 and 2004.

Conclusion: 2000–2004

Despite concerns over the outcome of the election generally, and the results in Florida specifically, Republicans George W. Bush and Dick Cheney were declared the winners in 2000, defeating Democrats Al Gore and Joe Lieberman. This was the first presidential election since 1952 which did not include a sitting president or vice president. Bush and Cheney won re-election in 2004, defeating John Kerry and John Edward, their Democratic challengers. Overall, these campaigns used acclaims more than attacks (only Bush in 2004 used more attacks than acclaims). These campaigns also stressed policy more than character.

BARAK OBAMA, AFRICAN-AMERICAN PRESIDENT: 2008, 2012

In 2008, candidates for the American presidency raised over one billion (Center for Responsive Politics, 2009). Senator Barack Obama Spent over $235 million on television advertising; Senator John McCain spent over $125 million (*New York Times*, 2008), a new record for presidential candidate advertising spending (Obama was the first candidate to every decline federal campaign funds for the general election, so he could spend more than the $84 million limit). Television spots have been an important element of presidential campaigns since 1952 and both candidates employed them extensively in 2012. Wilson (2012) reported that over a billion dollars was spent in the general election campaign by Obama, Romney, and outside groups. This is almost a half a billion dollars more than was spent on this race just four years earlier.

President Bush's popularity was low in 2008. This ad sponsored by Obama used guilt by association to attack McCain:

ANNCR: Barack Obama: endorsed by Warren Buffett and Colin Powell. And John McCain's latest endorsement?

CHENEY: I'm delighted to support John McCain and I'm pleased that he's chosen a running mate with executive talent, toughness and common sense, our next vice president, Sarah Palin.

ANNCR: And boy, did McCain earn it. He voted with Bush and Cheney 90 percent of the time. ("Delighted")

The attempt to link McCain with Bush continued in "Rearview Mirror":

ANNCR: Wonder where John McCain would take the economy? Look behind you. John McCain wants to continue George Bush's economic policies. As president, he'd provide no tax breaks to 101 million Americans but keep tax breaks for companies that ship our jobs overseas [IRS Statistics of Income; Vote #63, 3/17/05; Vote #83, 5/5/04]. He wants $4 billion in new tax breaks for Big Oil. And would tax your health care benefits for the first time ever [*Center For American Progress Action Fund*, 3/27/08; *ABC News*, 9/28/08; *New York Times*, 5/1/08]. Look behind you. [Photos of McCain and Bush in the rearview mirror] We can't afford more of the same.

This commercial offers both future plans and general goals and spans both domestic and foreign policy topics:

Here's what I believe we need to do. Reform our tax system to give a $1,000 tax break to the middle class instead of showering more on oil companies and corporations that out-source our jobs. End the "anything goes" culture on Wall Street with real regulation that protects your investments and pensions. Fast-track a plan for energy "made in America" that will free us from our dependence on mid-east oil in ten years and put millions of Americans to work. Crack down on lobbyists—once and for all—so their back-room deal-making no longer drowns out the voices of the middle class and undermines our common interests as Americans. And yes, bring a responsible end to the war in Iraq so we stop spending billions each month rebuilding their country when we should be rebuilding ours. ("Plan for Change")

The Obama campaign also questioned McCain's character. In this ad, the Republican nominee's expertise and judgment are criticized:

MCCAIN: "I'm going to be honest: I know a lot less about economics than I do about military and foreign policy issues. I still need to be educated" (*Wall Street Jour-*

nal, 11/26/05). "The issue of economics is not something I've understood as well as I should" (*Boston Globe Political Intelligence*, 12/18/07). "I might have to rely on a vice president that I select" for expertise on economic issues. (*GOP Debate*, 11/28/07)

ANNCR: His choice? [Photo of Sarah Palin on screen] ("His Choice")

These ads illustrate Obama's first campaign for the Oval Office.

McCain's campaign included discussion of policy, including ideas to help the auto industry: "Michigan families depend on the auto industry. John McCain and his congressional allies know it. Their plan: Loans to upgrade assembly lines, tax credits to boost sales of clean vehicles, offshore drilling to reduce the cost of gas and spur truck sales, and financial reforms to protect your retirement. Change is coming" ("Michigan Jobs"). This ad for McCain discussed his character and his policies:

CRIST: Hi. I'm Charlie Crist. Our next president will face enormous challenges. For me, the choice is clear. John McCain is an American hero. He's a conservative who knows to move America forward, we must work together. John McCain's uniquely qualified to lead our nature through a crisis. A reformer, a maverick, he'll fight out-of-control spending and keep our taxes down. John McCain never quits, and he'll always fight for you. Join me November 4 in voting for John McCain. ("Crist")

The McCain campaign criticized Obama's experience and his economic policies: "With crises at home and abroad, Barack Obama lacks the experience America needs. And it shows. His response to our economic crisis is to spend and tax our economy deeper into recession. The fact is, Barack Obama's not ready yet" ("TV Special"). This argument was reinforced with a statement made by Obama's running mate: "Biden: Mark my words. It will not be six months before the world tests Barack Obama. The world is looking. We're going to have an international crisis . . . to test the mettle of this guy. I guarantee you it's gonna happen" ("Ladies and Gentlemen"). These excerpts exemplify the Republican presidential campaign.

Obama criticized Romney's record as governor of Massachusetts in this spot from 2012:

ROMNEY: I speak the language of business. I know how jobs are created.

ANNCR: One of the worst economic records in the country. When Mitt Romney was governor, Massachusetts lost 40,000 manufacturing jobs—a rate twice the national average—and fell to forty-seventh in job creation, fourth from the bottom. Instead of hiring workers from his own state, Romney outsourced call-center jobs to India. He cut taxes for millionaires like himself, while raising them on the middle class. And left the state $2.6 billion deeper in debt. So now, when Mitt Romney talks about what he'd do as president . . .

ROMNEY: I know what it takes to create jobs.

ANNCR: Remember, we've heard it all before.

ROMNEY: I know how jobs are created.

ANNCR: Romney economics. It didn't work then, and it won't work now. ("We've heard it all Before")

Job creation was an important issue in this campaign. Romney's tax record was also criticized:

> As governor, Mitt Romney did cut taxes . . . on millionaires like himself. But he raised taxes and fees on everyone else: $1.5 billion. Over a thousand fee hikes: On health care. On school bus rides. On milk. On driver's licenses. On nursing homes. On lead poisoning prevention. On meat and poultry inspection. On fishermen and gun owners. On nurses. On electricians. On hospitals. On funeral homes. On mental health services. On hospice care. Romney economics didn't work then and won't work now. ("Mosaic")

The next advertisement began with character but moved quickly to Obama's record in office:

> The son of a single mom. Proud father of two daughters. President Obama knows women being paid 77 cents on the dollar for doing the same work as men isn't just unfair, it hurts families. So the first law he signed was the Lilly Ledbetter Fair Pay Act to help ensure that women are paid the same as men for doing the exact same work. Because President Obama knows that fairness for women means a stronger middle class for America. ("First Law")

These ads indicate the nature of Obama's campaign for re-election.

The Republican nominee criticized the president's character in this spot, which discussed Obama's negative campaigning:

> BOB SCHIEFFER, *Face the Nation* host: "When the president was elected, he talked about hope and change. Whatever happened to hope and change? Now it seems he's just coming right out of the box with these old fashioned negative ads."
>
> DAVID BROOKS, *New York Times* columnist: "By starting negative, by going extremely tough and extremely hard, looking conventional, and frankly running ads that are inaccurate."
>
> MARK HALPERIN, *Time* journalist: "Barack Obama's campaign and allies will run more negative ads against this Republican nominee in 2012 than have ever been run in the history of the world."
>
> SCHIEFFER: "Whatever happened to hope and change?" ("Hope and Change")

An advertisement sponsored by Romney took the president to task on welfare reform:

> In 1996, President Clinton and a bipartisan Congress helped end welfare as we know it by requiring work for welfare. But on July 12, President Obama quietly announced a plan to gut welfare reform by dropping work requirements. Under Obama's plan, you wouldn't have to work and wouldn't have to train for a job. They just send you your

welfare check. And welfare-to-work goes back to being plain old welfare. Mitt Romney will restore the work requirement because it works. ("Right Choice")

The ad ended with an acclaim of Romney's approach to welfare. This spot also made an unflattering contrast between Obama and Clinton. The challenger also discussed values in this campaign:

ANNCR: Who shares your values? President Obama used his health care plan to declare war on religion, forcing religious institutions to go against their faith. Mitt Romney believes that's wrong.

ROMNEY: In 1979, a son of Poland, Pope John Paul II, spoke words that would bring down an empire: Be not afraid.

ANOUNCER: When religious freedom is threatened, who do you want to stand with? ("Be Not Afraid")

These examples indicate the nature of Romney's advertising campaign.

Functions of Presidential Television Spots 2008–2012

These candidates attacked more than they acclaimed (the least common function was defense). For example, Obama's 2012 spot "Determination" illustrates an acclaim:

OBAMA: There's just no quit in America and you're seeing that right now. Over five million new jobs. Exports up forty one percent. Home values rising. Our auto industry back. And our heroes are coming home. . . .
Here's my plan for the next four years: Making education and training a national priority; building on our manufacturing boom; boosting American-made energy; reducing the deficits responsibly by cutting where we can, and asking the wealthy to pay a little more. And ending the war in Afghanistan, so we can do some nation-building here at home. That's the right path.

Ideas such as creating jobs, increasing exports, increasing home values, increasing domestic energy production, reducing deficits, and ending the war in Afghanistan would be seen as desirable by most voters. An attack is exemplified in Romney's commercial "Can't Afford Another Term":

ANNOUNCER: Gutted the work requirement for welfare, doubled the number of able bodied adults without children on food stamps, record unemployment, more women in poverty than ever before, borrowed from China, and increased the debt to over $16 trillion, passing the burden on to the next generation.

Weakening the program to move people from welfare to work, greater reliance on food stamps, higher unemployment, more women in poverty, borrowing from

China, and increasing the national debt would appear undesirable to many voters. Finally, Obama's advertisement "Dubious" is an example of a defense:

> ANNOUNCER: Seen this ad? Mitt Romney claiming the President would end welfare's work requirements. NBC calls this ad dubious and they're right. It's false. The *Washington Post* says, the Obama administration is not removing the bills work requirements at all.

This spot rejects Romney's attack that Obama weakened the welfare to work requirements.

Topics of Presidential Television Spots 2008–2012

These four presidential candidates discussed policy more than character in their ads. To illustrate these results, an advertisement from Obama in 2012 ("Remember") serves as an example of a policy discussion.

> Mitt Romney's plan rolls back regulations on the banks that crashed our economy. Medicare voucherized. Catastrophic cuts to education. Millionaires will get one of the largest tax cuts ever. While middle class families pay more.

These topics—bank regulations, Medicare, education, tax proposals—all address policy. In contrast, Romney's ad "American Needs a Leader" addresses character:

> ROMNEY: We need American leadership. Where is American leadership?
>
> RYAN: This is the moment where the moment and the man are meeting. We need someone who will be honest with us about our problems, who will not blame other people for the next 4 years, who will take responsibility, who will not duck the tough issues. . . . That's this man right here [Romney].

Leadership, honesty, and taking responsibility all concern character. A *chi-square goodness-of-fit* test shows that these topics occurred with different frequencies (χ^2 [df = 1] 84.82, $p < .0001$).

Forms of Policy and Character in Presidential Television Spots 2008–2012

Past deeds were discussed most (38 percent), followed by future plans (23 percent) and general goals (38 percent). For example, Obama's 2012 ad "Character" discussed his past deeds: Obama "helped rescue the auto industry." In contrast, Romney argued that Obama had the "worst job record since the Depression" ("Shame on You"). These themes both concern Obama's past deeds, or record in office. Romney's ad "Paid In" discussed one of his future plans; "The Romney–Ryan plan protexts Medicare benefits for today's seniors and strengthens the plan for the next generation." Obama criticized aspects of Romney's tax proposals: Romney "supports tax breaks for companies that ship jobs overseas." These two statements talk about means of implementing policy, or future plans. A spot from Romney ("Deficit Iowa") articulated one of his policy goals: Romney will "eliminate the deficit." Obama used a political TV spot to attack his opponent's goals: "Here's what he said as governor outside a coal-fired power plant: 'I will not create jobs or hold jobs that kill people, and that plant, that plant kills people'" (Obama, "Not One of Us").

Turning to the question of the relative proportions of the three forms of character in these presidential campaigns, personal qualities were discussed most often (69 percent), with ideals (17 percent) and leadership ability (14 percent) at similar levels. Romney illustrated a statement on personal qualities when his ad declared: "We need someone who believes in America" to be president ("These Hands"). Obama criticized his opponent's personal qualities in "The Question" when he declared that Romney "would be so out of touch with the average person in this country." The candidates also used their advertising to discuss their leadership abilities. Romney ("Strong Leadership") declared "Romney: the difference is strong leadership." Obama offered this critique of Romney's leadership ability: "Amateurish. . . . Even Republican experts said Romney's remarks were 'the worst possible reaction to what happened [in Libya].' If this is how he handles the world now just think what Mitt Romney might do as president" (Obama, "Policy"). Obama ad "First Law" explained that "President Obama knows that fairness for women means a stronger middle class for America." Fairness is an ideal. Romney ("Firms") attacked the president's ideology when he talked about "Obama and his liberal allies."

Conclusion: 2008–2012

A clear shift in emphasis acclaims to attacks occurred (Bush in 2004 used slightly more attacks and acclaims but in 2008 the percentage of attacks jumped dramatically). In 2008 the Democratic nominee, Barack Obama, became the first candidate to decline federal financing for the general election campaign. He believed, correctly as it turned out, that he could raise more money than the Federal Election Committee would give him ($84 million in this year). This meant that Obama had to raise money throughout the general election period and it appears that he did so by attacking furiously to excite his base. McCain probably attacked as a response to Obama's barrage of criticisms. Neither Obama nor Romney accepted federal funds in 2012 and they attacked at high levels because both candidates needed to appeal to their base to raise the funds needed for their campaigns. Although functions and topics are independent ideas, the large shift from acclaims to attacks that occurred in 2008 was not accompanied by a large shift in the topics of their TV spot utterances.

7

Primary Campaigns

Who Shall Lead Us?

The primary phase of the presidential campaign has been comparatively neglected in election research. A focus on the general election campaign makes sense, just as the greatest emphasis in sports is accorded to the championship (e.g., World Series in baseball or the Superbowl in football). Presidential primaries are an important way for party members to learn about their potential leaders and then select the candidate who will represent their party in the Fall. Still, primary campaigns are significant because they are an opportunity for party members to participate in democracy and exert influence on the direction their party will take. Davis (1997) observed that "in no other Western country do so many people take part in the party nominating process" (p. 2).

IMPORTANCE OF PRIMARY CAMPAIGNS

The primary campaign phase deserves attention for several reasons. First, in recent history, it has been essential for a presidential candidate to secure the nomination of the Republican or Democratic Party in order to win the White House. Various candidates—including George Wallace, John Anderson, Ross Perot, and Ralph Nader—have discovered the truth of this assertion. Davis explained that "the presidential nominating process narrows the alternatives from a theoretical potential candidate pool of . . . millions . . . to only two candidates, one Republican and one Democrat, with a realistic chance of winning the White House" (p. 1). So, winning the primary campaign and securing the Democratic or Republican party nomination for president is a necessary (although not a sufficient) condition for becoming president.

Second, the primary campaign has become increasingly important in recent years. Bartels (1988) summarized changes in the nomination process:

> The new system is dominated by candidates and by the news media; the old system was dominated by professional party politicians. The central decision-making mechanism in the new system is mass voting; the central mechanism in the old system was face-to-face bargaining. The locus of choice in the new system is the primary ballot box; the locus of choice in the old system was the convention backroom. (p. 13)

Because party bosses controlled the nomination in the past, obtaining the support of primary voters was a means to an end rather than an end in itself. Candidates did not run in primaries in order to win a majority of the delegates to the nominating conventions; they ran to demonstrate to party bosses that they had the *ability to garner votes*. For example, John F. Kennedy's West Virginia primary campaign was important "because it convinced powerful party leaders . . . that Kennedy [a Catholic] could win Protestant votes" (Bartels, 1988, p. 15). Levine observed that in the past "presidential hopefuls generally did not even need to campaign in primaries, which were relatively few in number" (1995, p. 56). As recently as 1968, Hubert Humphrey became his party's nominee without campaigning in a single primary (Levine, 1995), although he entered the race relatively late, waiting until after President Johnson dropped out of the campaign. In earlier years, the contests over who should be the party's nominee were often divisive—and they were broadcast over the national television. The Democratic National Convention in 1968, complete with televised riots, is a notorious example of a bitterly disputed convention that may have damaged the Democratic Party and contributed to a win by Republican Richard Nixon. To avoid contentious conventions and to decrease perceptions that party leaders rather than rank and file party members determined the nomination, both political parties increased their use of primaries and caucuses to select their nominees (Davis, 1997; Kendall, 2000).

Moreover, some years feature vulnerable incumbents, such as Ford in 1976, Carter in 1980, Bush in 1992, or Obama in 2012. It is possible that someone other than Jimmy Carter could have ousted President Gerald Ford in 1976, that another Republican besides Ronald Reagan could have unseated President Carter four years later, or that Bill Clinton was not the only Democrat who could have defeated President George Bush in 1992. However, because these three candidates won their parties' nominations, they were the only ones who were entitled to challenge those weak opponents. So, in a very real sense, the primary campaign may have decided who would ultimately become the president by determining who had the right to run against a vulnerable incumbent. To return to the sports metaphor used earlier, if one conference is weaker than the other, then the playoff game or games to determine the winner of the other stronger conference (semi-finals) may in a real sense determine the overall champion, because that game determines who gets to face the representative of the weaker conference.

Finally, messages in the primary campaign have the ability to influence voters. Bartels (1988) offers the following example to illustrate this point:

> At the beginning of 1976, Jimmy Carter was a relatively unknown one-term ex-governor of a medium-sized southern state. Although he had been running for president full-time for more than a year . . . [a] Gallup poll indicated that fewer than 5 percent of the Democratic party rank and file considered him their first choice for the party's nomination.
>
> Five months later, Carter was quite clearly about to become his party's nominee. . . . Carter was the first choice of an absolute majority of Democrats—leading his nearest rival by a margin of almost forty percentage points—and a winner by almost twenty percentage points in trial heats against the incumbent Republican president. (p. 3)

Carter's campaign, directly via his messages and indirectly as mediated by news coverage of his campaign, clearly influenced voters and made a difference. Presidential primary TV spots clearly deserve our attention.

DIFFERENCES BETWEEN PRIMARY AND GENERAL CAMPAIGNS

The idea that the primary phase merits scholarly attention is important because the two phases of a political campaign—primary and general—possess substantial differences. This section will discuss each of these factors, elucidate additional principles of the Functional Theory of Political Campaign Discourse that pertain to campaign phase, and compare campaign messages to test predictions about the nature of discourse produced in these two phases. There are several important differences between primary and general campaigns (see, e.g., Benoit, 2007a): I will discuss two of them here.

Party of Opponent

In contested primaries, when more than one candidate seeks the nomination of his or her political party, it is important to realize that those fellow party members are the immediate opponents. For example, Barack Obama and John McCain were opponents in the 2008 general election campaign, but, in a very real sense, they were not opponents in the primary. Senator Obama first had to defeat his Democratic rivals in the primary: Joe Biden, Hillary Clinton, John Edwards, Mike Gravel, Dennis Kucinich, and Bill Richardson. Senator McCain had to win the Republican nomination over his competitors: Sam Brownback, James Gilmore, Rudi Giuliani, Mike Huckabee, Duncan Hunter, Alan Keyes, Ron Paul, Mitt Romney, Tom Tancredo, Fred Thompson, and Tommy Thompson. A candidate must win his or her party's nomination first: In a 1980 primary debate in New Hampshire, Ronald Reagan discussed the "eleventh commandment," asserting that Republicans should not attack Republicans in the primary. However, primary candidates must distinguish themselves from immediate opponents, and they must convince voters that they are preferable to those opponents, and attacks on fellow party members are a means of achieving these goals.

For example, in the 1992 primaries, President Bush was still enjoying support from the success of Operation Desert Storm. However, Pat Buchanan challenged Bush for the Republican nomination and Bush had to survive Buchanan's attack and win the Republican nomination before he could run in the general campaign. Similarly, in the early part of the 2000 primary campaign it appeared as if George W. Bush did not fully appreciate this principle, looking past McCain, his most serious challenge, to Gore, mistakenly thinking that his real opponent was Gore at that point in time. McCain won primaries in New Hampshire and Michigan, and for a time threatened to win South Carolina as well (McCain also won Arizona, Connecticut, Massachusetts, Rhode Island, and Vermont). These events forced the Bush campaign to turn its attention to defeating McCain. The Bush camp refocused his campaign (e.g., his slogan became "A Reformer with Results" instead of a "Compassionate Conservative"). In 2012 President Obama did not need to use the primary phase of the election to fend off challengers from within his own party. The point is, if a political party's nomination is contested, the candidates' real or immediate opponents are fellow party members, rather than the presumed nominee of the other party.

The nature of one's opponent influences the nature of campaign discourse. For example, compare Bill Clinton's primary campaigns from 1992 and 1996. In his first presidential campaign, the Democratic nomination was sought by Clinton as well as by other Democrats such as Jerry Brown, Tom Harkin, and Paul Tsongas. Clinton mentioned his Democratic opponents in ten of forty primary spots and mentioned the presumed Republican nominee, President George Bush, in but four primary spots. Clinton also responded to attacks from his fellow Democrats in other spots. Here is just one example of these 1992 primary television spots, which focused on one of his Democratic opponents:

> Jerry Brown says he'll fight for we the people. Question is, which people? He says he for working families. But his tax proposal has been called a flat-out fraud. It cuts taxes for the very rich in half and raised taxes on the middle class. Jerry Brown says he'll clean up politics and limit campaign contributions. But a year ago he helped lead the fight that killed campaign reform and contribution limits in California. So the next time Jerry Brown says he's fighting for the people, ask him which people and which Jerry Brown. ("Which")

Thus, Clinton, who needed to defeat his Democratic opponents in the primary, could do little to help his general campaign in his 1992 primary messages. He had to wait until after he had secured the Democratic nomination before he could turn his attention to his likely Republican opponent.

In contrast, when Clinton sought re-election in 1996 his nomination was not contested in Democratic primaries. Thus, he could, and did, focus his primary campaign on attacking Dole (the presumptive Republican nominee) instead of other Democrats. For example, in this campaign, Clinton and Democratic National Committee (DNC) spots run during the primary season mentioned Dole or showed his picture in twenty-five out of forty television spots, such as this one:

> The Oval Office. If it were Bob Dole sitting here, he would have already cut Medicare $270 billion. Toxic polluters off the hook. No to the Brady Bill; sixty thousand criminals allowed to buy handguns. Slashed education. President Clinton stood firm and defended our values. But next year, if Newt Gingrich controls Congress and his partner, Bob Dole, enters the Oval Office, there'll be nobody there to stop them. ("Nobody")

Clearly, Clinton started his general campaign early with spots such as this one. He did not need to expend effort or money getting past a primary candidates from his own political party. As noted earlier, Buchanan challenged President Bush in 1992. At least five of Bush's primary television spots explicitly responded to Buchanan. Thus, except in the case of uncontested primaries, it is vital for candidates, as well as theorists and analysts, to focus on the candidate's immediate opponent (or opponents).

Target Audience

In the primary, the object is to win the most votes from fellow-party members (an exception would be McCain's appeal to non-Republicans to vote for him in "open" primaries in 2000). Primary votes determine how delegates to the parties' national nominating convention will vote (which candidate they support). This means that the target audience in this phase of the campaign should be members of one's own political party. This is precisely why conventional wisdom holds that presidential candidates run to the right (or left) in the primaries and then run to the center in the general campaign. Republican candidates need to secure the approval of their party members in the primary, on the right of the ideological spectrum, whereas Democratic candidates must persuade their party members, on the left. Of course, in an uncontested primary, as with Clinton in 1996, Bush in 2004, or Obama in 2012, candidates can essentially commence the general campaign early, appealing to other voters in addition to those in their own political party.

However, in the general campaign, the party nominees can count on the support of most of their party members. They may wish to try to increase the likelihood that their party members will actually vote on Election Day; they may also attempt to keep potential vote defectors from their own party from defecting, or try to attract potential vote defectors from the other party. But most effort in the general campaign should be directed toward winning the support of the independent and undecided voters who often cluster at the middle of the political spectrum. As established in chapter 1, no candidate can assure a win relying only on votes from his own political party because neither political party has the support of a majority of voters. Thus, the audience which matters most in a contested primary are members of one's own political party; in the general campaign, the target audience shifts to focus more on independent or undecided voters and potential vote defectors.

This analysis explains why candidates are sometimes said to "run to the right (or left) in primaries and then to the center in the general campaign." The principal audience in these two campaign phases is quite different. In order to obtain their party's nomination, a candidate must convince the majority of *his or her party members* that he or she is preferable to members of his own political party. For Republicans, this means emphasizing issues on the right of the political spectrum; for Democrats, it means stressing issues on the left of the political spectrum. However, after the party nominees have been selected and they turn to the general campaign, they can for the most part take for granted the votes of most partisans (worrying only about potential vote defectors). But to win the general phase of the election, candidates must appeal to *other groups of voters*—undecided, independent, and potential vote defectors—voters whose concerns may be quite different from those of committed partisans. Benoit and Hansen (2002) found that presidential candidates' television spots focus more on their own party's issues in the primary than the general campaign, evidence that message adaption by campaign phase does occur. Thus, candidates should emphasize different issues and take positions that lie more in the middle of the political spectrum in the general than the primary campaign. In other words, the shift in target audience explains a concomitant shift in the content campaign discourse. Of course, candidates cannot ignore their base in the general campaign but they widen their target audience after they secure their party's nomination.

Previous research on presidential primary campaign advertising is relatively sparse. Devlin (1994) provided his interesting insider's perspective on the 1992 New Hampshire primary. Payne, Marlier, and Baukus (1989) examined spots from 1988 using Diamond and Bates' (1992) four categories of identification, argumentative, negative, and resolution spots. Shyles (1983) identified the issues of the 1980 campaign from primary ads and later (1984) discussed the interrelationships of images, issues, and presentation in the same campaign. Pfau, Diedrich, Larson, and van Winkle (1993) conducted an experimental study of relational and competence perceptions of candidates in the 1992 primary. The most extensive study analyzed 1089 primary spots from 1960 to 1988 (Kaid and Ballotti, 1991); unfortunately, this study has not been published.

It was not always necessary to compete in the primary campaigns to secure a party's nomination. In fact, the first primaries occurred just after the turn of the century in Wisconsin, Pennsylvania, and South Dakota. The number of states with primaries hovered between thirteen and nineteen until 1972. As late as 1968, Hubert Humphrey was nominated without competing in a single primary (Levine, 1995). However, the riots and divisiveness of the Democratic National Convention in Chicago in 1968 (and other factors) prompted reforms in both parties which encouraged more primaries and earlier primaries. An important goal was to decide who would be the nominee well in advance of the convention so there would be time for the divisions that occur in a contested nomination to heal before the party's showcase event (the nominating convention) on national television. In 1992, there were 37 primary contests which selected about 80 percent of the delegates to the national conventions (Jackson and Crotty, 1996).

The earliest primary television advertisement I could locate, and very likely the first primary spot ever used in a presidential race, was by Eisenhower in 1952:

> What will Eisenhower do about cleaning up purveyors of influence in Washington? President Truman has made an abortive attempt to clean up the mess in Washington. Eisenhower will clean it up for real. Who will Eisenhower surround himself with if he becomes president? He will come to Washington without commitments. Keep in mind that in every step of his remarkable career he has surrounded himself with outstanding talent. And that throughout his life of significant accomplishments, he has won the determined cooperation of other great men. Thus, he brought in, in addition to military people, top civilian talent of the United States and Europe. What is Eisenhower's position on censorship in America? Eisenhower says, in my opinion, censorship is a stupid and shallow way to approach the solution to any problem. It is quite clear that if the freedom of the press should disappear, all other freedoms that we enjoy shall disappear. What is Eisenhower's definition of democracy? He says, for my own part, in seeking some definition for the word democracy, I believe this one satisfies me more than any other: Democracy is the political expression of a deeply felt religion. If General Eisenhower wins the nomination, what kind of a political campaign will he wage? Eisenhower has given us these words: If by any chance it should come about that the Republican Party does name me as its standard-bearer, I am determined to lead the entire organization into a fight in which there will be no cessation, no rest, and no lack of intensity until the final decision is made. ("Purveyors of Influence")

This commercial laments the mess in Washington and argues that the incumbent Democratic administration was incapable of solving it. It alludes to his status as a war hero (and leader). His ideals (freedom of speech, democracy, religion) are mentioned. It ends with a declaration of his intent to campaign hard. Of course, Eisenhower was nominated and won two terms in the White House.

In 1960, Senator Kennedy (from Massachusetts) entered the primaries to demonstrate his viability. Particular concerns had been expressed about his religion (no Catholic had been elected president to this point). He campaigned hard in West Virginia (not a Catholic stronghold) to dispel these fears.

> The question is whether I think that if I were elected president, I would be divided between two loyalties: my church and my state. There is no article of my faith that would in any way inhibit—I think it encourages—the meeting of my oath of office. And whether you vote for me or not because of my competence to be president, I am sure that this state of West Virginia, that no one believes that I'd be a candidate for the presidency if I didn't think I could meet my oath of office. Now you cannot tell me the day I was born it was said I could never run for president because I wouldn't meet my oath of office. I came to the state of West Virginia, which has fewer numbers of my

coreligionists than any state in the nation. I would not have come here if I didn't feel I was going to get complete opportunity to run for office as a fellow American in this state. I would not run for it if in any way I felt that I couldn't do the job. So I come here today to say that I think this is an issue. ("Loyalty")

This message draws upon the American Dream that anyone can grow up to be president when he declared that "you cannot tell me the day I was born it was said I could never run for president." Perhaps he could also have referred to freedom of religion (one's religion should not prohibit anyone from becoming president). Kennedy made his point and won the Democratic nomination—and, later that year, the presidency.

In 1964, Barry Goldwater developed a series of at least seven spots in a consistent format. These advertisements began with an image of Goldwater and a caption displayed upside down. The announcer introduced a topic and reported what "they" were saying about Barry Goldwater. Then he asked, "What did he really say?" and the image turned right-side up and Goldwater stated his actual position. Here is a typical example:

ANNOUNCER: They say Barry Goldwater is against social security [image of Goldwater upside down with label "Social Security" also upside down]. What did he really say? [image turns right-side up].

GOLDWATER: I want to strengthen social security, keep the security in it, so you can be paid in real American dollars that are still worth enough to buy the groceries.

ANNOUNCER: He said it, you vote it, Goldwater. ("Social Security")

This format suggests that Goldwater's critics are wrong (they have turned the truth upside down) and he used this approach to discuss such topics as Social Security, taxes, war, and civil rights. It clearly functions as defense, denying the accusations as well as acclaiming a general goal.

In 1968, Nixon ran several primary spots that were adapted to individual primary states (perhaps this had occurred earlier, but this campaign, including a spot for McCarthy, is the earliest such audience adaptation I found). For example, this commercial uses both ordinary citizens and a congressman to speak on his behalf in the Wisconsin primary:

[SUSANNE WILMETH, UW Madison]: Here at school a lot of the kids seem to think that America is just drifting, that we have no real leadership. I think that Dick Nixon could provide that leadership.

[MRS. DOROTHY KROHN, Oshkosh]: I don't feel safe in my own kitchen, any more, unless the front doors are locked. My neighbors feel the same way. And I think that's a tragedy in a country as great as ours. Mr. Nixon shares our concern and I know he will do something about this rising crime rate.

[CONGRESSMAN GLENN DAVIS]: My concern is with the careless use of the taxpayers' money. I know Dick Nixon well. I know of his dedication to efficient government and a sound dollar. I know of his repugnance to spending money which we do not have. I shall vote for Dick Nixon on April 2. ("Concerns")

Some of Nixon's spots mentioned other states and included other election dates. That same year, Eugene McCarthy challenged Bobby Kennedy to a primary debate. This is the earliest spot I found to attack another candidate for refusing to debate:

> I'm Eddie Albert. I'd like to ask you a question. Why is Bobby Kennedy afraid to debate Eugene McCarthy? McCarthy challenged him to a debate but Kennedy refused. After all it was Bobby's brother John Kennedy who challenged Nixon to a debate. That certainly helped the country make up its mind. I think a debate between the two candidates in California would give all of us a chance to decide which man would make the better president. You know I remember when Gene McCarthy decided the Vietnam War was wrong, and he had the guts to stand up in New Hampshire and take on President Johnson. Bobby Kennedy sat on the fence, and waited to see how Gene McCarthy would make out. It seems to me that Kennedy wouldn't face Johnson in New Hampshire, and now he won't face McCarthy in California. Now I admire courage, and that's just one of the reasons why I'm going to vote for Eugene McCarthy on June 4. ("Eddie Albert")

This spot, developed for the California primary, also used a celebrity, actor Eddie Albert, and an unusual form of reluctant testimony: the fact that Bobby's brother, John, had been willing to debate Nixon eight years earlier.

In 1972, Nixon ran for re-election. He used ordinary people in this primary spot to acclaim his first-term performance:

> WOMAN: I think President Nixon in his first-term has done an absolutely fantastic job.
>
> WOMAN: And he's getting our boys out of Vietnam, and that's very important, very important to me.
>
> MAN: President Nixon did exactly what he said he was going to do.
>
> WOMAN: He's turned the economy around.
>
> WOMAN: I certainly do approve of President Nixon's going to Peking.
>
> MAN: Without a doubt Mr. Nixon should be re-elected.
>
> MAN: I like him.
>
> WOMAN: You better believe it. I am going to vote for President Nixon. ("Approve")

These comments function to acclaim both his policy ("He's turned the economy around") and his character ("I like him").

In 1976, Ronald Reagan challenged Ford for the Republican nomination. In this spot, Reagan alludes generally to his record as governor of California:

> I believe that what we did in California can be done in Washington. If government will have faith in the people and let them bring their common sense to bear on the problems bureaucracy hasn't solved. I believe in the people. Now Mr. Ford places his faith in the

Washington establishment. This has been evident in his appointment of former congressmen and long-time government workers to positions in his administration. Well, I don't believe that those who've been a part of the problem are necessarily the best qualified to solve those problems. ("Record")

He also suggests that Ford is part of an entrenched establishment, attacking as well as acclaiming. When Edward Kennedy challenged Carter for the Democratic nomination in 1980, he used Carter's words and campaign promises against him:

KENNEDY: Everybody remembers the candidate who said in 1976, "I'll never mislead you, and you can depend on it." But do you remember what else he said? He said he would reduce inflation and unemployment to 4 percent by the end of his first-term, that he would never use high interest rates to fight inflation, that he would never decontrol the price of oil and natural gas, that nuclear power is the resource of last resort, that he would get the ERA passed during his first year in office, that he would balance the budget and reduce the size of government. But now he's secluded in the White House telling us to rally around his failure overseas. He refuses to discuss the issues, but America cannot afford to forget the problems President Carter has left behind. New Hampshire can change that. New Hampshire can make the difference in 1980. ("Promises")

He explicitly refers to Carter's broken promises and failures in both domestic and foreign policy.

In 1984, Democrat McGovern contrasted himself with Reagan, who was not challenged for the Republican nomination:

It'd be some fight all right. A classic. [McGovern pictured on left, Reagan on right]:

food for peace versus death squads
military cuts versus deficits
home mortgages versus tax breaks
social security versus insecurity
college loans versus B-1s
compassion versus indifference
a nuclear freeze versus space wars
negotiation versus name-calling
coexistence versus no existence

Who says George can't win—are you kidding? ("Some Fight")

Here, he assailed the incumbent, President Reagan. Perhaps McGovern should have concentrated more on his immediate opponent (Walter Mondale, the eventual Democratic nominee) during the primaries, giving Democrats a reason to prefer McGovern over Mondale.

In 1988, Vice President George Bush sought the Republican nomination. Senator Bob Dole was one of those who contested his nomination. In this spot, unlike the previous one from McGovern, Bush attacked his Republican opponent:

Bob Dole says that President Reagan calls him to get things done. But under Bob Dole's leadership we lost the Bork nomination. And in sixteen of the thirty-four votes Reagan lost in the Senate, Dole couldn't deliver even half of the Republicans. Senate Republican support for the president hit an all-time low in 1987, when even Senator Dole failed to support him almost 30 percent of the time. So when President Reagan wanted a vice president he could count on, he didn't call Bob Dole: He called George Bush. ("16 of 34—Dole Senate Record")

In addition to attacking Dole's record, notice how Bush tried to capitalize on his experience as vice president and on the support of the very popular Republican president, Ronald Reagan.

Clinton used a version of the "Which Barry Goldwater" spot Johnson ran in 1964 to attack one of the other Democratic candidates in the 1992 primary campaign:

[Brown's photo switches from left to right side]: Jerry Brown says he'll fight for we the people. Question is, which people? He says he is for working families. But his tax proposal has been called a flat-out fraud. It cuts taxes for the very rich in half and raises taxes on the middle class. Jerry Brown says he'll clean up politics and limit campaign contributions. But a year ago he helped lead the fight that killed campaign reform and contribution limits in California. So the next time Jerry Brown says he's fighting for the people, ask him which people and which Jerry Brown. ("Which")

This commercial suggests that Brown's actions do not match his campaign pledges. Voters want a candidate who will follow through with his promises.

That same year, in 1992, Pat Buchanan challenged Bush for the Republican nomination. Bush had won in 1988 in part based on his "Read my Lips—No new taxes" pledge. Several of these spots, like the next one, included a clip from Bush's famous pledge:

MAN [Nashua, NH]: The betrayal that I feel in George Bush is now the harder I work, the closer I come to losing my home.

MAN [Amherst, NH]: I remember that day he said read my lips, no new taxes and he went against his word.

WOMAN [Manchester, NH]: That does not go well with the people of New Hampshire because people in New Hampshire keep their word.

MAN [Nashua, NH]: And we have to suffer the consequences.

BUSH: Read my lips.

ANNOUNCER: Send a message.

PEOPLE: Read our lips. ("Betrayed")

This spot works from the same basic premise, that we want to be able to trust candidates to keep their campaign promises.

In 1996, Alexander used a more folksy approach to seek the Republican nomination in many of his primary television spots:

> This race for president is coming down to a zillionaire mudslinger, a grumpy Texan, and a Senator who's been in Washington since before I could vote. I'm Lamar Alexander, and I'm offering new Republican leadership to beat Bill Clinton. Here's my plan. Cut tax rates and unleash free enterprise to create good new jobs. Make our schools as good as our colleges. And replace Washington arrogance with community citizenship. So if you're ready for new leadership, I'm your candidate. ("New Leadership")

He begins with unflattering characterizations of his major opponents in the race. Then he describes three general proposals for improving life in America. The spot talks about leadership, but this claim is based on policy proposals. These examples give an indication of how primary spots use acclaims, attacks, and defense, on topics of policy and character.

In 2000, Vice President Al Gore and Senator Bill Bradley contended for the Democratic nomination, which Gore won. On the Republican side, television spots were broadcast by Gary Bauer (President of the Family Research Council), Governor George W. Bush, businessman Steve Forbes, Ambassador Alan Keyes, and Senator John McCain; Bush secured the nomination. For example, an advertisement from Gore declared that "We need to protect our oceans and beaches, and if elected president, I'll do that" ("Oceans"). Forbes offered this acclaim: "I will eliminate the current tax code and institute the flat tax. I will preserve Social Security for older Americans and offer a new system for working Americans. I will not be apologetic about restoring respect for human life" ("United"). McCain attacked fellow-Republican Bush in this ad:

> ANNOUNCER: This is George Bush's ad promising America he'd run a positive campaign.
>
> BUSH: I want to run a campaign that is hopeful and optimistic and very positive.
>
> ANNOUNCER: This is George Bush shaking hands with John McCain, promising not to run a negative campaign. This is George Bush's new negative ad, attacking John McCain and distorting his position. Do we really want another politician in the White House American can't trust? ("Can't Trust")

McCain defended against attacks from Bush about McCain's proposals: "Mr. Bush's attacks are wrong: My plan cuts taxes, secures social security, pays down the debt. There is no tax increase" ("Bush Negative"). This statement offers a straightforward denial of the accusation.

No Republican contested President Bush's nomination in 2004. Several Democrats contended to run against President Bush: General Wesley Clark, Governor Howard Dean, Senator John Edwards, Representative Dick Gephardt, Senator John Kerry, Representative Dennis Kucinich, and Senator Joe Lieberman. John Kerry won the Democratic nomination. Dean attacked Bush in this ad:

I'm Howard Dean. It's time for the truth, because the truth is that George Bush's foreign policy isn't making us safer. His tax cuts are ruining our economy and costing us jobs. And too many Democrats in Washington are afraid to stand up for what we believe in. Well, I believe it's time to put people back to work, to provide health insurance for every American, and time for Democrats to be Democrats again. That's why I'm running for president. That's why I approved this message. I'm Howard Dean, and it's time to take our country back. ("Straight Talk")

After criticizing the president's foreign and domestic policy he acclaimed his stance on health care. Lieberman acclaimed his character in this ad ("More and More"): "Choose experience and independence. Choose integrity. Choose a president—Joe Lieberman." Gephardt's ad "Jobs" attacked the incumbent president: "George Bush has lost more jobs than any president since Herbert Hoover. He's lost more jobs than the last eleven presidents. Bush's budget deficit is almost twice what it was under his father, and forty-one million Americans have no health insurance." Jobs, the budget deficit, and health insurance are all policy topics. A Republican ad run by the Club for Growth criticized Dean. Dean's ad "Club for Truth" defended against this by declaring that this Republican ad was "False."

In 2008 President Bush was term-limited and Vice President Dick Cheney decided not to run for president, making this the first presidential campaign since 1952 to feature neither a president nor a vice president. On the Democratic side, Senator Joe Biden, Senator Hillary Clinton, Senator Chris Dodd, Senator John Edwards, Senator Barack Obama, and Governor Bill Richardson ran TV spots; the race narrowed to Clinton and Obama and Obama won the primary. Seven Republicans vied for their party's nomination: Mayor Rudy Giuliani, Governor Mike Huckabee, Senator John McCain (who won the nomination), Representative Ron Paul, Governor Mitt Romney, Representative Tom Tancredo, and Senator Fred Thompson. Giuliani, for example, acclaimed accomplishments as major: "He cut taxes $9 billion, welfare 60 percent, crime in half" ("Challenges"). In Biden's ad "Cathedral," he declared that "we must end" the war in Iraq. McCain charged that Clinton wanted to "spend $1 million on the Woodstock concert museum" ("Tied Up"). In the spot "Candor," Obama charged that the other candidates were "dodging." McCain attacked Romney because Romney said he was not running on "Republican values" ("Trust").

President Obama had no challengers for the Democratic nomination in 2012. Representative Michele Bachmann, businessman Herman Cain, Representative Newt Gingrich, Governor Mike Huckabee, Governor Jon Huntsman, Representative Ron Paul, Governor Tim Pawlenty, Governor Rick Perry, Governor Mitt Romney, and Senator Rick Santorum ran TV spots seeking the Republican nomination; Romney won the primary. Gingrich provided an illustration of an acclaim when he declared in "Timid vs. Bold" that while in the House of Representatives he "balanced the budget, reformed welfare, helped create millions of new jobs." Paul attacked one of his opponents in this spot: "Santorum promised a balanced budget and then voted to raise the debt ceiling five times" ("Betrayal"). This statement criticizes his opponent in two ways (for voting to raise the debt ceiling and for breaking a promise), illustrating attacks. A spot sponsored by Paul ("Tea for Two") defended against an attack which claimed that he would take away Social Security by arguing that Paul is "actually the only candidate that has a real plan to save your social security." This spot identifies and rejects an attack, making it a defense.

Functions of Primary TV Spots

Overall, these spots devoted over two-thirds (72 percent) of their remarks to acclaiming. In two campaigns (1992, 2012), both Republican, acclaims and attacks occurred at the same rate. In the 1996 primary, for example, this commercial praised Alexander's accomplishments:

> A conservative governor who balanced eight budgets, kept taxes the fifth lowest of any state, reformed education, brought in the auto industry with Saturn, and later helped found a new business that now has 1,200 employees. Lamar Alexander: governor, businessman, Education Secretary, a Republican running for president from the real world. ("Real World")

Alexander had experience as an elected governor, an appointed cabinet member, and as a businessman. In the 2012 Republican primary campaign an advertisement for Newt Gingrich proclaimed that in the House he "balanced the budget, reformed welfare, helped create millions of new jobs" ("Timid vs. Bold"). These three achievements would appear desirable to fellow Republicans, making these three themes examples of acclaims. *Spearman rho* calculated on year and percentage of attacks was not significant. See table 7.1 for these data.

Attacks accounted for 28 percent of remarks in these primary advertisements. Dole provided an illustration of this function when attacked Forbes in this spot from the 1996 primary campaign:

> Have you heard about Steve Forbes' risky ideas? Forbes supports taxpayer supported welfare benefits for illegal aliens. Forbes opposes mandatory life sentences for criminals convinced of three violent felonies. Forbes' economic plan will add $186 billion a year to the deficit. No wonder Forbes opposes a constitutional amendment to balance the budget. ("Risky")

This commercial laid out several reasons (welfare, crime, the economy) to oppose Forbes. In 2012, Ron Paul criticized one of his opponents in this statement: "Santorum promised a balanced budget and then voted to raise the debt ceiling five times" ("Betrayal"). This utterance functions to criticize his opponent in two ways—first for voting to raise the debt ceiling and second for breaking a promise—clearly illustrating an attack. Although not as common as acclaims in this sample, attacks were used frequently in presidential primary spots.

Defenses in primary advertisements were relatively rare at 1 percent. In 1992, for example, Tsongas used denial in this spot to respond to charges that he would

Table 7.1.   Functions and Topics of Presidential Primary TV Spots

	Functions			Topics	
	Acclaims	Attacks	Defenses	Policy	Character
1952 R	**47 (87%)**	7 (13%)	0	17 (31%)	**37 (69%)**
1960 D	**63 (73%)**	20 (23%)	3 (3%)	39 (47%)	**44 (53%)**
1964 R	**8 (57%)**	2 (14%)	4 (29%)	**6 (60%)**	4 (40%)
1968 D	**34 (65%)**	18 (35%)	0	17 (35%)	**32 (65%)**
1968 R	**34 (68%)**	15 (26%)	1 (2%)	26 (38%)	**42 (62%)**
1972 D	**127 (66%)**	65 (34%)	0	**114 (59%)**	78 (41%)
1972 R	**30 (100%)**	0	0	**17 (57%)**	13 (43%)
1976 D	**56 (59%)**	36 (38%)	3 (3%)	37 (40%)	**55 (60%)**
1976 R	**154 (82%)**	26 (14%)	8 (4%)	78 (43%)	**102 (57%)**
1980 D	**167 (59%)**	117 (41%)	1 (0.4%)	122 (43%)	**162 (57%)**
1980 R	**299 (76%)**	97 (24%)	0	134 (34%)	**262 (66%)**
1984 D	**246 (70%)**	104 (30%)	0	162 (46%)	**188 (54%)**
1988 D	**244 (89%)**	31 (11%)	0	**151 (55%)**	124 (45%)
1988 R	**126 (70%)**	54 (30%)	0	**104 (58%)**	76 (42%)
1992 D	**297 (67%)**	138 (31%)	11 (2%)	**286 (66%)**	149 (34%)
1992 R	92 (50%)	92 (50%)	0	**109 (59%)**	75 (41%)
1996 D	**180 (62%)**	108 (37%)	4 (1%)	**252 (87%)**	36 (13%)
1996 R	**466 (59%)**	312 (39%)	13 (2%)	382 (49%)	**396 (51%)**
2000 D	**318 (87%)**	46 (13%)	1 (0.3%)	**238 (65%)**	126 (35%)
2000 R	**495 (84%)**	85 (15%)	6 (1%)	290 (50%)	290 (50%)
2004 D	**624 (78%)**	171 (21%)	1 (0.1%)	**485 (61%)**	310 (39%)
2008 D	**746 (80%)**	192 (20%)	0	**534 (57%)**	404 (43%)
2008 R	**514 (82%)**	114 (18%)	0	**374 (60%)**	254 (40%)
2012 R	367 (50%)	368 (50%)	2 (0.3%)	368 (50%)	367 (50%)
Total	**5734 (72%)**	2218 (28%)	58 (1%)	**4342 (54%)**	3626 (46%)

Source: Benoit, 1999; Benoit and Compton, in press; Benoit, et al. 2003; Benoit et al. 2007; Benoit and Rill, 2012.
Functions: χ^2 (df = 2) = 6147.92, $p < .0001$; attacks and year *rho* (n = 24) = .17, $p > .2$, *ns*
Topics: χ^2 (df = 1) = 64.34, $p < .0001$; policy and year *rho* (n = 24) = .54, $p < .005$

threaten Social Security if elected: "Now, Bill Clinton is distorting Paul Tsongas's record on Social Security, trying to scare people. But Bill Clinton knows that for ten years in the Congress, Paul Tsongas fought to protect Social Security, to extend Medicare coverage, and to end age discrimination" ("Record"). This spot clearly denies Clinton's attack. It also manages to criticize Clinton for knowingly distorting Tsongas' policy on this issue. In 1996, Gramm used this spot to defend against an accusation from Forbes, although no specific issue is mentioned here: "Phil Gramm's team starts to roll [Gramm bus]. Billionaire Steve Forbes starts negative commercials [Forbes in an ad]. One problem: They're not true [red FALSE over Forbes' face]. Bob Smith called Forbes' ads deceitful" ("False"). Even though no specific allegation is cited, Gramm labels Forbes' attacks as false. This is a clear illustration of a primary commercial's use of simple denial to respond to an attack. Figure 7.1 illustrates the functions of presidential primary advertisements over time. A *chi-square goodness-*

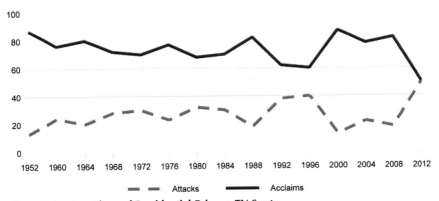

Figure 7.1. Functions of Presidential Primary TV Spots

Source: Benoit, 1999; Benoit and Compton, in press; Benoit, et al. 2003; Benoit et al. 2007; Benoit and Rill, 2012.

of-fit test revealed that these differences were significant (χ^2 [*df* = 2] = 6147.92, *p* < .0001). In no campaign did attacks outnumber acclaims; twice these two functions occurred at the same rate (1992, 2012).

Topics of Primary TV Spots

Policy was a common topic in these commercials (54 percent). However, five Democratic and five Republican campaigns discussed character more than policy. Baker provided an example of an acclaim on his agricultural policy in this 1980 spot: "We should start a new trade offensive in our foreign produce. And I want a vice president who knows how to promote farm exports to run the programs" ("Farm"). That same year, Bush attacked President Carter's domestic and foreign policy: "President Carter, what you don't seem to understand is people are really fed up. If we don't get tough with inflation, we're going down the drain. If we don't build up our military capability, we're going to get stung, again. America is in trouble, at home, abroad, with itself. The job has to be done now" ("Fed Up"). The last line lends some urgency to the appeal: We need to correct our domestic and foreign policy shortcomings immediately. Rick Perry discussed policy in this theme in the 2012 election: "You know my record, creating a million jobs" ("Win Iowa'). Job creation clearly concerns policy (see table 7.1 for these data). *Spearman rho* indicates that policy utterances increased over time (*rho* [*n* = 24] = .54, *p* < .005).

Character appeals (46 percent) were almost as common in primary spots as policy themes. In 1996, this advertisement acclaimed Dole's character: "This courageous man, who understands so much about the privilege and the price of what it is to be an American" ("Courage"). Courage is a laudable quality in a presidential candidate. Buchanan used a disillusioned voter to charge that Dole was untrustworthy in this spot from 1992:

WOMAN [Nashua, NH]: Now I don't believe a word that the president says. I don't believe anything that comes out of his mouth anymore. I think it's all double talk, and I just I suspect anything that he says and I don't trust him and I'll never, ever get the trust that I had for Mr. Bush when I elected him, when I voted for him. I'll never get that trust back. ("Trust")

Trust and integrity are other important qualities for a president to possess. Michele Bachmann ran a spot in 2012 ("Voices Part 1") which declared that "Whenever she speaks there's like, there's a passion with her and it's real." Discussing the candidate's passion illustrates a character utterance. Thus, many primary commercials addressed questions of character. A *chi-square goodness-of-fit* test revealed that these differences were significant (χ^2 [df = 1] = 64.34, p < .0001). Figure 7.2 shows how these topics varied over time; inspection of table 7.1 shows that twelve data sets discussed policy more than character, ten discussed character more than policy, and two used these topics at the same rate (a data set is defined here as ads from one party in one campaign).

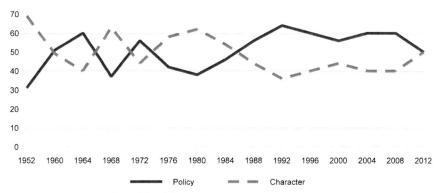

Figure 7.2. Topics of Presidential Primary TV Spots

Source: Benoit, 1999; Benoit and Compton, in press; Benoit, et al. 2003; Benoit et al. 2007; Benoit and Rill, 2012.

I also looked at the relative frequency of acclaims and attacks on the two topics, policy and character. In this sample more acclaims addressed character than policy (76 percent to 69 percent) and so more attacks concerned policy than character (31 percent to 24 percent). A *chi-square test of cross-classification* confirmed that these differences were significant (χ^2 [df = 1] = 50.2, p < .0001, φ = .08).

Forms of Policy and Character in Primary TV Spots

Primary spots focused primarily on general goals (46 percent) when they discussed policy topics. For example, in 1996, Alexander explained his goals to viewers: "I thought I'd take a minute to tell you what I'd actually do as president. I'd cut taxes, and unleash free enterprise to create good, new jobs. I'd help parents make our school as good as our colleges. And I'd help us learn to expect less from Washington and more from ourselves" ("Expectations"). Alexander acclaims three separate goals in this message. Kerry touted his goals in the 1992 primaries: "As president, I'll force open Japanese markets. That will mean almost three thousand jobs a day, a million jobs a year, and help put America back to work" ("Markets"). Although he does not indicate specifically how he will achieve this goal, he does spell out the desirable consequences of his proposal. These data are displayed in table 7.2.

Discussions of past deeds occurred almost as often as general goals in these advertisements (40 percent). Edward Kennedy attacked President Carter's energy policies in 1980: "You pay 98 cents a gallon for home heating oil. Gasoline, now a dollar-sixteen a gallon. Elderly people face a cruel choice between heat for their homes and food on their tables. And oil refiners' profits went up 800 percent last year. Jimmy Carter decontrolled the price of oil, so you pay while the oil companies profit" ("Energy"). Note how Kennedy explicitly links these problems with Carter's action of decontrolling the price of oil. In 1972, Humphrey acclaimed by reminding viewers of several of his past accomplishments: "So many people are seeking the Democratic nomination it's hard to tell the players without a scorecard. Who created Medicare? Humphrey. The job corps? Humphrey. The food stamp program? Humphrey. The first water control bill? Hubert Humphrey, and again, and again and again" ("Scorecard"). This commercial acclaims Humphrey by listing three specific deeds for which he is responsible and alludes to others as well.

Relatively fewer remarks from these commercials address the topic of future plans (13 percent). In this spot for Bush in 1992, he acclaimed his proposal for a balanced budget amendment: "To get our economy moving faster, we have to reduce the huge federal deficit by cutting spending. The only way to do that with certainty, is to pass the balanced budget amendment" ("Spending"). That same year, Clinton attacked the future plans of Brown and Tsongas: "Who's going to fight for us? Jerry Brown? Citizens for Tax Justice said 'Jerry Brown's national tax proposal would cut taxes for the rich in half, raise taxes for the middle class, and create a new 13 percent national sales tax.' And Paul Tsongas? He proposes another capital gains tax break for the rich, and up to a fifty-cent hike in the gas tax over ten years for the rest of us" ("Fights for Us"). Clinton clearly refers to and rejects specific taxation proposals advanced by his opponents Brown and Tsongas in this advertisement. Thus, future plans were at times the topics of both acclaims and attacks in primary spots.

When these spots discussed character, they were most likely to address personal qualities (54 percent). This advertisement for Bush in 1980 acclaimed his personal qualities: "George Bush has the ability and the integrity to earn the complete trust of the American people" ("Integrity"). In 1976, Wallace praised his own character and background in this commercial:

> I came up the hard way. I came up like the average Southerner came up in the years came up in the depression, and therefore I recognize and know for instance what poverty

Table 7.2. Forms of Policy in Presidential Primary TV Spots

	Past Deeds		Future Plans		General Goals	
	Acclaims	Attacks	Acclaims	Attacks	Acclaims	Attacks
1952 R	4	1	0	1	8	3
	5 (29%)		1 (6%)		**11 (65%)**	
1960 D	8	9	14	0	8	0
	17 (44%)		14 (36%)		8 (21%)	
1964 R	0	1	0	0	5	0
	1 (17%)		0		**5 (83%)**	
1968 D	0	3	2	1	10	1
	3 (18%)		3 (18%)		**11 (65%)**	
1968 R	0	15	2	0	9	0
	15 (58%)		2 (8%)		9 (35%)	
1972 D	8	41	7	1	48	9
	49 (43%)		8 (7%)		**57 (50%)**	
1972 R	16	0	0	0	1	0
	16 (94%)		0		1 (6%)	
1976 D	1	14	1	4	17	0
	15 (41%)		5 (14%)		**17 (46%)**	
1976 R	45	19	0	0	14	0
	64 (82%)		0		14 (18%)	
1980 D	34	51	0	5	30	2
	85 (70%)		5 (4%)		32 (26%)	
1980 R	8	33	14	3	66	10
	41 (31%)		17 (13%)		**76 (57%)**	
1984 D	15	45	11	2	80	9
	60 (37%)		13 (8%)		**89 (55%)**	
1988 D	50	9	4	2	80	6
	59 (39%)		6 (4%)		**86 (57%)**	
1988 R	10	16	7	1	46	24
	26 (25%)		8 (8%)		**70 (67%)**	
1992 D	46	38	43	42	107	10
	84 (28%)		85 (30%)		**117 (41%)**	
1992 R	7	26	14	8	42	12
	33 (30%)		22 (20%)		**54 (50%)**	
1996 D	46	42	31	42	77	14
	88 (35%)		73 (29%)		**91 (36%)**	
1996 R	47	118	64	15	116	22
	165 (43%)		79 (21%)		**138 (36%)**	
2000 D	28	18	35	6	144	7
	46 (19%)		41 (17%)		**151 (63%)**	
2000 R	38	26	39	10	165	12
	64 (22%)		49 (17%)		**177 (61%)**	
2004 D	97	102	25	2	243	16
	199 (41%)		27 (6%)		**259 (53%)**	

(continued)

Table 7.2.   (continued)

	Past Deeds		Future Plans		General Goals	
	Acclaims	Attacks	Acclaims	Attacks	Acclaims	Attacks
2008 D	104	123	42	4	255	6
	227 (43%)		46 (9%)		**261 (49%)**	
2008 R	111	83	21	0	150	9
	194 (52%)		21 (6%)		159 (42%)	
2012 R	50	156	37	5	85	32
	206 (56%)		42 (12%)		117 (32%)	
Total	742	978	404	154	1776	199
	1720 (40%)		558 (13%)		**1975 (46%)**	

Source: Benoit, 1999; Benoit and Compton, in press; Benoit, et al. 2003; Benoit et al. 2007; Benoit and Rill, 2012.
$\chi^2 \ (df = 2) = 804.88$, $p < .0001$

is. I have seen it. I have felt it. I have smelt it. I know it when I see it. I'm not like one of these limousine liberals who has never seen or knows what poverty is unless he reads it in the dictionary, because he was born with a silver spoon in his mouth, wants to be the president of the United States and wants to run the country, but he has no feel of actually what the average citizen feels and understands when he suffers inflation, unemployment, and no income. Because I have suffered every one of those—no income, low income, inflation, no employment. ("Silver Spoon")

He argues that his background prepares him to better understand the plight of the ordinary citizen. He also attacks his (unnamed) opponents for lacking the ability to identify with voters. Muskie acclaimed his likability and trustworthiness in this 1972 spot: "Ed Muskie has always had a strong sense of community. He's been liked and trusted and involved here for a long time" ("Community"). Thus, primary spots frequently addressed the candidates' personal qualities. These data are reported in table 7.3.

These advertisements also discussed leadership ability (26 percent). In this spot from 1992 Bush's exceptional leadership ability was acclaimed: "Perhaps no president in our history has shown the world such strong leadership" ("Leadership"). In 1984, this commercial for Mondale stressed his vast experience in government: "A lifetime of leadership. Attorney General of Minnesota, U.S. Senator, vice president" ("Service"). In the 1976 campaign, a spot promised explicitly that Reagan will "provide the strong new leadership America needs." Gary Hart in 1984 explained that "The South can once more change the course of history, by voting for new leadership, new ideas, and a fresh start for America" ("History"). Of course, Hart offers these very qualities. So, primary candidates acclaimed their qualifications to be leader of the free world.

Discussions of ideals constituted the least common form of character (20 percent). In 1972, Wallace attacked the ideals of his opponents: "There are six Senators in the race for the presidential nomination in Florida. In the Senate of the United

Table 7.3. Forms of Character in Presidential Primary TV Spots

	Personal Qualities		Leadership Ability		Ideals	
	Acclaims	Attacks	Acclaims	Attacks	Acclaims	Attacks
1952 R	9	1	20	1	6	0
	10 (27%)		**21 (57%)**		6 (16%)	
1960 D	13	9	4	2	16	0
	22 (50%)		6 (14%)		16 (36%)	
1964 R	1	1	0	0	2	0
	2 (50%)		0		2 (50%)	
1968 D	9	6	4	3	9	1
	15 (47%)		7 (22%)		10 (31%)	
1968 R	14	0	18	3	7	0
	14 (33%)		**21 (50%)**		7 (17%)	
1972 D	22	10	7	4	35	0
	32 (41%)		11 (14%)		**35 (45%)**	
1972 R	10	0	3	0	0	0
	10 (77%)		3 (23%)		0	
1976 D	13	13	19	3	14	2
	26 (41%)		22 (34%)		16 (25%)	
1976 R	35	2	53	4	7	1
	37 (36%)		**57 (56%)**		8 (8%)	
1980 D	48	20	22	37	33	2
	68 (42%)		59 (36%)		35 (22%)	
1980 R	99	30	81	17	31	4
	129 (50%)		98 (38%)		31 (12%)	
1984 D	42	28	62	18	36	2
	79 (37%)		**80 (43%)**		38 (20%)	
1988 D	61	12	31	2	14	0
	73 (61%)		33 (28%)		14 (12%)	
1988 R	27	12	27	1	9	0
	39 (51%)		28 (37%)		9 (12%)	
1992 D	72	40	17	6	12	2
	112 (75%)		23 (15%)		14 (8%)	
1992 R	7	43	15	3	7	0
	50 (67%)		18 (24%)		7 (9%)	
1996 D	3	10	1	0	22	0
	13 (36%)		1 (3%)		**22 (61%)**	
1996 R	115	114	48	21	76	22
	229 (58%)		69 (17%)		98 (25%)	
2000 D	82	13	19	2	10	0
	95 (75%)		21 (17%)		10 (8%)	
2000 R	132	31	41	0	80	6
	163 (56%)		41 (14%)		86 (30%)	
2004 D	148	37	57	10	54	4
	185 (60%)		67 (22%)		58 (19%)	

(continued)

Table 7.3.   (continued)

	Personal Qualities		Leadership Ability		Ideals	
	Acclaims	Attacks	Acclaims	Attacks	Acclaims	Attacks
2008 D	187	56	116	3	42	0
	243 (60%)		119 (29%)		42 (10%)	
2008 R	73	13	79	3	80	6
	86 (34%)		82 (32%)		86 (34%)	
2012 R	102	126	36	17	57	29
	228 (62%)		53 (14%)		86 (23%)	
Total	1324	637	780	160	659	81
	1961 (54%)		940 (26%)		740 (20%)	

Source: Benoit, 1999; Benoit and Compton, in press; Benoit, et al. 2003; Benoit et al. 2007; Benoit and Rill, 2012.
χ^2 (df = 2) = 706.75, $p < .0001$

States a vote was taken on freedom of choice. All six of them voted against freedom of choice" ("Choice"). It is clear that Wallace considered freedom of choice to be an important ideal, unlike his opponents. In 1996, an advertisement for Bob Dole acclaimed both his ideals and his personal qualities: "Bob Dole's conservative convictions and character will lead an American renewal" ("Renewal"). Obviously, conservative ideals should appeal to his Republican audience. These examples illustrate how primary candidates addressed the various forms of character appeals.

Functional Theory predicts that both general goals and ideals will be used more often to acclaim than to attack. It is easier to praise than criticize goals such as reducing unemployment or ideals such as freedom. In these ads, 90 percent of general goals were acclaims and 10 percent were attacks (χ^2 [df = 1] = 1259.2, $p < .0001$). When discussing ideals, these presidential primary spots also acclaimed much more than they attacked (89 percent to 11 percent; χ^2 [df = 1] = 451.45, $p < .0001$).

Conclusion: Primary TV Spots

These primary advertisements generally prefer acclaims (72 percent) to attacks (28 percent). Table 7.4 compares Kaid and Ballotti's results with the data reported here. Although the figures for some years are quite close (e.g., acclaims in 1984: 69 percent, 70 percent; in 1988: 80 percent, 82 percent), others are fairly discrepant (e.g., acclaims in 1968: 98 percent, 72 percent; in 1976: 94 percent, 77 percent). These differences could be a result of their coding method, which determines the "dominant focus" of an ad (which I think is most likely; this idea was discussed in chapter 2, or because their sample includes more spots than my sample, or because my sample includes more campaigns than theirs. Defenses occurred, but are relatively infrequent in primary spots (1 percent; Kaid and Ballotti did not code for defenses).

Table 7.4. Comparison of Kaid and Ballotti (1991) and Benoit Results

Campaign	Acclaims (Benoit)	Positive* (Kaid and Ballotti)	Attacks (Benoit)	Negative (Kaid and Ballotti)
1968	72%	98%	24%	2%
1972	73%	86%	27%	14%
1976	77%	94%	23%	6%
1980	68%	76%	32%	24%
1984	70%	69%	30%	31%
1988	82%	80%	18%	20%
Total	74%	78%	26%S	22%

*positive = image + issue

There is only a slight edge for policy topics (54 percent) over character (46 percent). This is roughly similar to Kaid and Ballotti's findings: 48 percent issue and 32 percent image and 3 percent combination (exact comparisons between their results and mine are difficult because their approach also classified spots as negative—18 percent—although we cannot tell if these negative spots discussed policy or character). Discussion of general goals (46 percent) and past deeds (40 percent) are more common than future plans (13 percent). When character is addressed, these spots tend to discuss personal qualities most often (54 percent), with leadership (26 percent) and ideals (20 percent) less frequently discussed.

8

Political Television Spots from Third-Party Candidates

Another Choice

In the modern era, presidential campaigns have been dominated by the two major political parties. However, third-party candidates regularly seek the presidency. Democrat Hubert Humphrey decided to attack George Wallace (who was running as a third-party candidate in 1968) in several of his spots, whereas Republican Richard Nixon advertisement cautioned citizens against "wasting" their vote on a third-party candidate. In an interesting twist to this argument, in 1996 Ross Perot urged "Don't waste your vote on politics as usual." Perot clearly exerted an influence on the 1992 campaign, and was selected to participate in the presidential debates. Ralph Nader ran in 2000 and won 2 percent of the vote in Florida, where eventually Bush won over Gore (both had 49 percent of the vote; InfoPlease, 2000). Of course we have no idea what would have happened if Nader had not run, but the Florida results that year determined who became president. Despite a few prominent examples, third-party candidates and their spots are relatively uncommon. I located 66 spots from six campaigns (1968, 1980, 1992, 1996, 2000, 2012) and six candidates (Wallace, Anderson, Perot [twice], Browne, Nader, and Johnson). Although this is a much more limited than the sample for either general or primary spots, I was unable to locate any study in the literature that focused on third-party spots (of course, third-party candidates are sometimes mentioned in articles devoted to a single campaign).

The earliest third-party candidate for whom I located television spots was George Wallace, who ran in the 1968 campaign (he also competed in Democratic primaries later). His spots hammered away at issues like forced public school busing, crime and violence, and foreign aid. Another theme was that he has the courage to lead America in the proper direction. Here is one of his advertisements:

> ANNOUNCER [1968; scenes of riots, poverty, violence]: 1968, a time of international crisis and domestic chaos. In times like these we need a president who can meet the challenges of America. A man of sufficient courage to return the nation to its proper course.

WALLACE: And the most recent mistake they made was when Castro was in the hills of Cuba, the *New York Times* wrote that he was the Robin Hood of the Caribbean. He was introduced on nationwide television as being the George Washington of Cuba.

ANNOUNCER: At informal discussions designed to seek an upward revision of Cuba's sugar quota, it was Mr. Nixon who said, quote: "The United States is nationally interested in working with Cuba." Is this the kind of man we want to trust with the future of America? ("1968")

This spot uses a quotation from and a picture of Nixon. Especially given Nixon's history as an opponent of Communism, this was a potentially damaging attack.

In 1980, John Anderson ran against Jimmy Carter and Ronald Reagan. This spot illustrates his approach:

Fact: Former President Gerald Ford once said of John Anderson, "He's the smartest guy in Congress, but he insists on voting his conscience instead of his party." *Fact*: 69 percent of Americans believe John Anderson has the courage to talk straight [ABC News-Harris Survey, October 8, 1980]. *Fact*: The *LA Times* poll shows John Anderson ahead of Carter when he is given a chance to win [*LA Times*–National Poll, October 15, 1980]. So we can have a president we respect. Don't we need more than a Jimmy Carter or a Ronald Reagan now? Don't we really need John Anderson? ("Fact 1")

Repetition of the word "fact" is surely intended to provide more force to these claims. Because the major parties have dominated presidential politics for so long, it is important for third-party candidates to establish their viability in the election that a vote for them would not be wasted. This spot argues strongly that Anderson is a credible candidate.

Ross Perot ran in the 1992 election. Many of his advertisements focused on the huge federal debt. However, he also discussed our country's potential for improvement under his leadership:

ANNOUNCER: Ross Perot on what this country can be.

PEROT: We can be a country whose people are working hard at their jobs instead of working hard just to find a job. We can be a country where once again the diversity of our people is our greatest strength, instead of division being our greatest weakness. We can be a country leading the way instead of a country falling behind. We can be all of these things tomorrow if we would just make the tough choices today. ("What This Country Can Be")

Perot juxtaposes the problems of today (unemployment, division, falling behind) with the goals that he would help achieve if elected.

In his 1996 campaign, Perot focused on two other themes: complaints about being omitted from the presidential debates, and the problem of special interests in Washington. This spot illustrates the latter argument:

[The video metamorphoses through a series of ordinary people]: Don't throw your vote away on politics as usual. Just vote for Ross. We can make the twenty-first century the greatest in our history. We can take our country back from the special interests. Just vote for Ross.

PEROT: Because it is your country. ("Your Country")

Perot attacks special interests (and, implicitly, the politicians who cater to them) and promises great things for our next century if he is elected president.

The most radical of the third-party candidates for whom I found spots was Harry Browne, the Libertarian candidate for president in 1996. This advertisement illustrates his campaign:

BROWNE: Social Security is headed for collapse, yet neither Bill Clinton nor Bob Dole will admit it. We must get the government completely out of Social Security by selling off federal assets and using the proceeds to buy a private annuity for everyone who needs it. And then you will be free forever from that 15 percent tax that you know is just money down the drain. I'm Harry Browne, the Libertarian candidate for president. This year, vote for freedom. Vote to get your life back. Vote for Harry Browne. ("Social Security")

He offers proposals for change that are quite different from those advocated by the major party candidates.

Ralph Nader ran ads in 2000. One was a spoof of a commercial from Master Card giving prices for some purchases suggesting that a woman could make her ex-boyfriend feel jealous and concluding that there were some things money can't buy, but for everything else there is Mastercard. Nader's commercial "Priceless" was modeled after a commercial for Mastercard:

Grilled tenderloin for fundraiser: $1000 per plate [picture of Bush]. Campaign ads filled with half-truths: $10 million [Gore ad]. Promises to special interest groups: over $10 billion [pictures of Bush and Gore]. Finding out the truth: priceless [Nader working at desk]. There are some things money can't buy. Without Ralph Nader in the presidential debates, the truth will come in last. Find out how you can help: go to votenader.com. Vote Ralph Nader for president.

This spot clearly suggested that Nader's principal opponents could be bought but Nader's search for truth was without price.

Gary Johnson, who served as Governor of New Mexico, represented the Libertarian Party in the 2012 election. One of the two ads I found for Johnson was called "Imagine."

[music, on screen, no announcer] IMAGINE Balanced Budget in 2013. Less taxes taken from your paycheck [$] No more inflation: Gas, food, tuition. Health care entrepreneurs unleashed on a free market. Real national defense not nation building.

An administration for who LGBT is not a four letter word. Imagine President Gary Johnson. Join Team Johnson.

He hit several issues—inflation, health care, national defense, GLBT rights—and used more acclaims than attacks. Johnson's other ad in this sample had video of a drone, over which he declared that "Right now in Iran, a lot of little kids are about to die. I'm gonna be the only candidate that does not want to bomb Iran." This makes you wonder whether future ads will feature drones—and whether they will reject or support the use of this weapon. These commercials illustrate the third-party campaigns in this study.

FUNCTIONS OF THIRD PARTY POLITICAL TV SPOTS

Third party candidates acclaimed in 66 percent of their spot utterances; only one candidate in this sample (Nader, 2000) used more attacks than acclaims. For example, in 1968, Wallace announced that "As president, I shall within the law turn back the absolute control of the public school systems to the people of the respective states." Forced busing was a heated topic of discussion during that campaign, and Wallace acclaimed his goal on this issue. A spot for Anderson in 1980 reported that "My purpose in running for president is not to weaken the two party system in America. Rather, it is to strengthen that system in the future by making it aware that it must respond to the people." Surely we want our political system to be responsive to our will. Perot acclaimed his ideals in 1992 in this commercial: "If you want a government that comes from the people instead of at the people, let your vote say so." In 1996, Browne proposed this solution for financing the government: "Let's repeal the income tax and replace it with nothing. Let's make the government live by the Constitution and pass the savings on to you." Although this proposal might seem radical, some voters would surely embrace it. Thus, these candidates acclaimed extensively in their campaigns (see table 8.1).

Table 8.1. Functions and Topics of Third Party Political TV Spots

	Functions		Topics	
	Acclaims	*Attacks*	*Policy*	*Character*
Wallace 1968	**18 (56%)**	14 (44%)	**24 (75%)**	8 (25%)
Anderson 1980	**80 (95%)**	4 (5%)	27 (32%)	**57 (68%)**
Perot 1992	**59 (54%)**	50 (46%)	**65 (60%)**	44 (40%)
Perot 1996	**46 (70%)**	20 (30%)	25 (38%)	**41 (62%)**
Browne 1996	**21 (55%)**	17 (45%)	**33 (75%)**	11 (25%)
Nader 2000	2 (15%)	**11 (85%)**	3 (28%)	**10 (77%)**
Johnson 2012	**8 (80%)**	2 (20%)	**8 (80%)**	2 (20%)
Total	**234 (66%)**	118 (34%)	**185 (52%)**	173 (48%)

No defenses occurred in these spots.

These candidates attacked in 34 percent of their remarks. Wallace attacked foreign aid in this advertisement: "Watch your hard-earned dollars sail away to anti-American countries [video of ship sailing off]." Anderson argued that in 1980: "Our nation faces deep problems, and this year's presidential campaign is one of them. Issues are being ignored, problems papered over, personal attacks, easy promises, easy answers, and none of it feels true. What does it mean for a great democracy when the two major candidates for our highest elected office refuse to face up to the crucial issues?" Here, he managed to allude to policy problems while attacking the character of both Carter and Reagan. In 1996, Perot complained bitterly that he had been left out of the presidential debates: "Why are they [Dole and Clinton video] desperate to keep Ross Perot out of the debate when 76 percent of the voters want him?" Browne attacked his Republican opponent in this spot: "Bob Dole wants to give you a tiny tax cut, but he has no plans to reduce the size of government." Thus, attacks were common in these spots. None of these third-party candidates used defenses in their advertisements, probably because attacks on third-party candidates are quite rare.

TOPICS OF THIRD PARTY POLITICAL TV SPOTS

Third party candidates addressed policy topics (52 percent) at essentially the same race as character (48 percent). The ads for three candidates (Anderson, 1980; Perot, 1996; and Nader, 2000) emphasized character more than policy. An example of a policy utterance can be found in this ad from Wallace in 1968: "As president, I will stand up for your local police and firemen in protecting your safety and property." In 1980, Anderson acclaimed his record on several important issues: "He has fought for equal rights, campaign reform [leader in fight for campaign reform], a strong economy, and John Anderson's proposed a bold new energy program for America [leader for energy independence]." Perot directed our attention to the federal budget deficit in this advertisement from 1992: "Our children dream of the world that we promise them as parents, a world of unlimited opportunity. What would they say to us if they knew that by the year 2000, we will have left them with a national debt of eight trillion dollars?" Browne focused on governmental spending in this 1996 advertisement: "The major issue in this election is whether we're going to stop the Democratic and Republican organizations from taking your money and throwing it away. From stealing your freedoms while promising you benefits they can't deliver. From destroying our cities, our schools, our health care system, and our country." He accuses both major parties of complicity in these problems. Thus, third-party spots are replete with policy appeals (see table 8.1).

Character was about as common in these advertisements as policy. In 1968, one spot noted that "Wallace has the courage to stand up for America," acclaiming his personal quality. An advertisement for Anderson asked voters, "Don't we really need that independence, that intelligence, that conscience in a president? Don't we really need John Anderson now?" These are three desirable qualities in a president. In

1996, this commercial for Perot declared: "I'm voting for the only candidate who is not for sale at any price. I'm voting for Ross. He has never taken a penny of special interest money. Never will." Clearly integrity is an important trait for a candidate for president to possess. Browne acclaimed his ideals in this advertisement: "This year, vote for freedom. Vote to get your life back. Vote for Harry Browne." Thus, these spots devoted a good deal of their time to addressing character issues.

FORMS OF POLICY AND CHARACTER IN THIRD PARTY POLITICAL TV SPOTS

When third-party commercials discussed policy topics, they focused most on general goals (52 percent), then on past deeds (39 percent), and least often on future plans (10 percent). For example, Wallace acclaimed this goal, should the Paris peace talks fail to resolve the Vietnam War: "As your president, I shall call upon the Joint Chiefs of Staff to bring a military conclusion to the war with conventional weapons and bring American servicemen home and turn the security of South Vietnam over strictly to the South Vietnamese forces." In 1996, this spot mentioned Perot's "pledge to reform campaign spending [reform campaign spending] and influence peddling by lobbyists [reform influence peddling by lobbyists]." Browne appealed to past deeds in this spot: "Your paycheck is being ravaged by the income tax. Your retirement is being subverted by a fraudulent scheme called Social Security, and your city is being destroyed by an insane war on drugs." Clearly he sees these problems as reasons to turn away from the traditional parties. Anderson attacked plans for tax reduction from the other candidates: "Multi-billion dollar tax cuts, proposed by my opponents, sound good. I can't support them. They will increase inflation, the cruelest tax of all." In 1992, Perot rejected his opponents' plans to reduce the federal debt: "We have a national debt of four trillion dollars. . . . This is a bomb that is set to go off and devastate the economy, destroy thousands and thousands of jobs. The other two candidates have told you to ignore the ticking. They've given you plans that will only delay dealing with the issue. But I've spelled out a solution that will fix this problem starting now." He attacks Bush's and Clinton's future plans while acclaiming his own proposal in this commercial. Thus, these spots illustrate use of the three forms of policy topics (see table 8.2).

When third-party spots addressed character topics, they emphasized personal qualities most (60 percent), followed by ideals (23 percent), and then by leadership ability (17 percent). Anderson spoke out against certain religious figures, basing his objection on an important ideal: "I'm repelled by those television preachers who call themselves a moral majority. They want to tell us how to vote, influence legislation, and reveal whose prayers God listens to. That's not for me. It violates a basic constitutional principle that I believe in: separation of church and state." In 1992, Perot explained simply that "I want you to have the American dream," a declaration of one of his ideals. In 1980, Anderson acclaimed his experience in

Table 8.2. Forms of Policy in Third Party Political TV Spots

Candidate	Past Deeds		Future Plans		General Goals	
	Acclaims	Attacks	Acclaims	Attacks	Acclaims	Attacks
Wallace 1968	0	13	0	0	11	0
Anderson 1980	10	0	8	0	9	0
Perot 1992	0	28	0	3	34	0
Perot 1996	5	1	0	0	19	0
Browne 1996	0	11	2	4	11	5
Nader 2000	0	2	0	0	1	1
Johnson 2012	0	2	1	0	5	0
Total	15	57	11	7	90	7
	72 (39%)		18 (10%)		97 (52%)	

government: "He served on the powerful House Rules Committee." Wallace acclaimed both his leadership ability and his personal qualities in this advertisement: "In times like these we need a president who can meet the challenges of America. A man of sufficient courage to return the nation to its proper course." These excerpts reveal how these third-party candidates used the three forms of character utterances in their spots. See table 8.3 for these data.

CONCLUSION: THIRD PARTY POLITICAL TV SPOTS

No third-party candidate has won the presidency during the modern era (during which television spots played a role in the campaign, 1952–2012). I take this as evidence of the continued importance of the two major political parties.

However, this does not necessarily mean that third-party candidates are irrelevant. For example, Perot in 1992 focused attention on the federal debt. Furthermore, Benoit and Wells (1996) argue that his presence influenced the course of the presidential

Table 8.3. Forms of Character Third Party Political TV Spots

Candidate	Personal Qualities		Leadership Ability		Ideals	
	Acclaims	Attacks	Acclaims	Attacks	Acclaims	Attacks
Wallace 1968	5	1	1	0	1	0
Anderson 1980	34	4	11	0	8	0
Perot 1992	2	14	15	3	8	2
Perot 1996	13	19	0	0	9	0
Browne 1996	0	1	0	0	8	2
Nader 2000	1	9	0	0	0	0
Johnson 2012	0	0	0	0	2	0
Total	55	48	27	3	36	4
	103 (60%)		30 (17%)		40 (23%)	

debates because he tended to attack Bush more than Clinton—and neither candidate devoted many attacks to Perot (hoping not to alienate Perot's followers, who might have voted for Bush or Clinton at the last minute).

These spots from third-party candidates were more likely to acclaim (66 percent) than attack (34 percent) and did not contain defenses. They used topics of policy (51 percent) and character (49 percent) at almost exactly the same rate. When they addressed policy, they focused on general goals (51 percent) most often, followed by past deeds (39 percent), and, least often, on future plans (10 percent). When discussing character, they addressed personal qualities most frequently (60 percent), followed by ideals (22 percent), and leadership least often (18 percent). These advertisements relied more heavily on others (67 percent) than on the candidates themselves (33 percent).

III

OTHER CAMPAIGNS

9

Other Theories and Political Television Spots

Data from the study of political advertising have been used to investigate two theories that were developed in political science: Issue Ownership and Functional Federalism. These theories and the associated data will be discussed in this chapter. The data for research on Issue Ownership and Functional Federalism were generated with computer content analysis. One study (Petrocik, Benoit, and Hansen, 2003–2004) produced a list of words (generated from American presidential TV spots) of words for various issues such as jobs, education, crime, foreign policy, and health care. These topics were divided into issues owned by Democrats and Republicans (for Issue Ownership) and into national and state issues (for Functional Federalism). The transcripts of political debates were edited to eliminate all statements that were not made by candidates; for issue ownership separate files were created for statements by Democratic and Republican candidates. Software counted the number of times the words in each issue list (national, state/local; Democratic, Republican) occurred in a file (Concordance, 2012).

ISSUE OWNERSHIP

Petrocik (1996) focuses on policy problems (issues) and argues that a political party has an advantage it can exploit when voters believe that it is better able to handle a particular problem than the opposing party. Ownership of an issue can arise in two different ways. First, over time, political parties can acquire ownership of an issue:

> Party constituency ownership of an issue is much more long-term (although it can change and occasionally exhibits fluctuation) because its foundation is (1) the relatively stable, but different social bases, that distinguish party constituencies in modern party systems and (2) the link between political conflict and social structure. (p. 827)

Second, the "record of the incumbent creates a handling advantage when one party can be blamed for current difficulties" (p. 827). Such difficulties as "wars, failed international or domestic policies, unemployment and inflation, or official corruption" can provide the out party with a "'lease'—short-term ownership—of a performance issue" (p. 827). Although the forms of issue ownership vary in the length of advantage they confer on a political party, owning or leasing an issue has the same potential advantage.

Petrocik notes that "the campaigns waged by the candidates increase the salience of some problems, and, in doing so, cause voters to use their party linkage perception of the issue handling ability of the candidates to choose between (or among) them" (p. 827). Fundamentally, the idea is that when a candidate stresses an issue during the campaign such emphasis should have an agenda-setting effect (see, e.g., McCombs, 2004; McCombs and Shaw, 1972), increasing the perceived importance of that issue for voters. Presumably, issues of higher salience will exert a greater influence on voting behavior. An ABC news poll (9/23–26/2002) reported that 51 percent of respondents believed that Republicans could do a better job handling crime compared with 30 percent who believed Democrats fought crime better than Republicans. In the same poll people said that Democrats did a better job handling Social Security than Republicans, 50 percent to 33 percent. If the attitudes reported in this poll were held by voters on Election Day in 2004, President Bush would have a decided advantage over Senator Kerry if crime was uppermost in the minds of citizens. In contrast, Kerry would have enjoyed a distinct advantage if Social Security mattered most to the electorate on the day they voted. So, candidates have a reason to stress the issues owned by their party in messages hoping that those issues will become more important to voters, advantaging them at the polls.

Damore (2005) discusses the concept of "issue convergence," the notion that opposing candidates often discuss the same issues in their campaign messages (see also Pfau and Kenski, 1990 or Sigelman and Buell, 2004). Although some view this as a criticism of Issue Ownership Theory, Petrocik did not argue that political candidates only addressed the issues owned by their own political party; he claimed that Democratic and Republican candidates *emphasized* different issues. The data reported here clearly shows that candidates from both political parties discuss many of the same issues (as advocates of issue convergence claim) but that Democratic candidates are prone to emphasize Democratic issues more, and Republican issues less, than Republican candidates (as Issue Ownership predicts).

Literature Review

Several studies offer evidence pertinent to Issue Ownership theory. Petrocik (1996) provided public opinion polls from 1988–1991 on a number of issues to indicate which parties owned those issues at that point in time.

Democrats are seen as better able to handle welfare problems. Perceptions of the parties on moral issues (e.g., crime and protecting moral values) favor the GOP. The data also document the GOP's hold on foreign policy and defense through the late 1980s. Opinions were mixed on economic matters, but were generally a GOP asset (by an average of about 13 points). Government spending, inflation, and taxation were also Republican issues. (p. 831)

The data confirmed the existence of issue ownership patterns among voters during this time period.

Petrocik (1996) investigated the question of whether candidates tend to use campaigns to stress issues owned by their own political party. Content analysis of *New York Times* coverage of the presidential campaign from 1952–1988 revealed that "presidential candidates emphasize issues owned by their party, although there are notable election and party differences" (p. 833). Petrocik, Benoit, and Hansen (2003–2004), employing data from 1952–2000, found that both nomination acceptance addresses and general television spots confirm issue ownership predictions (although they noted a tendency for presidential candidates to emphasize Republican issues more than Democratic issues overall, arguing that Republicans tend to own more national issues than Democrats). Similarly, presidential candidates show a tendency to stress their own party's issues even more in the primary than the general campaign (Benoit and Hansen, 2002). Other research reveals issue ownership patterns in nonpresidential spots (Benoit and Airne, 2005; Brazeal and Benoit, 2008) and in *New York Times'* coverage of nonpresidential spots (Brasher, 2003). Benoit (2014) reviews data from content analysis of political debates that support Issue Ownership's prediction. Thus, various data confirm the prediction of Issue Ownership Theory that candidates exhibit a tendency to emphasize the issues owned by their own political party in their campaign messages.

Other research has studied the effects of issue ownership on voters. Ansolabehere and Iyengar (1994) found that messages on Democratic issues were more effective when they were attributed to Democratic than Republican sources (and messages on GOP issues were more persuasive when the sources was a Republican rather than a Democrat). Simon (2002) reported that candidates were less persuasive when they engaged in "dialogue" on the other party's issues. Finally, Petrocik, Benoit, and Hansen (2003/2004; see also Petrocik, 1996) report that there is a strong relationship "between the vote and the issue ownership bias of the problems of concern to the electorate" (p. 617; see also Benoit, 2007c). Issue Ownership, therefore, has been found to influence voters and voting behavior.

Sample of Political TV Spots

The presidential TV spots employed in this analysis are from 1952–2000. Nonpresidential advertisements (gubernatorial, senate, house, and local) are from 1980–2002.

Results

Overall, Democratic candidates discussed issues owned by their party 60 percent of the time and Republican issues 40 percent of the time. Republicans had the opposite distribution: 60 percent Republican-owned issues and 40 percent Democratically-owned issues. Statistical analysis using a *chi-square test of cross-classification* confirmed that these differences were significant (χ^2 [df = 1] = 652.91, p < .0001, φ = .2). This pattern—a greater emphasis on the issues owned by the candidate's own political party—occurred in all three sets of data. All three sub-samples—presidential primary, presidential general, and nonpresidential debates—found the expected contrast. Notice that these data provide support for both issue convergence and issue ownership. In these ads candidates from both political parties discussed Democratic issues and Republican issues (convergence); however, Democrats treated Democratic issues more often, and Republican issues less often, than Republicans (issue ownership). These data are reported in table 9.1.

Table 9.1. Issue Ownership in Political TV Spots

	TV Spot Issues	
Candidate's Party	Democratic	Republican
Presidential General TV Spots		
Democrat	**1070 (51%)**	1009 (49%)
Republican	653 (36%)	**1142 (64%)**
Presidential Primary TV Spots		
Democrat	**1025 (65%)**	543 (35%)
Republican	860 (39%)	**1341 (61%)**
Governor, Senate, House, Local		
Democrat	**2789 (63%)**	1658 (37%)
Republican	1598 (42%)	**2174 (58%)**
Total		
Democrat	**4884 (60%)**	3210 (40%)
Republican	3111 (40%)	4657 **(60%)**

President: Petrocik, Benoit, and Hansen, 2003–2004; Senate and House: Brazeal and Benoit, 2008; Governor, Senate, House, and Local: Benoit and Airne, 2005
Pres 1952–2000; Senate and House 1980–2000; Governor, Senate, House, and Local 1980–2002
χ^2 (df = 1) = 652.91, p < .0001, φ = .2

FUNCTIONAL FEDERALISM

America has adopted a federalist system of government, which means that different levels of government have responsibilities for different areas. For example, the federal government does not collect garbage or fight fires; state government does not make treaties or fight wars with other countries. Peterson (1995) explained that "each level of government had its own independently elected political leaders and its own separate taxing and spending capacity" (p. 10). He distinguished between two groups of issues, developmental (state) and redistributive (national). "Developmental programs provide the physical and social infrastructure necessary to facilitate a country's economic development" (p. 17). Developmental policies concern transportation, sanitation, and public utilities (physical infrastructure), as well as police, fire, public health, and education (social infrastructure). In contrast, he explained that "Redistributive programs reallocate societal resources from the 'haves' to the 'have-nots'" (p. 17). These include welfare programs for the elderly, the poor, the unemployed, single-parent families, and those who are ill. Peterson argued that the national government has primary responsibility for redistributive policies whereas state and local government mostly implement developmental policies. Some areas of overlap exist (e.g., both state and federal governments fight crime); still, state and local government spends about twice as much as the federal government on developmental policies; the federal government, in contrast, spends about three times as much as state and local government on redistributive policies.

Atkeson and Partin (2001) discussed the implications of Functional Federalism for political campaign messages:

> National-level politicians should emphasize in their work and communications with citizens . . . a more heavily redistributive and international agenda. In contrast, state leaders and state elected officials should emphasize in their work and communications with citizens . . . a more localized, state agenda oriented around developmental policies such as education, taxes, infrastructure, and crime. (p. 796)

Similarly, Stein (1990) argued that, in general, citizens understand these governmental functions:

> Voters are aware of the differences in functional responsibilities assigned to local, state, and federal governments. Specifically, they understand that responsibility for state economic conditions depends significantly on the actions of the national government and market factors. Unemployment, interest rates, [and] economic growth . . . are largely, if not exclusively, the domain and responsibility of the national government. (p. 34)

Stein offered opinion poll data which shows that economic issues are thought by voters to be important reasons for senatorial, but not gubernatorial, vote choice. He also indicated that in the 1982 elections that "Senatorial voting exhibits clear and unambiguous economic voting" (p. 50) but the evidence for economic voting in gubernatorial elections is less strong.

Literature Review

Atkeson and Partin (2001) analyzed Senate and gubernatorial television advertisements broadcast in 1986, reporting that developmental issues, such as education, were more likely to be found in political spots for gubernatorial than senatorial candidates. On the other hand, redistributive issues such as the elderly and foreign policy were more likely to be employed in senatorial than gubernatorial ads. They also reported that newspaper coverage tended to follow the predictions of functional federalism (stories on governor's races stressed state issues; stories on senate races emphasized national issues). Tidmarch, Hyman, and Sorkin (1984) examined newspaper coverage in 1982, concluding that "the national policy agenda, while visible, is a demonstrably smaller presence in gubernatorial campaign coverage than in House and Senate coverage" (p. 1239). Benoit (2014) reports data from political campaign debates supporting this theory (see Henson and Benoit, 2007). So, Functional Federalism predicts that:

H1. *Candidates for Senate will use discuss national issues more, and local issues less, than candidates in gubernatorial races.*

However, this theory can also be extended to address presidential campaign messages along with senate and gubernatorial messages. The president serves the entire United States; the constituency for a senator is a single state. This suggests that presidents will tend to stress national issues even more than senators. Accordingly, I also predict that:

H2. *Candidates for president will discuss national issues even more than candidates for Senate.*

Sample of Political TV Spots

The political TV spots employed in this analysis included gubernatorial, senate, and house ads from 2002–2004 and presidential TV spots from 1980–2004.

Results

Analysis revealed that, as predicted, ads from candidates for governor stressed local issues more (54 percent to 37 percent and 36 percent) and national issues less (46 percent to 63 percent and 64 percent) than spots for House and Senate Races. Presidential ads stressed national issues more than local issues (66 percent to 34 percent). Statistical analysis confirmed that these differences were significant (χ^2 [$df = 3$] = 373.84, $p < .0001$, $V = .17$). These data are reported in table 9.2.

Table 9.2.   Functional Federalism in American Political TV Spots

	State/Local	National
Gubernatorial	**1812 (54%)**	1526 (46%)
House	952 (37%)	**1603 (63%)**
Senate	1328 (36%)	**2405 (64%)**
Presidential	1404 (34%)	**2670 (66%)**

χ^2 ($df = 3$) = 373.84, $p < .0001$, $V = 0.17$.
Gubernatorial, Senate, House ads from 2002–2004; Presidential ads from 1980–2004. Benoit and Airne, 2005; Brazeal and Benoit, 2008

CONCLUSION

This chapter examines two theories developed in political science using data from political TV spots. The predictions of Issue Ownership theory (Petrocik, 1986) on relative emphasis of Democratic and Republican issues were confirmed in presidential, gubernatorial, senate, house, and local TV spots. The predictions related to Functional Federalism (Peterson, 1995)—that gubernatorial ads stress state issues most and national issues least, presidential ads discuss national issues most and state issues least, with senate and house ads in the middle—were also confirmed with these data. These theories supplement Functional Theory in understanding political television advertisements.

10

Nonpresidential and Non-U.S. Television Spots

Thus far, this book has focused mainly on presidential TV spots (chapter 9 is an exception, but does not focus on functions and topics). However, political television advertising is used frequently in campaigns for nonpresidential offices and in campaigns for offices in other countries. This chapter focuses on these two sites for political advertising.

NONPRESIDENTIAL TV SPOTS

Campaign consultants and candidates alike are convinced that televised political advertising is a vital element component of successful campaigns (Jenkins, 1997; Sinclair, 1995). A meta-analysis (Benoit, Leshner, and Chattopadhyay, 2007) found that televised political advertising increased issue knowledge, influenced perceptions of the candidates' character, altered attitudes, affected candidate preference; influenced agenda-setting, and altered vote likelihood (turnout). Billions of dollars are spent on political advertising. Bachman (2012) indicated that total ad spending in 2012 would top $5 billion. Although the presidential campaign constitutes the lion's share of this spending, millions of dollars are devoted to nonpresidential ads as well. And, of course, millions are spent on advertising in off-year elections in the United States. For example, TNS Media Intelligence (2004) reported that congressional candidates spent $379.4 million on television advertising in 2004. The Center for Responsive Politics (2010) reported that the ten most expensive U.S. Senate races in 2008 (Minnesota, Kentucky, North Carolina, Georgia, Texas, Colorado, Oregon, Massachusetts, New Hampshire, and Louisiana) together spent over $243 million. Meg Whitman established a new record for spending in gubernatorial elections, spending $27 million in eleven weeks during the primary campaign (Rotheld and

McGreevy, 2010). It is not surprising that political campaign spending continues un-
abated. The huge amount of money spent on gubernatorial and congressional races
is not wasted: Research confirms that television spots influence election outcomes
at all levels (Joslyn, 1981; Wanat, 1974). However, most content analytic research
on political advertising focuses at the presidential level: Books on presidential television advertising include Benoit (1999), Diamond and Bates (1992), Dover (2006),
Jamieson (1996), Kaid and Johnston (2001), and West (2014). Although some research investigates both presidential and nonpresidential advertising (Ansolabehere
and Iyengar, 1995; Johnson-Cartee and Copeland, 1991, 1997; Kern, 1989; Nelson
and Boynton, 1997; Schultz, 2004; Thurber, Nelson, and Dulio, 2000), few books
focus exclusively on nonpresidential advertising (e.g., Kahn and Kenney, 1999; Lau
and Pomper, 2004; Maisel and West, 2004; Nesbit, 1988) and none examine gubernatorial commercials. However, political advertising is unquestionably important in
nonpresidential races because the news lavishes most attention on the presidential
contest. Political advertising, which has been shown to inform the electorate (Benoit,
Leshner, and Chattopadhyay, 2007), may have a disproportionate impact in nonpresidential races where less information is usually available about these candidates
and their issue positions from other sources, such as the news.

Furthermore, a presidential campaign occurs once every four years. In sharp
contrast, the United States is the scene for thousands of other political campaigns,
some of which are held as frequently as every two years. Nonpresidential spots are
also important because the news focuses on horse race rather than policy or character when reporting on these races. Furgerson, Sargardia, Seifert, and Benoit (2013)
analyzed news coverage of 2010 Senate and 2010 gubernatorial campaigns. Horse
race (43 percent) was the most frequent topic of stories about these campaigns,
followed by character (30 percent), and policy (26 percent). Clearly, the study of
nonpresidential political advertising is justified by the large amounts of money
spent on this medium, the sheer number of candidates and offices involved, as well
as the number of voters who constitute the audience for these messages. First, I
review the literature on nonpresidential television spots. Existing research into the
nature of nonpresidential television advertising addresses two variables, function
(acclaims, attacks, defenses) and topic (policy and character). Studies investigating
each concept in such ads will be reviewed. Then discuss data which investigate the
content of these spots.

Several authors have examined the functions of political commercials. Negative
advertising was used frequently in the North Carolina Senate race between Helms
and Hunt (Kern, 1989). Challengers frequently use attack ads, as in the Maryland
Senate race between Mikulski and Chavez (Sheckels, 1994) and in the Boschwitz-
Wellstone race (Pfau, Parrott, and Lindquist, 1992). Benze and Declerq (1985)
reported that congressional candidates attacked about half the time: 47 percent for
male candidates, and 44 percent for female candidates. Kahn and Kenney's (1999)
study of the 1988, 1990, and 1992 Senate campaigns reported that 18 percent of the
ads in their sample criticized the general policy priorities of the opposing candidate,
17 percent criticized a specific policy position, and 20 percent blamed an opponent

for a negative policy outcome. Weaver-Lariscy and Tinkham (1996) surveyed candidates for the U.S. House of Representatives: 48 percent reported that they ran partly or mainly negative campaigns in 1982 whereas 35 percent said their campaign was partly or mainly negative in 1990. Ansolabehere et al. (1994), who analyzed newspaper coverage rather than ads, indicated that 51 percent of U.S. Senate campaigns in 1992 were mainly negative (newspaper coverage of campaigns are consistently and significantly more negative than the candidates themselves: see, e.g., Benoit, Hemmer, and Stein, 2010; Benoit, Stein, and Hansen, 2005). Several studies of specific congressional races in 2002 found more positive than negative ads (Brewer, 2004; Ezra, 2004; Larson, 2004; Petterson, 2004; cf. Busch, 2004; Prysby, 2004). Two studies reported that challengers attacked more than incumbents (Petterson, 2004; Shockley, 2004) and four indicated that candidate ads were more positive than ads from other sponsors (Brewer, 2004; Larson, 2004; Petterson, 2004; Shockley, 2004). It is unfortunate that none of these studies of the 2002 congressional races reported statistical analyses to indicate whether these differences were significant.

Lau and Pomper (2004), relying on newspaper reports of campaigns (not ads), concluded that about one-third of U.S. Senate races from 1992–2002 were negative. Brazeal and Benoit (2006) analyzed TV spots from the U.S. Senate and House of Representatives between 1980 and 2004; the themes in these ads used more acclaims (69 percent) than attacks (31 percent) and few defenses (0.5 percent). Benoit (2000), analyzing a variety of races in the state of Missouri in 1998, reported that candidates acclaimed 67 percent of the time and attacked 31 percent of the time in their television spots (2 percent of utterances were defenses against attacks). Airne and Benoit (2005) analyzed U.S. Senate, U.S. House, and gubernatorial ads from the 2000 campaign. Acclaims dominated the ads for all three offices (Senate, 71 percent; House, 62 percent, governor, 76 percent). Attacks were roughly one-quarter to one-third of the ad content (Senate, 29 percent; House, 37 percent, governor, 23 percent) and defenses were again uncommon (Senate, 0.5 percent; House, 0.7 percent, governor, 1 percent). Cooper and Knotts (2004) reported that gubernatorial ads in 2000 were 50 percent positive, 28 percent attack, and 22 percent contrast (combination of positive and negative). Benoit and Airne (2009) found that gubernatorial, U.S. Senate, and U.S. House ads in 2004 acclaimed more than they attacked (72 percent to 27 percent; 1 percent of the themes were defenses). Gubernatorial and senate ads from 2008 were content analyzed by Benoit, Delbert, Sudbrock, and Vogt (2010). Ads for governor acclaimed (68 percent) more than they attacked (31 percent) and rarely defended (1 percent). Senate spots offered the same distribution of functions (59 percent acclaims, 40 percent attacks, and 1 percent defenses).

It is difficult to summarize this diverse work, in part because articles use different categories when they report results (e.g., Kahn and Kenney [1999] do not report total attacks, but only attacks on various aspects of policy; Cooper and Knotts [2004] report positive, attack, and contrast ads). Still, attacks in nonpresidential races seem to range from about 25–50 percent, with acclaims making up most of the rest of ad content. One important limitation is that most studies focus on U.S. congressional advertising, ignoring gubernatorial advertising.

Studies have also looked into the incidence of policy (issues) and character (image) in congressional advertising. Earlier studies seemed to support the contention that character is discussed more often than policy. Joslyn (1980) found that 24 percent of Senate spots mentioned policy positions and 40 percent of those spots mentioned the candidates' character. Benze and Declerq (1985), investigating congressional ads in California, found that advertisements usually addressed policy (68 percent) but they discussed character even more frequently (82 percent by female candidates, 90 percent by male candidates). A study by Payne and Baukus (1988) investigated Republican senate ads, finding roughly equal emphasis of policy and character. Johnston and White (1994) analyzed spots by female candidates in 1986 senate races, reporting that women tended to emphasize "issues more than image in their ads" (p. 325). Kahn and Kenney (1999) reported that 80 percent of their ads mentioned, and 36 percent emphasized, policy. Brazeal and Benoit's (2006) study of ads from the Senate and House found that themes in ads were almost equally divided between policy (51 percent) and character (49 percent). However, the ads after 1992 stressed policy more than character. Benoit's (2000) analysis of nonpresidential television advertising found that 66 percent of utterances concerned policy and 34 percent addressed character. Cooper and Knotts' (2004) study of gubernatorial ads from 2000 reported that policy ads predominated (59 percent), followed by ads discussing both policy and character (31 percent), and character only (10 percent). Airne and Benoit (2005) also reported a preference for policy discussion in 2000 political advertising (Senate, 62 percent to 38 percent; House, 55 percent to 45 percent, governor, 69 percent to 31 percent). Benoit and Airne (2009), investigating Senate, House, and gubernatorial ads from 2004, found that the topics were roughly equally addressed in themes (52 percent policy, 49 percent character). Benoit, Delbert, Sudbrock, and Vogt (2010) reported that in 2008 gubernatorial ads stress policy over character (61 percent to 39 percent), as did senate advertisements (69 percent to 31 percent).

Again, summarizing this work is a challenge because of the diverse ways they report results (e.g., some studies report figures for mentioning or emphasizing a topic; Cooper and Knotts, 2004, on the other hand, report figures for policy, character, and both). It appears, though, that research which uses ads as the unit of analysis indicate that character or image ads predominate; studies using themes as the unit of analysis suggest that policy comments can outnumber character remarks, particularly in more recent elections. Most of this research focuses on U.S. Senate advertising, neglecting campaign advertising for other offices.

Sample of Nonpresidential TV Spots

This sample investigated here includes ads for governor: 1974–1998 (Pier, 2002); 2000 (Airne and Benoit, 2005); 2002 (Benoit and Airne, 2013); 2004 (Benoit and Airne, 2009); and 2008 (Benoit, Delbert, Sudbrock, and Vogt 2010). Senate spots included several campaigns: 2000 (Airne and Benoit, 2005); 2002 (Benoit and Airne, 2013); 2004 (Benoit and Airne, 2009); 2008 (Benoit, Delbert, Sudbrock, and Vogt, 2010). House: 2000 (Airne and Benoit, 2005); 2004 (Benoit and Airne, 2009). Congressional ads (House and Senate) from 1980–2004 (Brazeal and Benoit, 2006). Finally, local ads from 1998 were part of the sample (Benoit, 2000).

Functions of Nonpresidential TV Spots

Acclaims were the most common function in these samples of U.S. nonpresidential TV commercials: acclaims (70 percent), attacks (30 percent), and defenses (1 percent). This ordering of functions occurred in every office (governor, Senate, House, and local) across time. Statistical analysis using a *chi-square goodness-of-fit* test confirms that these functions were used with different frequencies (χ^2 [*df* = 2] = 16222.5, *p* < .0001). These data can be found in table 10.1.

Topics of Nonpresidential TV Spots

The most common topic of these ads was policy (54 percent) and then character (46 percent). The sample of U.S. congressional ads 1980–2004 was nearly equal (51 percent policy, 49 percent character) but in no sample did character themes outnumber policy themes. A *chi-square goodness-of-fit* test established that the difference was statistically significant (χ^2 [*df* = 1] = 106.62, *p* < .0001). These data are also reported in table 10.1.

Table 10.1. Functions of U.S. Nonpresidential TV Spots

	Functions			Topics	
	Acclaims	*Attacks*	*Defenses*	*Policy*	*Character*
Governor					
1974–1998	**1131 (71%)**	450 (29%)	1 (1%)	**1046 (66%)**	547 (34%)
Governor 2000	**313 (76%)**	94 (23%)	4 (1%)	**262 (69%)**	119 (31%)
Governor 2002	**2095 (73%)**	765 (27%)	10 (.3%)	**1620 (57%)**	1240 (43%)
Governor 2004	**985 (70%)**	496 (29%)	14 (1%)	**720 (52%)**	671 (48%)
Governor 2008	**610 (68%)**	272 (31%)	9 (1%)	**534 (61%)**	347 (39%)
US Senate 2000	**1003 (71%)**	422 (29%)	7 (0.5%)	**872 (62%)**	542 (38%)
US Senate 2002	**840 (68%)**	392 (43%)	7 (0.5%)	**637 (54%)**	565 (46%)
US Senate 2004	**1973 (70%)**	823 (29%)	24 (1%)	**1526 (55%)**	1270 (45%)
US Senate 2008	**632 (59%)**	431 (40%)	15 (1%)	**724 (69%)**	328 (31%)
US House 2000	**361 (62%)**	215 (37%)	4 (0.7%)	**315 (55%)**	262 (45%)
US House 2004	**1891 (75%)**	624 (25%)	9 (0.3%)	**1243 (51%)**	1276 (51%)
US Congress					
1980–2004	**3481 (69%)**	1568 (31%)	28 (0.5%)	**2572 (51%)**	2477 (49%)
Local					
1998–2000	**393 (67%)**	181 (31%)	9 (2%)	**349 (61%)**	225 (39%)
Total	**15708 (70%)**	6733 (30%)	141 (1%)	**11374 (54%)**	9869 (46%)

Governor: 1974–1998: Pier, 2002; 2000: Airne and Benoit, 2005; 2002: Benoit and Airne, 2013; 2004: Benoit and Airne, 2009; 2008: Benoit, Delbert, Sudbrock, and Vogt (2010). Senate: 2000: Airne and Benoit, 2005; 2002: Benoit and Airne, 2013; 2004: Benoit and Airne, 2009; 2008: Benoit, Delbert, Sudbrock, and Vogt (2010). House: 2000: Airne and Benoit, 2005; 2004: Benoit and Airne, 2009. Congress: 1980-2004: Brazeal and Benoit (2006). Local: 1998: Benoit, 2000.
Functions: χ^2 (*df* = 2) = 16222.5, *p* < .0001, Topics: χ^2 (*df* = 1) = 106.62, *p* < .0001

Statistical analysis using a *chi-square test of cross classification* confirmed that attacks occurred more frequently when the candidates discussed policy rather than character (χ^2 [*df* = 1] = 19.82, *p* < .0001, φ = .04).

Incumbent candidates acclaimed more (77 percent to 60 percent) and attacked less (22 percent to 39 percent) than challengers. A *chi-square test of cross-classification* confirmed that these differences were statistically significant (χ^2 [*df* = 1] = 304.49, *p* < .0001, φ = .18). See table 10.2 for these data. This finding is consistent with past studies by Sheckels (1984) and Pfau, Parrott, and Lindquist (1992). Open-seat candidates fell in between, with 60 percent acclaims and 33 percent attacks.

Table 10.2. Functions of U.S. Nonpresidential Political TV Spots by Incumbency

	Acclaims	Attacks	Defenses
Governor 1974–1998			
Incumbent	**368 (81%)**	89 (19%)	0
Challenger	253 (59%)	**170 (40%)**	6 (1%)
Open-Seat	813 (54%)	682 (45%)	6 (0.4%)
Governor 2000			
Incumbent	**71 (85%)**	13 (15%)	0
Challenger	33 (72%)	**13 (28%)**	0
Open Seat	199 (73%)	68 (25%)	4 (1%)
Governor 2002			
Incumbent	**499 (74%)**	167 (25%)	4 (0.6%)
Challenger	233 (64%)	**131 (36%)**	2 (0,5%)
Open Seat	401 (69%)	179 (31%)	3 (0.5%)
Governor 2008			
Incumbent	**194 (85%)**	35 (15%)	0
Challenger	53 (52%)	**44 (44%)**	4 (4%)
Open Seat	195 (67%)	89 (31%)	5 (2%)
US Senate 2000			
Incumbent	**296 (70%)**	123 (29%)	3 (1%)
Challenger	275 (68%)	**123 (31%)**	4 (1%)
Open-Seat	242 (73%)	89 (27%)	0
US Senate 2008			
Incumbent	**171 (58%)**	117 (40%)	3 (2%)
Challenger	143 (55%)	**113 (43%)**	6 (2%)
Open-Seat	146 (40%)	62 (40%)	1 (0.5%)
Gubernatorial, US Senate, and House 2004			
Incumbent	**869 (78%)**	231 (21%)	12 (1%)
Challenger	550 (65%)	**299 (35%)**	0
Open-Seat	1738 (70%)	720 (29%)	20 (1%)

	Acclaims	Attacks	Defenses
	US House 2000		
Incumbent	**112 (63%)**	63 (35%)	3 (2%)
Challenger	65 (50%)	**65 (50%)**	1 (1%)
Open-Seat	128 (63%)	76 (37%)	0
	US Congress 1980–2000		
Incumbent	**1121 (76%)**	354 (24%)	8 (0.5%)
Challenger	825 (56%)	**633 (43%)**	11 (1%)
Open-Seat	950 (70%)	399 (29%)	7 (0.5%)
	Local 1998		
Incumbent	**47 (92%)**	4 (8%)	0
Challenger	31 (63%)	**16 (33%)**	2 (4%)
Open-Seat	15 (63%)	9 (38%)	0
	Total		
Incumbent	**3748 (77%)**	1085 (22%)	33 (0.7%)
Challenger	2461 (60%)	**1607 (39%)**	36 (1%)
Open-Seat	4827 (66%)	2373 (33%)	46 (0.6%)

Governor: 1974–1998: Pier, 2002; 2000: Airne and Benoit, 2005; 2002: Benoit and Airne, 2013; 2008: Benoit, Delbert, Sudbrock, and Vogt (2010). Senate: 2000: Airne and Benoit, 2005; 2008: Benoit, Delbert, Sudbrock, and Vogt (2010). House: 2000: Airne and Benoit, 2005. Governor, Senate, and House 2004: Benoit and Airne, 2009; Congress: 1980–2004: Brazeal and Benoit (2006). Local: 1998: Benoit, 2000.
Incumbents versus Challengers, acclaims versus attacks: χ^2 $(df = 1) = 304.49$, $p < .0001$, $\varphi = .18$

Forms of Policy and Character in Nonpresidential TV Spots

The candidates in these samples used past deeds most (54 percent), followed by general goals (35 percent) and future plans (11 percent). A *chi-square goodness-of-fit* test showed that these were significantly different (χ^2 $[df = 2] = 2183.59$, $p < .0001$). General goals were used more to acclaim (89 percent) than attack (1 percent), a significant difference (χ^2 $[df = 1] = 1658.82$, $p < .0001$). Incumbent candidates acclaimed more (76 percent, 30 percent) and attacked less (24 percent, 70 percent) than challengers when discussing past deeds or record in office. A *chi-square test of cross classification* revealed that these frequencies were significantly different (χ^2 $[df = 1] = 580.02$, $p < .0001$, $\varphi = .46$). In contrast, when the candidates addressed future plans, incumbents attacked more (32 percent, 19 percent) and acclaimed less (81 percent, 69 percent) than challengers. These differences were also significant (χ^2 $[df = 1] = 10.72$, $p < .005$, $\varphi = .15$). These data are displayed in table 10.3.

In these ads personal qualities were the most common character topic (65 percent), followed by leadership ability (24 percent) and ideals (11 percent). These differences were significant (χ^2 $[df = 2] = 3040.59$, $p < .0001$). As anticipated, ideals were used for acclaims more often than for attacks (χ^2 $[df = 1] = 390.92$, $p < .0001$).

Table 10.3. Forms of Policy in Nonpresidential TV Spots

	Past Deeds		Future Plans		General Goals	
	Acclaims	Attacks	Acclaims	Attacks	Acclaims	Attacks
Governor 1974–1998						
Incumbent	168	18	10	15	56	14
Challenger	23	88	16	0	105	8
Open-Seat	104	107	40	4	242	18
Total	295	213	66	19	403	40
Governor 2002						
Incumbent	262	44	10	5	64	13
Challenger	4	54	10	6	81	8
Open-Seat	91	73	30	4	153	16
Total	357	171	50	15	298	37
Governor, Senate, House 2004						
Incumbent	284	110	22	3	215	25
Challenger	87	189	5	0	177	19
Open-Seat	252	297	37	34	518	69
Total	623	596	64	37	910	113
Governor 2008						
Incumbent	132	13	20	0	47	13
Challenger	12	27	0	0	32	6
Open-Seat	53	51	20	2	131	36
Total	197	91	40	2	210	55
Senate 2008						
Incumbent	56	76	5	3	28	9
Challenger	34	77	18	2	37	4
Open-Seat	48	39	21	6	36	6
Total	138	192	44	11	101	19
Congress 1980–2004						
Incumbent	370	139	120	63	152	11
Challenger	180	351	118	31	179	8
Open-Seat	192	179	140	67	223	38
Total	742	669	388	161	554	58
Grand Total						
Incumbent	**1272**	400	187	**89**	562	85
	(76%)	(24%)	(68%)	**(32%)**	(87%)	(13%)
Challenger	340	**786**	**167**	39	611	53
	(30%)	**(70%)**	**(81%)**	(19%)	(92%)	(8%)
Open-Seat	740	746	288	117	1303	183
	(50%)	(50%)	(71%)	(29%)	(88%)	(12%)
Total	2352	1932	642	245	2476	321
	(55%)	(45%)	(72%)	(28%)	(89%)	(11%)
	4284 (54%)		887 (11%)		2797 (35%)	

Governor: 1974–1998: Pier, 2002; 2000: Airne and Benoit, 2005; 2002: Benoit and Airne, 2013; 2008: Benoit, Delbert, Sudbrock, and Vogt (2010). Senate: 2000: Airne and Benoit, 2005; 2008: Benoit, Delbert, Sudbrock, and Vogt (2010). House: 2000: Airne and Benoit, 2005. Governor, Senate, and House 2004: Benoit and Airne, 2009; Congress: 1980–2004: Brazeal and Benoit (2006). Local: 1998: Benoit, 2000.
Forms of Policy: χ^2 ($df = 2$) = 2183.59, $p < .0001$
Incumbents versus Challengers, Acclaims versus Attacks on Past Deeds: χ^2 ($df = 1$) = 580.02, $p < .0001$, $\varphi = .46$
Incumbents versus Challengers, Acclaims versus Attacks on Future Plans: χ^2 ($df = 1$) = 10.72, $p < .005$, $\varphi = .15$
Functions of General Goals: χ^2 ($df = 1$) = 1658.82, $p < .0001$

Incumbents in these spots were more likely to acclaim (94 percent, 80 percent) less likely to attack (6 percent, 20 percent) than challengers. A *chi-square test of cross-classification* demonstrated that these differences were significant (χ^2 [*df* = 1] = 35.22, *p* < .0001, φ = .21). These data are displayed in table 10.4.

Sponsor of political television advertisements has an influence on content. First, TV spots sponsored by candidates used acclaims more (73 percent to 25 percent) and attacks less (26 percent to 74 percent) than ads sponsored by political parties. A *chi-square test of cross classification* confirmed that these differences were significant (χ^2 [*df* = 1] = 901.29, *p* < .0001, φ = .31). This relationship occurred on each sample of nonpresidential ads. Candidates focused more on character (46 percent to 34 percent) and less on policy (54 percent to 61 percent) than ads from parties. These differences were also statistically significant (χ^2 [*df* = 1] = 10.38, *p* < .005, φ = .03). The ads from 2004 were an exception to this relationship. See table 10.5 for these data.

Table 10.4.   Forms of Character in Nonpresidential TV Spots

	Personal Qualities		Leadership Ability		Ideals	
	Acclaims	Attacks	Acclaims	Attacks	Acclaims	Attacks
Governor 1974–1998						
Incumbent	28	20	28	6	7	3
Challenger	46	42	22	19	8	0
Open-Seat	96	78	112	9	20	1
Total	170	140	162	34	35	4
Governor 2002						
Incumbent	68	96	62	5	33	4
Challenger	71	56	38	5	29	2
Open-Seat	63	70	36	13	28	1
Total	202	222	136	23	90	7
Governor, Senate, House 2004						
Incumbent	166	84	130	4	52	5
Challenger	143	66	107	24	31	1
Open-Seat	564	280	254	22	113	18
Total	873	430	491	50	196	25
Governor 2008						
Incumbent	30	15	10	0	54	4
Challenger	11	20	3	1	8	0
Open-Seat	58	44	31	17	54	6
Total	99	79	44	18	116	10
Senate 2008						
Incumbent	45	13	29	7	9	7
Challenger	27	21	15	4	8	4
Open-Seat	10	6	28	0	19	10
Total	82	40	72	11	36	21

(*continued*)

Table 10.4. *(continued)*

	Personal Qualities		Leadership Ability		Ideals	
	Acclaims	*Attacks*	*Acclaims*	*Attacks*	*Acclaims*	*Attacks*
			Congress 1980–2004			
Incumbent	470	152	141	4	54	10
Challenger	315	258	123	24	45	17
Open-Seat	426	168	135	19	88	18
Total	1211	588	399	47	187	45
			Grand Total			
Incumbent	807 (68%)	380 (32%)	**400 (94%)**	26 (6%)	209 (86%)	33 (14%)
Challenger	613 (57%)	463 (43%)	308 (80%)	**77 (20%)**	129 (84%)	24 (16%)
Open-Seat	1217 (65%)	646 (35%)	596 (88%)	80 (12%)	322 (86%)	54 (14%)
Total	2637 (64%)	1489 (36%)	1304 (88%)	183 (12%)	**660 (86%)**	111 (14%)
	4126 (65%)		1487 (24%)		711 (11%)	

Governor: 1974–1998: Pier, 2002; 2000: Airne and Benoit, 2005; 2002: Benoit and Airne, 2013; 2008: Benoit, Delbert, Sudbrock, and Vogt (2010). Senate: 2000: Airne and Benoit, 2005; 2008: Benoit, Delbert, Sudbrock, and Vogt (2010). House: 2000: Airne and Benoit, 2005. Governor, Senate, and House 2004: Benoit and Airne, 2009; Congress: 1980–2004: Brazeal and Benoit (2006). Local: 1998: Benoit, 2000.
Forms of Character: χ^2 $(df = 2) = 3040.59$, $p < .0001$
Acclaims versus attacks on ideals: χ^2 $(df = 1) = 390.92$, $p < .0001$
Incumbents versus challengers, acclaims versus attacks on leadership ability: χ^2 $(df = 1) = 35.22$, $p < .0001$, $\varphi = .21$

Table 10.5. **Functions and Topics of Nonpresidential TV Spots by Sponsor**

	Functions			Topics	
	Acclaims	*Attacks*	*Defenses*	*Policy*	*Character*
			US Senate 2000		
Candidate	**927 (78%)**	255 (21%)	5 (0.4%)	711 (60%)	**471 (40%)**
Party	76 (32%)	**256 (67%)**	2 (1%)	**161 (69%)**	71 (31%)
			US House 2000		
Candidate	**318 (70%)**	135 (29%)	4 (1%)	238 (53%)	**208 (47%)**
Party	23 (30%)	**54 (70%)**	0	**49 (58%)**	36 (42%)
		Governor, Senate, House 2004			
Candidate	**4706 (74%)**	1648 (26%)	43 (0.7%)	3291 (52%)	3063 (48%)
Party	78 (43%)	**102 (55%)**	3 (2%)	92 (52%)	86 (48%)
			Governor, Senate 2008		
Candidate	**297 (58%)**	205 (40%)	7 (1%)	506 (61%)	**324 (39%)**
Party	57 (55%)	**44 (42%)**	3 (3%)	**14 (64%)**	8 (36%)
			Total		
Candidate	**6248 (73%)**	2243 (26%)	59 (0.7%)	4746 (54%)	**4066 (46%)**
Party	234 (25%)	**688 (74%)**	8 (1%)	**316 (61%)**	201 (39%)

Governor: 1974–1998: Pier, 2002; 2000: Airne and Benoit, 2005; 2002: Benoit and Airne, 2013; 2008: Benoit, Delbert, Sudbrock, and Vogt (2010). Senate: 2000: Airne and Benoit, 2005; 2008: Benoit, Delbert, Sudbrock, and Vogt (2010). House: 2000: Airne and Benoit, 2005. Governor, Senate, and House 2004: Benoit and Airne, 2009; Congress: 1980–2004: Brazeal and Benoit (2006). Local: 1998: Benoit, 2000.
Acclaims versus attacks: χ^2 $(df = 1) = 901.29$, $p < .0001$, $\varphi = .31$
Policy versus Character: χ^2 $(df = 1) = 10.38$, $p < .005$, $\varphi = .03$

NON-U.S. POLITICAL TV SPOTS

Kaid and Holtz-Bacha (1995b) report the results of studies of political advertisements in three countries (Italy, 1992; France, 1988, Germany, 1990): They report significant changes (not always favorable to the candidate) in candidates' images, after exposure to television spots, for three of the eight candidates involved. This shows that political advertising can, but will not necessarily, affect perceptions of candidates in other countries. Advertising in other countries is also important because campaign news emphasizes horse race rather than policy or character. Benoit, Compton, and Phillips (2013) examined news coverage of political campaigns in Australia (2010), Canada (2011), and the United Kingdom (2010). They found that the most common topic was horse race (51 percent), followed by character (27 percent), and policy (22 percent). Again, voters can use information from candidate advertising to supplement what is available in the news.

Sample of Non-U.S. Political TV Spots

This analysis uses data from televised advertisements broadcast in Britain 1992, 1997; France 1988; Germany 1992, 1994; Greece 1996; Israel 1992; Italy 1992; Netherlands 2006; Poland 1995; Russia 1996; South Korea 1963-1992 (includes newspaper ads), 2002; Taiwan 1996, 2000; Turkey 1995 (Chang, 2000; Kaid, 1999; Kaid and Holtz-Bacha, 1995b; Lee and Benoit, 2004; Tak, Kaid, and Lee, 1997; Walter and Vliegenthart, 2010; Wen, Benoit, and Yu, 2004). Only Lee and Benoit and Wen, Benoit, and Yu used Functional Theory and looked for defenses.

Functions of Non-U.S. Political TV Spots

Several studies have investigated the functions and topics of television spots for presidents and prime ministers of other countries. Functional Theory predicts acclaims will be more common than attacks. The percentage of positive ads ranges from 58 percent (Israel, 1992) to 93 percent (Poland, 1995; see table 10.6). The mean percentage of positive ads (all studies but Wen, 2002, and Lee and Benoit, 2004, which used the entire spot as the coding unit) 72 percent; attacking ads were 27 percent of the sample. This difference is significant (χ^2 [df = 1] = 194.67, $p <$ .0001) and every study is consistent with this prediction.

Topics of Non-U.S. Political TV Spots

Functional Theory predicts that policy will be a more frequent topic of campaign messages than character. Overall, table 10.6 indicates that 59 percent of the ads addressed policy and 41 percent concern character. The difference was statistically significant (χ^2 [df = 1] = 231.43, $p <$ .0001). However, ads were divided evenly between the two topics in Israel and Korea (2002) and in four cases (Germany, Greece, Russia,

Table 10.6. Functions and Topics of Non-U.S. Political TV Spots

	Functions		Topics	
	Acclaims	*Attacks*	*Policy*	*Character*
Britain 1992, 1997	**11 (69%)**	4 (31%)	**14 (88%)**	2 (12%)
France 1988	**15 (75%)**	5 (25%)	**20 (100%)**	0
Germany 1992	**26 (68%)**	12 (32%)	12 (32%)	26 **(68%)**
Germany 1994	—	—	**36 (69%)**	16 (31%)
Greece 1996	**55 (71%)**	23 (29%)	32 (42%)	44 **(58%)**
Israel 1992	**35 (58%)**	25 (42%)	30 (50%)	30 (50%)
Italy 1992	**35 (85%)**	6 (15%)	**29 (71%)**	12 (29%)
Korea 1963–1992	**295 (67%)**	145 (33%)	**286 (65%)**	154 (35%)
Netherlands 2006	**262 (67%)**	129 (33%)	**364 (93%)**	27 (7%)
Poland 1995	**75 (93%)**	6 (7%)	**53 (66%)**	28 (34%)
Russia 1996	**26 (72%)**	10 (28%)	**21 (58%)**	15 (42%)
Taiwan 1996	**16 (81%)**	4 (19%)	—	—
Turkey 1995	**8 (89%)**	1 (11%)	3 (33%)	6 **(67%)**
Subtotal†	**859 (70%)**	370 (30%)	**900 (71%)**	360 (29%)
Taiwan 2000	**195 (63%)**	109 (35%)	97 (32%)	207 **(68%)**
Korea 2002	**89 (72%)**	33 (27%)	62 (50%)	61 (50%)
Grand Total	**74%**	26%	**61%**	39%

*These samples included newspaper ads.
†Functions: χ^2 (*df* = 1) = 194.67, *p* < .0001; Topics: χ^2 (*df* = 1) = 231.43, *p* < .0001
Chang (2000), Kaid (1999), Kaid and Holtz-Bacha (1995b), Tak, Kaid, and Lee (1997), Walter and Vliegen-thart, 2010, Lee and Benoit (2004), Wen, Benoit, and Yu (2004). The last two studies included defenses, which are excluded from this table.

Taiwan) character was discussed more often than policy. This means the predicted rela-tionship obtained in eight of the fourteen samples, so this relationship is not consistent.

Forms of Policy and Character in Non-U.S. Political TV Spots

In this sample of political TV spots (South Korea and Taiwan), when candidates discussed policy they talked about past deeds in 50 percent of themes, 38 percent of themes were general goals and 12 percent were about future plans. This distribution of forms of policy was significant (χ^2 [*df* = 2] = 33.92, *p* < .0001). These candidates were more likely to acclaim than attack (79 percent to 21 percent) when they dis-cussed general goals (χ^2 [*df* = 1] = 18.29, *p* < .0001). See table 10.7 for data on forms of policy in non-U.S. advertisements.

When addressing character these candidates discussed personal qualities (50 per-cent) most often, followed by leadership ability (25 percent) and ideals (24 percent). These frequencies were significantly different (χ^2 [*df* = 2] = 36.18, *p* < .0001). They were more likely to acclaim than attack when talking about ideals (79 percent to 21 percent). Statistical analysis confirms that these are significantly different (χ^2 [*df* = 1] = 21.88, *p* < .0001). These data can be found in table 10.8.

Table 10.7. Forms of Policy in Non-U.S. Political TV Spots

	Past Deeds		Future Plans		General Goals	
	Acclaims	*Attacks*	*Acclaims*	*Attacks*	*Acclaims*	*Attacks*
	South Korea					
Incumbent	0	3	3	0	4	2
Challenger	2	21	0	3	20	2
	Taiwan					
Incumbent	22	5	8	4	15	7
Challenger	6	14	1	0	14	1
	Total					
Incumbent	**22 (73%)**	8 (27%)	11 (73%)	4 (27%)	10 (53%)	9 (47%)
Challenger	8 (19%)	**35 (81%)**	1 (25%)	3 (75%)	34 (92%)	3 (8%)
Grand Total	30 (41%)	43 (59%)	12 (63%)	7 (37%)	44 (79%)	12 (21%)
	73 (50%)		18 (12%)		56 (38%)	

South Korea: Lee and Benoit (2004); Taiwan: Wen, Benoit, and Yu (2004).
Forms of Policy: χ^2 ($df = 2$) = 33.92, $p < .0001$
Acclaims versus Attacks on General Goals: χ^2 ($df = 1$) = 18.29, $p < .0001$
Incumbents versus Challengers, acclaims versus attacks on past deeds: χ^2 ($df = 1$) = 21.87, $p < .0001$, $\varphi = .55$
Note. Expected frequencies for incumbents versus challengers, acclaims versus attacks on future plans, were too small to calculate *chi-square*.

Table 10.8. Forms of Character in Non-U.S. Political TV Spots

	Personal Qualities		Leadership Ability		Ideals	
	Acclaims	*Attacks*	*Acclaims*	*Attacks*	*Acclaims*	*Attacks*
	South Korea					
Incumbent	12	11	5	5	16	8
Challenger	0	0	1	2	2	2
	Taiwan					
Incumbent	19	41	20	10	14	1
Challenger	39	15	17	8	20	3
	Total					
Incumbent	31	52	25	15	30	9
Challenger	39	15	18	10	22	5
Grand Total	70 (51%)	67 (49%)	43 (63%)	25 (37%)	52 (79%)	14 (21%)
	137 (50%)		68 (25%)		66 (24%)	

South Korea: Lee and Benoit (2004); Taiwan: Wen, Benoit, and Yu (2004)
Forms of Character: χ^2 ($df = 2$) = 36.18, $p < .0001$
Acclaims versus Attacks on Ideals: χ^2 ($df = 1$) = 21.88, $p < .0001$

In this sample, incumbents did not differ from challengers on acclaims and attacks: Both groups of candidates produced 57 percent acclaims and 43 percent attacks. Functional Theory anticipates that incumbents will be more likely to acclaim than attack on past deeds. When candidates discussed their records in office (past deeds), incumbents were more likely to acclaim (73 percent to 19 percent) and less likely to attack (27 percent to 81 percent) than challengers. A *chi-square test of cross classification* confirmed that these differences were significant (χ^2 [df = 1] = 21.87, $p < .0001$, φ = .55). See table 10.8 for these data. Consistent with this prediction, Kaid and Holtz-Bacha (1995b) report that in four of five countries (France, German, Italy, Israel, but not Britain), more ads by incumbent candidates emphasized their own accomplishments than attacked record of the opponent. In contrast, in four of five countries (Germany, Italy Britain, Israel, but not France), more challenger spots attacked the opponent's record than emphasized their own accomplishments. This result is consistent with this prediction.

CONCLUSION

This chapter has investigated the functions and topics of political advertising in nonpresidential and non-U.S. election campaigns. Research from many American nonpresidential candidates, several offices, and several years use acclaims more than attacks and attacks more often than defenses. Policy is discussed more often than character. Incumbents acclaim more, and attack less, when discussing record in office. Acclaims are used more than attacks when talking about general goals and ideals. Ads sponsored by candidates acclaim more, and attack less, than ads from political parties. Party ads stressed policy more (and character less) than candidate ads. When we look at ads from other countries, they consistently acclaim more than they attack. Most non-U.S. ads, but not all, address policy more than character. Incumbents acclaim more, and attack less, than challengers when they discuss record in office. Candidates acclaim more and attack less when talking about general goals and ideals. Thus, the patterns found in U.S. presidential ads tend to occur in advertising for other offices and in other countries.

IV

COMPARISONS

11

Trends and Contrasts of Political Television Spots

This chapter will explore eight topics based on the results of the analyses presented in earlier chapters. First, I will discuss the number of themes addressed in general presidential television spots. Second, I will address the average length of these advertisements. Then, I take up the topic of the functions of political television commercials. Fourth, I will contrast these spots' reliance on policy and character topics. Then I will also discuss use of the three forms of policy and the three forms of character. The seventh topic is the effect of incumbency on political advertising. Next, I contrast ads from the two campaign phases, primary and general. This is followed by a discussing of ads from winners versus losers. Finally, I discuss how the nature of the source influences the functions of political advertising.

INCREASING DENSITY: NUMBER OF THEMES PER PRESIDENTIAL TV SPOT

A trend emerged over time for candidates to use more themes in their spots (the first two analyses are based on presidential general election spots from 1952–1996). The initial sample for this project had a goal of obtaining thirty minutes of spots for each candidate in every campaign, which was not possible (thirty minutes of ads for every presidential candidate do not survive today; some candidates likely did not make thirty minutes of ads). In order to better investigate this trend I conducted an analysis in which I adjusted the totals for number of themes in those campaigns for which I had obtained less than thirty minutes of spots to reflect the number of themes that probably would have occurred if I had located thirty minutes of spots. I divided the number of seconds of the advertisements I had into 1,800 (thirty minutes) and multiplied the result by the number of acclaims, attacks, and defenses observed (totals which were within twenty seconds of 1,800 were not adjusted). This produced an estimate for the number of each kind of utterance the candidate probably would have used had each one made thirty minutes of spots. Controlling this way for sample size, the number of themes per thirty minutes of spots has increased steadily over time for both parties, from 236 in 1952 to 843 in 1996. Statistical analysis reveals a significant positive correlation (*Spearman rho* [df = 12] = .958, p < .0001). In the last three election years, however, the increase is especially dramatic for Democrats. To illustrate this phenomenon, contrast a thirty-second spot from McGovern in 1972 with a thirty-second spot from Clinton in 1996:

> President Nixon has received ten million dollars in secret campaign contributions from men and interests whose names Mr. Nixon refuses to reveal to the American people. Who are these men, and what do they want? (McGovern, "Secret Nixon Contributions")

> The facts Bob Dole ignores in his negative attacks. The deficit cut 60 percent. Ten million new jobs. Family income up $1,600. Health insurance you don't lose when changing jobs. President Clinton: moving our economy ahead, helping families. Now a plan to cut taxes for college tuition: $500 per child tax credit. Break up violent gangs. Move one million from welfare to work. Dole resorts to desperate negative attacks. President Clinton is protecting our values. (Clinton, "Ignores")

The McGovern ad articulates only one theme: that Nixon accepts huge secret campaign contributions. In contrast, in the same amount of time the Clinton spot hurriedly mentions nine themes: Dole's negative attacks, the deficit, jobs, family income, health insurance, college tuition tax credit, gangs, welfare, and values. We do not know whether there is more benefit from focusing entirely on one theme (depth) or mentioning several themes (breadth)—but there is no doubt that political spots are moving in the direction of saying less and less about more and more topics.

SOUND BITES: AVERAGE LENGTH
OF PRESIDENTIAL TV SPOTS

I will also mention a related finding on presidential television spots from 1952–1996, although surely a less surprising one. After candidates experimented with this new kind of campaign message in the 1950s, most television spots in the 1960s and in 1972 were sixty seconds long. In the mid-1970s and 1980s the length of spots gradually shifted to thirty seconds, until by the 1990s the majority of television spots were thirty seconds in length. A *chi-square* confirms that the shift in length of ads over time is statistically significant (χ^2 [df = 1] = 344.73, p < .0001, ϕ = .54).

Thus, there is a trend toward producing shorter spots. Surely the cost of producing and broadcasting television spots has fueled this trend to shorter spots—although with today's computer capabilities, producing ads is easier and less expensive than ever. Similarly, the fact that the news media have been quoting shorter and shorter bits of candidate statements (Hallin, 1992) has probably also encouraged the move toward shorter messages.

FUNCTIONS OF POLITICAL TV SPOTS

Political candidates in every group of spots acclaimed more than they attacked and rarely defended. In American presidential primary ads, acclaims were 72 percent, attacks 28 percent, and defenses 1 percent. General election presidential ads acclaimed in 54 percent of themes, attacked in 45 percent, and defended in 1 percent. Third party ads for the Oval Office in this sample acclaimed twice as often as they attacked (66 percent to 34 percent) and used no defenses. U.S. nonpresidential spots used acclaims more than attacks (70 percent to 30 percent) and rarely attacked (1 percent). In non-U.S. television spots, acclaims were 74 percent and attacks 26 percent (most studies of non-U.S. ads did not code for defenses). Overall, the average number of acclaims is 67 percent, attacks 33 percent, and defenses 1 percent. These data are reported in table 11.1. This does not mean that every single candidate used more acclaims than attacks, but candidates who did so were rare (and defenses were the least common function for every candidate in these samples).

For example, in 1984, Reagan boasted of his first term accomplishments: "Today, inflation is down, interest rates are down. We've created six and a half million new jobs. Americans are working again, and so is America." He discusses three successes experienced during his first term in office (all dealing with policy): reducing inflation, reducing interest rates, and creating jobs. In 1960, in contrast, this ad from Nixon stressed his experience:

> Above everything else, the American people want leaders who will keep the peace without surrender for America and the world. Henry Cabot Lodge and I have had the opportunity of serving with President Eisenhower in this cause for the last seven and a half years. We both know Mr. Krushchev. We have sat opposite the conference table with him.

Table 11.1. Functions and Topics of Political Television Spots

	Functions			Topics	
	Acclaims	*Attacks*	*Defenses*	*Policy*	*Character*
Primary	**5734 (72%)**	2218 (28%)	58 (1%)	**4342 (54%)**	3626 (46%)
General	**3851 (54%)**	3174 (45%)	87 (1%)	**44342 (62%)**	2702 (38%)
Third Party	**234 (66%)**	118 (34%)	0	**185 (52%)**	173 (48%)
Nonpresident	**15708 (70%)**	6733 (30%)	141 (1%)	**11374 (54%)**	9869 (46%)
Non-U.S.*	**74%**	26%	—	**61%**	39%
Average	**67%**	33%	1%	**57%**	43%

Data from chapters 3–6, 8–10
*Some studies analyzed spots, some themes, so only percentages are reported here.

This acclaim stresses the character of the Republican ticket, in the form of boasting of their leadership ability. Every candidate repeatedly used acclaiming in their television commercials, with the least self-praise at 27 percent (Obama in 2012). The more desirable a candidate appears to voters, the more likely that candidate will seem preferable to opponents.

Attacks also occurred with frequency: attacks in these ads ranged from 28 percent to 70 percent. Given that Obama acclaimed at the lowest level of any candidate during his 2012 campaign it is no surprising that his ads used the most attacks in presidential campaign history (Eisenhower's first campaign in 1952 used virtually the same level of attacks, 69 percent). The less desirable an attacked opponent appears to voters, the more likely the sponsoring candidate will seem preferable. For example, in one of his "Eisenhower Answers America" spots, Eisenhower responded to this prompt: "General, the Democrats are telling me I never had it so good" by attacking the past deeds of the current, Democratic, administration: "Can that be true when America is billions in debt, when prices have doubled, when taxes break our backs, and we are still fighting in Korea?" He attacks on policy grounds here, leveling four separate criticisms, bemoaning the federal debt, inflation, taxation, and the Korean War. In 1988, Dukakis attacked his opponent's character: "The other side has pursued a campaign of distortion and distraction, of fear and of smear." These are not the actions of an honorable person. Every presidential candidate used at least some attacks in their television spots, although in 1956 Eisenhower attacked in but 2 percent of his remarks and Nixon in 1960 used just 9 percent attacks.

In general, acclaims occur more often than attacks. Both strategies have the potential to improve a candidate's apparent preferability, acclaims by making the candidate appear better and attacks by making an opponent look worse. However, voters profess to dislike mudslinging (Merritt, 1984; Stewart, 1975). There is some concern that attacks could create backlash with some voters. Thus, it is perfectly reasonable to expect that acclaims will usually be more frequent than attacks, as this data reveals. However, figure 11.1 suggests that (after a highly negative campaign in 1952) the percentage of acclaims in general election presidential TV spots is slowly dropping while the proportion of attacks is growing over time. In 1992, the overall

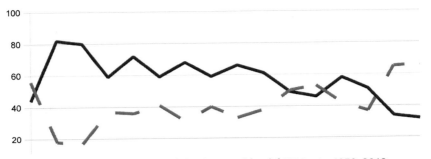

Figure 11.1.   Functions of General Election Presidential TV Spots, 1952–2012.
Source: Data from chapters 3–6 and table 11.9

percentage of attacks was higher than the percentage of acclaims for the first time since 1952 (and that distribution held true in 1996 as well). Statistical analysis of the percentage of attacks in presidential TV spots over time revealed a significant positive trend: r ($n = 16$) = .71, $p < .001$. Chapter 7 presented data that presidential primary spots are not becoming significantly more negative over time. Brazeal and Benoit (2006) examined the functions of congressional (U.S. Senate and House) ads from 1980–2004. They found that acclaims were more common at the beginning and end of their sample (a stretched out "V"), indicating no linear trend over time.

Defenses were also used in presidential television spots beginning in 1960, the third presidential campaign to employ television advertising, but this function occurs far less frequently than acclaims or attacks: Defenses accounted for only 1 percent of the total utterances in these advertisements (third party candidates for the U.S. president in this sample used no defenses). For example, in 1984, Reagan spots accused Mondale of wanting to increase taxes, declaring that "Walter Mondale thinks you can squeeze more money out of your budget." A Mondale advertisement used a woman to defend against to this attack: "I think you've got it all wrong. Mondale thinks I'm paying too much." This utterance clearly denies Reagan's attack. If candidates can effectively dissipate attacks, threats to their desirability can be reduced or eliminated with defense. This increases the likelihood that a candidate will seem preferable.

However, there are three reasons for defenses to be consistently less frequent than acclaims or attacks. First, a defense must identify an attack before it can refute that accusation; candidates may not wish to risk reminding or informing voters of attacks of their potential weaknesses. Second, candidates may wish to "stay on message." Typically, each campaign has a theme and a set of issues to emphasize which is different from the opponent's theme and issues. For example, in 1996 Clinton discussed education more than Dole, and Dole talked about his proposed tax cut more than Clinton talked about taxes. Presumably, opponents will attack on the issues that favor them, so to defend against an attack means the candidate must spend time on the opponent's issue. Finally, candidates may prefer to appear proactive rather than reactive. These factors are not equally important for all types of campaign messages. For example, in a presidential debate, there is no question that the audience has been exposed to an attack (it may also be more difficult to resist the impulse to respond to attacks in a live confrontation than when writing the script for a spot). Benoit (2007b) reports that defenses are more common in debates than in other message forms, such as TV spots, acceptance addresses, or direct mail brochures.

TOPICS OF POLITICAL TV SPOTS

Overall, candidates discussed policy matters in more utterances than character concerns: policy themes accounted for 52–62 percent of the themes in this sample (see table 11.1). Policy accounted for 54 percent of the utterances in American presidential primary ads, 62 percent of American general presidential spots, 52 percent of third party ads, 54 percent of U.S. nonpresidential advertisements, and 61 percent of non-U.S. political commercials. This does not mean every candidate discussed policy more than character; indeed the proportions of these two topics were fairly similarly in primary, third party, and nonpresidential ads. Still, policy was more common than policy overall in political television advertising. The five most recent presidential campaigns (1996–2012) average 67 percent policy and 33 percent character. For example, in 1960 Kennedy discussed federal aid to education:

> But I believe in the passage by this Congress and I hope the next administration, of a federal aid to education bill, which would provide assistance to the various states for school construction and for teachers' salaries. And we want good classrooms. And we want each child to have an advantage of getting the best education he can get. So I strongly support federal aid to education.

This is clearly an acclaim based on policy. Similarly, this spot for Nixon in 1972 acclaimed his policy accomplishments:

> He has brought home over 500,000 men from the war, and less than 40,000 remain. None engaged in ground combat. He has overhauled the draft laws and made them fair for everyone, black and white, rich and poor. He certified an amendment giving eighteen-year-olds the right to vote. He has created an economy that is growing faster than at any time in years. The rate of inflation has been cut in half. He has taken a strong stand for equal education but against massive busing as a means to accomplish it. He has named common sense judges to the Supreme Court. He's gone to China to talk peace with Mao Tse Tung. He's gone to the Soviet Union to talk peace with Leonid Breshnev.

The Vietnamese war, the right to vote, the economy, education and busing, judicial appointments, and foreign policy topics are all touched on in this spot.

In sharp contrast, this 1976 Ford commercial acclaimed his personal qualities: "Sensitivity and concern. A willingness to listen and to act." Similarly, this television advertisement for Bush in 1992 attacked Clinton's character:

> MAN: I don't believe him. I don't believe him one bit.
>
> WOMAN: I don't believe him.
>
> WOMAN: Trust.

In 1976, this Ford commercial acclaimed his personal qualities: "Sensitivity and concern. A willingness to listen and to act." Although policy was discussed more often than character in these spots, the data establish that character was a frequent topic for these candidates (at least 38 percent of themes). Thus, these television spots addressed both policy and character.

Figure 11.2 reveals that from 1952 through 1976, campaigns sometimes focused more on policy and sometimes more on character. Starting with 1980, however,

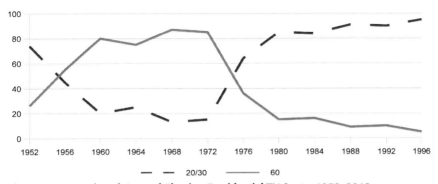

Figure 11.2. Topics of General Election Presidential TV Spots, 1952–2012.
Data from chapters 3–6 and table 11.9

there has been a persistent trend toward heavier reliance on policy than character; statistical analysis reveals a significant increase in the percentage of policy in presidential ads over time (r [n = 16] = .49, p < .05). Figure 7.2 shows a similar pattern, delayed a few years, with policy and character alternating as most common topic until 1992, when policy becomes more common.

Candidates did not acclaim (or attack) on policy and character equally. Acclaims were more common than attacks on both topics, but attacks more frequently addressed policy (36 percent) than character (30 percent; χ^2 [df = 1] = 129.67, φ = .07). It is possible that candidates are responding to voter preferences (voters are more likely to disdain attacks on policy than on character; see Johnson-Cartee and Copeland, 1986). Benoit (2004a) found that as a group, candidates who win elections are more likely to attack on policy, and less likely to attack on character, than losers.

FORMS OF POLICY AND CHARACTER IN POLITICAL TV SPOTS

Policy utterances are sub-divided into three sub-forms: past deeds (record in office), future plans (specific proposals for future policy), and general goals (proposed ends for future policy). The most common form of policy utterance is past deeds, which accounted for 49 percent of policy utterances. For example, in 1972, a citizen attacked Nixon's record in this spot for McGovern: "I voted for Nixon in 1968. I never voted for a Republican before until he came along and says he's gonna stop this war. But he didn't." General goals were the second most common kind of policy remark at 37 percent. In 1960, Kennedy adopted these goals: "We will build and expand our forest programs. We will cleanse our rivers of pollution. We will carry out reclamation and conservation programs on our land. And we will try to move ahead in those areas which have been cut back." Finally, specific future plans comprised 14 percent of the utterances in these television spots. In 1964, a Johnson spot declared that "Even his running mate William Miller admits

Table 11.2. Forms of Policy in Political TV Spots

	Past Deeds		Future Plans		General Goals	
	Acclaims	*Attacks*	*Acclaims*	*Attacks*	*Acclaims*	*Attacks*
Primary	742	978	404	154	1776	199
General	783	1474	431	480	1129	243
Third Party	15	57	11	7	90	7
Nonpres.	2352	1932	642	245	2476	321
Non-U.S.	30	43	12	7	44	12
Total	3922	4484	1500	893	5515	782
	(47%)	(53%)	(63%)	(37%)	(88%)	(12%)
	8406 (49%)		2393 (14%)		6297 (37%)	

Data from chapters 3–6, 8–10
Functions of General Goals χ^2 ($df = 1$) = 3557.45, $p < .0001$

that Senator Goldwater's voluntary plan would destroy Social Security," attacking Goldwater's future plan. See table 11.2 for these data.

Joslyn (1986) analyzed 506 spots from 1960–1984. He found that 37 percent concerned future policy. This is similar to the combined total of utterances devoted to future plans and general goals: 43 percent. He also discovered that past governmental policy accounted for 60 percent of the spots in his sample. This figure is quite close to the percentage of utterances devoted to past deeds: 58 percent.

Character remarks are also subdivided into themes addressing personal qualities (character traits), leadership ability (experience in office), and ideals (values and principles). The most common kind of character utterance addressed personal qualities, at 59 percent. For example, President Ford acclaimed his character in 1976: "So tonight it is not the power and the glamour of the Presidency that leads me to ask for another four years. It is something every hard working American will understand: the challenge of a job well begun but far from finished." This utterance talks about his character rather than policy. The candidates talked about leadership ability in 25 percent of the remarks. In 1968, this Nixon spot acclaimed his leadership ability, particularly in foreign affairs: "Well, I think Richard M. Nixon probably is more qualified in world affairs than anyone else that I know." The smallest group of character utterances concerning the candidates' ideals accounted for 16 percent of their character comments. An example of this topic occurs in this 1980 spot for Carter: "And I would like to serve eight years in the White House and have our nation stay at peace, but at the same time enhance the quality of life of people in other nations and promote freedom and human rights and democratic principles as well." Table 11.3 displays these data.

A few studies have quantified the frequency with which candidates addressed personal qualities. Joslyn (1986), for example, reported that 57 percent of the spots from 1960 to 1984 mentioned personal qualities. West (1997) reported that personal qualities were used in 30 percent of spots. The data reported here (59 percent personal qualities) are closer to Joslyn's figures than West's (recall from chapter 2 that West's sample has important limitations).

Table 11.3.   Forms of Character in Political TV Spots

	Personal Qualities		Leadership Ability		Ideals	
	Acclaims	Attacks	Acclaims	Attacks	Acclaims	Attacks
Primary	1310	615	746	159	652	81
General	667	875	587	181	386	108
Third Party	55	48	27	3	36	4
Nonpres.	2637	1489	1304	183	660	111
Non-U.S.	70	60	43	25	52	14
Total	4739	3087	2707	551	1786	318
	(61%)	(39%)	(83%)	(17%)	(85%)	(15%)
	7826 (59%)		3258 (25%)		2104 (16%)	

Data from chapters 3–6, 8–10
Functions of Ideals χ^2 $(df = 1) = 697.84$, $p < .0001$

Functional Theory predicts that candidates will acclaim more often than they attack when they address general goals and ideals. Goals such as keeping American safe from terrorism or ideals such as justice are easier to praise than criticize. In these data general goals were used more often as the basis of acclaims than attacks (88 percent to 12 percent). A *chi-square goodness-of-fit* test confirms that these differences are statistically significant (χ^2 [$df = 1$] = 3557.45, $p < .0001$); these data can be found in table 11.2. The same pattern occurred on ideals: 85 percent acclaims and 15 percent attacks, a difference which was also significant (χ^2 [$df = 1$] = 697.84, $p < .0001$). See table 11.3.

Benoit and McHale (2003) developed a typology of personal qualities. Starting with the texts of presidential TV spots (1952–1996), they applied Glaser and Strauss's (1967) method of constant comparison to themes which had been coded as representing personal qualities. This analysis resulted in a list of personal qualities (and a list search terms for each that could be used in computer content analysis): morality, empathy, sincerity, and drive. They applied this typology (Benoit and McHale, 2004) to presidential primary and general ads (1952–2000) as well as to congressional ads (1984–2000). Table 11.4 reports the results of this analysis. Overall, candidates in this sample of spots discussed morality most often (31 percent), followed by drive (26 percent), and then empathy and sincerity (21 percent each). A *chi-square goodness-of-fit* test shows that these frequencies are significantly different (χ^2 [$df = 3$] = 158.66, $p < .0001$).

Table 11.4.   Forms of Personal Qualities in Political TV Spots

	Morality	Empathy	Sincerity	Drive
Presidential Primary (1952–2000)	639	528	446	602
Presidential General (1952–2000)	934	477	583	718
Congress (1984–2000)	76	102	66	68
Total	1649	1107	1095	1388
	(31%)	(21%)	(21%)	(26%)

Source: Benoit and McHale (2004)
χ^2 $(df = 3) = 158.66$, $p < .0001$

INCUMBENTS VERSUS CHALLENGERS
IN POLITICAL TV SPOTS

At times the elected president runs for re-election, for example, Dwight Eisenhower in 1956, Richard Nixon in 1972, Jimmy Carter in 1980, Ronald Reagan in 1984, George Bush in 1992, Bill Clinton in 1996, George W. Bush in 2004, and Barack Obama in 2012. In other elections the Vice President seeks the Oval Office (e.g., Richard Nixon in 1960, Hubert Humphrey in 1968, George Bush in 1988, Al Gore in 2000). Two people who were not elected as president ran for election as president after 1952 (Lyndon Johnson became President when John Kennedy was assassinated; Gerald Ford was appointed Vice President when Spiro Agnew resigned and then Ford became President upon Nixon's resignation). In 1952 Democratic Governor Stevenson of Illinois ran to succeed Democrat Harry Truman in the White House. The 2008 election was the first truly "open" presidential election since 1952: President George W. Bush had served two terms and could not serve another; Vice President Dick Cheney chose not to seek the presidency after President Bush's second term in office (and Cheney's second term as Vice President).

Between 1952 and 2012, incumbent party candidates won half of the elections. However, if we look only at those candidates who were elected to the Oval Office and sought a second term, seven won and only two lost. Petrocik (2004) offers data that at all levels of office incumbents win 98 percent of primary campaigns and 94 percent of general elections over the last fifty years. The incumbency advantage is important in presidential elections, but even more so at lower levels of offices.

Salamore and Salamore (1985) indicate that the most important advantages for incumbents are recognition, ability to raise campaign funds, and the ability to begin campaigning early. It seems very likely that the incumbent party candidate will be better known than the challenger party candidate, particularly if the incumbent party candidate is an incumbent president running for re-election. If challengers are less well-known, the beliefs about and attitudes toward a candidate are probably easier to change for challengers than incumbents. This means that campaign messages should have more influence on knowledge and perceptions for challengers than incumbents, particularly in early stages of the campaign. Incumbents are likely to receive more attention from the press than challengers (see, e.g., Trent and Trent, 1974, 1995). Smith (Smith 2005; Smith and Mansharamani, 2002) and Dover (2006) discuss incumbency in presidential campaigns.

The nomination from the challenging party is always contested, but one advantage many incumbents have is that they do not have to fight for their party's nomination. For example, Reagan in 1984, Clinton in 1996, Bush in 2004, and Obama in 2012 were not contested when they sought their party's nomination for a second term in office. This means that they are not subjected to attacks from others in their own party. In sharp contrast, in 1980 Senator Ted Kennedy challenged President Jimmy Carter for the Democratic nomination. One of Kennedy's ads sharply criticized his fellow Democrat: "This man has misled the American public into the worst economic crisis since the Depression. He's broken promises and cost New York a billion dollars a year. In his latest foreign policy blunder he betrayed Israel at the UN." Similarly, in 1992 Pat Buchanan challenged President Bush for the Republican nomination. His ads also attacked the president, beginning with Bush's dramatic promise in 1988 that he would not raise taxes (which he broke): "Bush promised. Bush: Read my lips, no new taxes. Bush promised to cut spending, but our national debt has bone up 1.1 trillion dollars. Bush promised us jobs, but our unemployment has tripled. Now Bush is promising to fix the recession. Can we afford four more years of broken promises?" Incumbents have a substantial advantage when they are not challenged in the primary and subjected to attacks such as these.

The fact that incumbents who are not challenged in the primary also means that they can spend more time undermining their opponent. For example, in twenty-one of Republican Bob Dole's 1996 primary ads, two attacked President Bill Clinton and eleven attacked other Republicans. Bill Clinton in 1996 did not have any Democratic opponents to criticize, so he could focus his attacks on Dole, the Republican front-runner.

Importantly, only the incumbent candidate has a record in the office sought. A record in the office sought in an election is, arguably, the best evidence of how a candidate will do if elected (or re-elected). For this reason, both incumbents and challengers talk about the incumbent's record more than about the challenger's record. Incumbents and challengers use this information quite differently: Incumbents acclaim when they discuss their own record whereas challengers attack when they discuss the incumbent's record.

In the general election TV spots examined here, incumbents acclaimed more than challengers (64 percent to 56 percent). Challengers, on the other hand, attacked more than incumbents (43 percent to 31 percent; see table 11.7). A *chi-square* calculated on function (acclaims and attacks) versus incumbency was significant ($df=1$, $\chi^2 = 290.61$, $p < .0001$, $\phi = .13$; defenses were excluded from the calculations because there were so few of them). See table 11.5 for these data.

Kaid and Johnston (1991) found only slight differences between incumbents and challengers: There were only a few more positive incumbent than challenger spots (72 percent to 70 percent), and there were just a few more negative challenger than incumbent spots (30 percent to 28 percent). This discrepancy may well be related to the difference in our coding procedures, discussed earlier. Previous research on nomination acceptance addresses, debates, and direct mail advertising also found that incumbent's acclaim more and attack less than challengers (Benoit, 2007a).

An important difference between incumbents and challengers is that incumbents have a record in the very office sought. This may be a cross-cultural phenomenon, for Kaid and Holtz-Bacha (1995b) reported that "The most consistent strategies used across countries for incumbents were emphasizing accomplishments and stressing competency of the government office occupied." On the other hand,

Table 11.5. Incumbency and Functions of Political TV Spots

	Acclaims	Attacks	Defenses
	Presidential		
Incumbents	**2078 (58%)**	1474 (41%)	57 (2%)
Challengers	1773 (51%)	**1700 (49%)**	30 (1%)
	Nonpresidential		
Incumbents	**3748 (77%)**	1085 (22%)	33 (0.7%)
Challengers	2461 (60%)	**1607 (39%)**	36 (1%)
	Non-U.S.		
Incumbents	129 (55%)	97 (42%)	7 (3%)
Challengers	122 (63%)	71 (36%)	2 (1%)
	Total		
Incumbents	**5955 (68%)**	2656 (31%)	97 (1%)
Challengers	4356 (56%)	**3378 (43%)**	68 (1%)

Data from chapters 3–6, 9–10
χ^2 (df = 2) = 290.61, p < .0001, V = .13

"Challengers consistently called for change, took the offensive on issues, and attacked the record of the opponent in their spots" (p. 214). Thus, incumbents tend to acclaim more, and attack less, on past deeds than challengers. Although it would be a mistake for an incumbent to declare that no improvements would be possible if elected to another term, every future plan (means for achieving policy improvements) is at least implicitly a criticism of the *status quo* presided over by the incumbent. Accordingly, we should expect to see that challengers acclaim more, and attack less, on future plans than incumbents. Finally, as noted, only an incumbent has served in the office at stake in an election, only the incumbent has leadership experience *in that office*. Thus, we expect that incumbents would acclaim more frequently, and attack less often, than challengers when the candidates discuss their leadership experience. Data from general election campaigns for presidential, nonpresidential, and non-U.S. TV spots confirm these three predictions (see table 11.6). When discussing past deeds (record in office), incumbents acclaim more (65 percent to 25 percent) and attack less (35 percent to 75 percent) than challengers. Discussion of future plans show the opposite results (as predicted): Challengers acclaim more (60 percent to 52 percent) and attack less (40 percent to 48 percent) than incumbents. When they talk about leadership ability, both groups of candidates are more likely to acclaim. Still, incumbents acclaim more (86 percent to 75 percent) and attack less (14 percent to 25 percent) than challengers. All of these differences are statistically significant (incumbents versus challengers and functions of: past deeds χ^2 (df = 1) = 809.5, p < .0001, φ = .4; future plans χ^2 (df = 1) = 8.82, p < .005, φ = .08; leadership ability χ^2 (df = 1) = 32.06, p < .0001, φ = .14). The political TV spots produced by incumbents have clear and significant differences from ads made by challengers.

Table 11.6. Incumbency and Functions of Political TV Spots on Past Deeds, Future Plans, and Leadership Ability

	Past Deeds	
	Acclaims	Attacks
Presidential Incumbent	**542 (49%)**	568 (51%)
Presidential Challenger	241 (21%)	**906 (79%)**
Nonpresidential Incumbent	**1272 (76%)**	400 (24%)
Nonpresidential Challenger	340 (30%)	**786 (70%)**
Non-U.S. Incumbent	**22 (73%)**	8 (27%)
Non-U.S. Challenger	8 (19%)	**35 (81%)**
Total Incumbent	**1836 (65%)**	976 (35%)
Total Challenger	589 (25%)	**1727 (75%)**
	Future Plans	
Presidential Incumbent	180 (42%)	**253 (58%)**
Presidential Challenger	**251 (59%)**	337 (47%)
Nonpresidential Incumbent	187 (68%)	**89 (32%)**
Nonpresidential Challenger	**167 (81%)**	39 (19%)
Non-U.S. Incumbent	11 (73%)	4 (27%)
Non-U.S. Challenger	1 (25%)	3 (75%)
Total Incumbent	378 (52%)	**346 (48%)**
Total Challenger	**419 (60%)**	279 (40%)
	Leadership Ability	
Presidential Incumbent	**375 (81%)**	89 (19%)
Presidential Challenger	212 (70%)	**92 (30%)**
Nonpresidential Incumbent	**400 (94%)**	26 (6%)
Nonpresidential Challenger	308 (80%)	**77 (20%)**
Non-U.S. Incumbent	25 (62%)	15 (38%)
Non-U.S. Challenger	18 (64%)	10 (36%)
Total Incumbent	**800 (86%)**	130 (14%)
Total Challenger	538 (75%)	**179 (25%)**

Data from chapters 3–6, 10
Functions of Past Deeds, Incumbents versus Challengers: χ^2 ($df = 1$) = 809.5, $p < .0001$, $\varphi = .4$
Functions of Future Plans, Incumbents versus Challengers: χ^2 ($df = 1$) = 8.82, $p < .005$, $\varphi = .08$
Functions of Leadership Ability, Incumbents versus Challengers: χ^2 ($df = 1$) = 32.06, $p < .0001$, $\varphi = .14$

PRIMARY VERSUS GENERAL CAMPAIGN TV SPOTS

Table 11.7 contrasts the percentage of attacks and percentage of policy in TV spots from presidential candidates for whom we have ads from primary and general campaigns In twenty-one of twenty-two cases, these candidates attacked more in their general ads than their primary ads. In eighteen of twenty-two cases (one was a tie), these candidates discussed policy more in their general ads than their primary ads. Table 11.8 reports data primary versus general ads for all presidential candidates as well as for candidates for senate, governor and house in 2008 and for senate and governor in 2008. Overall, these ads acclaimed more (72 percent to 59 percent) and attacked less (28 percent to 41 percent) in the primary than the general campaign (χ^2 [$df = 1$] = 450.4, $p < .0001$, $\phi = .14$). Both groups of ads discussed policy more than character; however, the candidates in these samples discussed policy less (52 percent to 61 percent) and character more (48 percent to 39 percent) in the primary than the general campaign (χ^2 [$df = 1$] = 164.56, $p < .0001$, $\phi = .08$).

Table 11.7.   Percent of Attacks and of Policy in Primary and General Presidential TV Spots

	Attacks		Policy	
Candidate/Year	*Primary*	*General*	*Primary*	*General*
Eisenhower 1952	13%	**69%**	31%	**86%**
Kennedy 1960	23%	**27%**	47%	**50%**
Goldwater 1964	14%	**34%**	**60%**	48%
Nixon 1968	27%	**29%**	35%	**54%**
Nixon 1972	0	**22%**	57%	**62%**
Ford 1976	0	**22%**	37%	**43%**
Carter 1976	36%	**41%**	29%	**50%**
Reagan 1980	36%	**42%**	55%	**67%**
Carter 1980	29%	**37%**	35%	**42%**
Mondale 1984	27%	**45%**	35%	**71%**
Bush 1988	26%	**39%**	22%	**58%**
Dukakis 1988	14%	**37%**	51%	**63%**
Bush 1992	33%	**56%**	**73%**	63%
Clinton 1992	32%	**49%**	66%	66%
Dole 1996	47%	**62%**	52%	**64%**
Clinton 1996	39%	**47%**	**88%**	82%
Gore 2000	9%	**30%**	71%	**72%**
Bush 2000	12%	**20%**	65%	**69%**
Kerry 2004	17%	**44%**	64%	**66%**
Obama 2008	20%	**68%**	54%	**62%**
McCain 2008	19%	**62%**	36%	**54%**
Romney 2012	**72%**	66%	54%	**67%**

Data from chapters 3–6, 9

Table 11.8. Functions and Topics of Primary versus General TV Spots

	Acclaims	Attacks	Policy	Character
		Presidential		
Primary	5630	2186	4253	3563
General	3983	3361	4540	2894
		2004 Senate, Governor, House		
Primary	2601	920	1683	1838
General	2137	898	1730	1309
		2008 Senate, Governor		
Primary	423	195	271	242
General	807	495	868	427
		Total		
Primary	**8654 (72%)**	3301 (28%)	6207 (52%)	**5643 (48%)**
General	6927 (59%)	**4754 (41%)**	**7138 (61%)**	4630 (39%)

Data from chapters 3–6, 9
Functions of Primary versus General TV Spots: χ^2 (df = 1) = 450.4, p < .0001, ϕ = .14
Topics of Primary versus General TV Spots: χ^2 (df = 1) = 164.56, p < .0001, ϕ = .08

Kaid and Ballotti (1991) studied 1,089 primary television spots from 1968 through 1988. They found that 48 percent were issue ads (focusing on the sponsor's policy stances), 32 percent were image ads (focusing on the sponsor's characteristics or qualifications), 18 percent were negative ads (focusing on the opponent or comparing the sponsor and the opponent), and 3 percent were combinations (no dominant focus). Although our categories are not identical, their study suggests that primary spots are less negative than the data obtained here (18 percent to 32 percent). These discrepancies are akin to the ones between my study of general spots and that of Kaid and Johnston (1991), discussed above.

There are four possible explanations for these somewhat discrepant results. The first and second potential explanations concern the sample and coding definitions of "acclaim," "positive," "attack," and "negative." The arguments made above about Kaid and Johnston (1991) apply here as well. Third, primary spots have gotten more negative over time and I included primary spots from 1992–2012, after their study was completed. For this reason I broke out just the primary spots in my sample from 1968 to 1988 (omitting defenses) to make my data directly comparable to Kaid and Ballotti's results. For those years 73 percent of the presidential primary ad utterances were acclaims, and 27 percent were attacks. Thus, the fact that more recent primaries are somewhat more negative than the ones in the campaigns studied by Kaid and Ballotti does not entirely account for the discrepancy in the results of these two studies.

The final possible explanation is that some of the discrepancy occurs from our different methods of analysis: Their method classifies entire spots according to their "primary focus" whereas I analyze each theme separately. Consider these two primary spots from 1980. The italicized portions are attacks; the romanized parts are acclaims. The first spot is from Edward Kennedy's primary campaign:

[CARROLL O'CONNOR]: *Friends, I've seen some oddities off stage as well as on, but never anything odder than Jimmy Carter in a Democratic primary, because he may be the most Republican president since Herbert Hoover. And he may give us a depression that'll make Hoover's look like prosperity. Our money is worth less and less every day because of runaway prices. Soon it won't be worth the paper used to print it. We're looking at industrial lay-offs and unemployment in all parts of the country. We have a foreign policy nobody understands. And Jimmy stays in Washington making warm-hearted speeches. Maybe that's a smart political strategy, but I hope it doesn't fool too many people.* I hope you'll support a man who's out there facing problems. I mean my friend Senator Ted Kennedy. I've always liked him politically and personally, and I believe in his friends, in every way. So let's give him our vote, and give ourselves the best chance for a future with confidence and security. Thank you.

The following advertisement is from George Bush's Republican primary campaign that same year:

I'm George Bush. *In 1976, candidate Jimmy Carter said we didn't have an energy policy. We still don't.* Sure we have to conserve, but let's be more specific about what we have to do: get the government out of the energy business, tax dollars would go into research, not more bureaucracy. We've got to produce more energy; that means coal, safe nuclear, solar. We've pulled together before; we can do it now.

It is misleading to classify either advertisement as entirely positive or as negative. Each ad contains both positive (acclaiming) and negative (attacking) elements. The first example is clearly more negative than positive, whereas the second is more positive than negative. Even classifying them as "comparative" advertisements is misleading, because neither one is divided equally into positive (acclaiming) and negative (attacking) components. Again, their research is an extremely important contribution to the literature, but I believe that the most accurate way to analyze political television spots is by theme.

Why would general spots rely more heavily on attacks than primary spots? It seems likely that this is a function of the differences in a candidate's opponents in each stage of the campaign. In the primaries, a candidate runs against other members of his (again, all of these candidates were male) own party. Although there are differences among Republicans (and among Democrats), for the most part two candidates of the *same party* should have more in common—and therefore possess fewer differences to attack—than two candidates from *different parties*. Of course, there are differences between candidates from the same party, and these can develop into areas for attack. The point is that there are comparatively fewer differences between members of the same party than between members of different parties.

There are also considerations which encourage candidates not to attack too much in the primaries. Candidates know that if they win their party's nomination, they will want their primary opponents to endorse them, if not actively campaign on their behalf, in the general campaign. Thus, savvy primary candidates may wish to avoid alienating their primary opponents by attacking them too much. Perhaps more importantly, primary contenders may wish to avoid alienating opponents' *supporters*. In 2012 Mitt Romney may have moderated his attacks against, for example, Newt Gingrich, hoping that Gingrich's fans would support Romney if he won the Republican nomination. Also, we have seen that attacks from the primaries can be used by the other party in the general campaign. In 1964, for instance, Johnson used statements from Goldwater's primary opponents to attack Goldwater, and in 1980 Reagan spots used clips from Edward Kennedy's primary ads attacking Jimmy Carter. This could be another factor which moderates to a certain extent the amount of attack in primary campaigns. Of course, attacks are still quite common in the primaries; they are just less frequent at that stage than in the general campaign.

West (1997) reported that personal qualities were a more common topic in primary (39 percent) than in general campaigns (31 percent). The sample reported here indicates that the percentage of personal qualities appeals (out of total character utterances) was 51 percent in the primaries and 49 percent in the general campaign. Thus, I do not agree that there is a significant difference in use of personal qualities by stage of the campaign (recall reservations about West's sample, expressed in chapter 2).

WINNERS VERSUS LOSERS

Overall, winners and losers acclaimed (54 percent, 55 percent), attacked (46 percent, 44 percent), and defended (1 percent, 2 percent) at about the same rate in these presidential television spots (χ^2 [df = 1] = 1.5, *ns*). Thus, winners are not distinguished from losers based on the functions employed in their television advertisements. These data are displayed in table 11.9.

In order to further explore the relationship between outcomes and functions, I decided to conduct a different analysis that considered whether the presidential race was close throughout the campaign. I used *Gallup Opinion Index* and polls obtained from the Internet to locate tracking polls and divided the candidates into three groups.

> ➤ Candidates who led throughout the campaign: Eisenhower: 1952, 1956; Johnson: 1964; Nixon: 1972; Reagan: 1984; Clinton: 1992, 1996.
> ➤ Candidates who trailed throughout the campaign (opponents of the candidates in the first group): Stevenson: 1952, 1956; Goldwater: 1964; McGovern: 1972; Mondale: 1984; Bush: 1992; Dole: 1996.
> ➤ Candidates who participated in closely contested races: Nixon and Kennedy: 1960; Nixon and Humphrey: 1968; Ford and Carter: 1976; Reagan and Carter: 1980; Bush and Dukakis: 1988; Bush and Gore: 2000; Bush and Kerry: 2004; Obama and McCain: 2008; and Obama and Romney: 2012.

When these data are broken out in this fashion, some interesting differences emerge. Acclaiming was most common among candidates led throughout the campaign (61 percent), followed by those in tight races (54 percent) and those who trailed throughout the campaign (48 percent). The least attacks were employed by those who led (38 percent), then those in close races (45 percent), and the most attacks were from candidates who trailed throughout the campaign (51 percent). A two by three *chi-square* calculated on function (acclaims and attacks) by type of race (leaders, trailers, and close) was significant at the .001 level (χ^2 [df = 2] = 42.44, p < .0001, V = .08) (see table 11.10).

It is possible that the functions addressed in television spots do not cause election outcomes as much as they respond to situational differences facing candidates. Those candidates who trail throughout the campaign may feel forced to attack more than other groups of candidates. Attacks do attract attention, and they can reduce the apparent favorability of their target. Of course, there is the risk of a backlash from voters, many of whom profess to dislike mudslinging as noted earlier. However, those candidates who are clearly losing the election may be willing to run this risk if there is a chance that negative ads can "move the [poll] numbers" in their favor. Thus, I would argue that the candidates' position in the race (front-runner, close, trailer) is an important determinant of political advertising function.

A difference did emerge in the topics of TV spots from winners versus losers. Those who won general presidential election campaigns discussed policy more (65 percent to 58 percent) and character less (35 percent to 42 percent) than losers (χ^2 [df = 1] = 36.68, p < .0001, ϕ = .07). As indicated earlier, voters indicate that policy is a more important determinant of their vote for president than character (Benoit, 2003).

Table 11.9. Functions of Presidential TV Spots by Winners and Losers

		Functions			Topics	
Year	Candidate	Acclaims	Attacks	Defenses	Policy	Character
1952	Eisenhower W	22 (31%)	48 (69%)	0	60 (86%)	10 (14%)
	Stevenson L	30 (64%)	17 (46%)	0	23 (49%)	24 (51%)
1956	Eisenhower W	78 (98%)	2 (2%)	0	35 (44%)	45 (56%)
	Stevenson L	41 (62%)	25 (38%)	0	37 (56%)	29 (44%)
1960	Kennedy W	105 (73%)	38 (27%)	0	71 (50%)	72 (50%)
	Nixon L	140 (85%)	14 (9%)	10 (6%)	56 (36%)	98 (64%)
1964	Johnson W	59 (58%)	42 (42%)	0	66 (65%)	35 (35%)
	Goldwater L	98 (60%)	55 (34%)	11 (7%)	73 (48%)	80 (52%)
1968	Nixon W	71 (71%)	29 (29%)	0	54 (54%)	46 (46%)
	Humphrey L	119 (73%)	36 (23%)	5 (3%)	67 (43%)	88 (57%)
1972	Nixon W	124 (78%)	35 (22%)	0	98 (62%)	61 (38%)
	McGovern L	58 (39%)	90 (60%)	1 (1%)	94 (64%)	54 (36%)
1976	Carter W	126 (59%)	89 (41%)	0	108 (50%)	107 (50%)
	Ford L	200 (75%)	59 (22%)	8 (3%)	112 (43%)	147 (57%)
1980	Reagan W	129 (58%)	93 (42%)	0	148 (67%)	74 (33%)
	Carter L	112 (61%)	68 (37%)	5 (3%)	75 (42%)	105 (58%)

Year	Candidate	Functions			Topics	
		Acclaims	Attacks	Defenses	Policy	Character
1984	Reagan W	202 (77%)	59 (23%)	0	177 (68%)	84 (32%)
	Mondale L	132 (54%)	110 (45%)	2 (1%)	173 (71%)	70 (29%)
1988	Bush W	121 (61%)	78 (39%)	0	115 (58%)	84 (42%)
	Dukakis L	206 (61%)	125 (37%)	4 (1%)	209 (63%)	122 (37%)
1992	Clinton W	167 (49%)	168 (49%)	5 (1%)	222 (66%)	113 (34%)
	Bush L	70 (44%)	90 (56%)	0	100 (63%)	60 (37%)
1996	Clinton W	225 (53%)	200 (47%)	3 (1%)	349 (82%)	76 (18%)
	Dole L	111 (37%)	185 (62%)	1 (.5%)	189 (64%)	107 (36%)
2000	Gore W*	120 (69%)	53 (30%)	1 (0.6%)	125 (72%)	48 (28%)
	Bush L*	101 (79%)	26 (20%)	1 (0.8%)	87 (69%)	40 (31%)
2004	Bush W	135 (48%)	141 (50%)	7 (2%)	184 (67%)	92 (33%)
	Kerry L	235 (55%)	202 (44%)	5 (1%)	300 (66%)	155 (34%)
2008	Obama W	133 (32%)	281 (68%)	2 (0.5%)	256 (62%)	158 (38%)
	McCain L	137 (38%)	224 (62%)	1 (0.3%)	196 (54%)	165 (46%)
2012	Obama W	109 (27%)	278 (70%)	12 (3%)	250 (65%)	137 (35%)
	Romney L	135 (32%)	214 (66%)	3 (1%)	233 (67%)	116 (33%)
Winners		1926 (54%)	1634 (46%)	30 (1%)	**2318 (65%)**	1242 (35%)
Losers		1925 (55%)	1540 (44%)	57 (2%)	2024 (58%)	**1460 (42%)**

Data from chapters 3–6
*Gore is considered the winner because he received more votes (although of course he lost in the Electoral College)
Functions (acclaims versus attacks): χ^2 ($df = 1$) = 1.5, $p > .2$; Topics: χ^2 ($df = 1$) = 36.68, $p < .0001$, $\varphi = .07$

Table 11.10.   Functions of Presidential TV Spots by Closeness of the Race

Candidate	Acclaim	Attack	Defense
Led Throughout Race			
1952 Eisenhower	22 (31%)	48 (69%)	0
1956 Eisenhower	78 (98%)	2 (2%)	0
1964 Johnson	59 (58%)	42 (42%)	0
1972 Nixon	124 (78%)	35 (22%)	0
1984 Reagan	202 (77%)	59 (23%)	0
1992 Clinton	167 (49%)	168 (49%)	5 (1%)
1996 Clinton	225 (53%)	200 (47%)	3 (1%)
Led Race	**877 (61%)**	554 (38%)	8 (0.5%)
Close Races			
1960 Nixon	140 (85%)	14 (9%)	10 (6%)
1960 Kennedy	105 (73%)	38 (27%)	0
1968 Nixon	71 (71%)	29 (29%)	0
1968 Humphrey	119 (73%)	36 (23%)	5 (3%)
1976 Ford	200 (75%)	59 (22%)	8 (3%)
1976 Carter	126 (59%)	89 (41%)	0
1980 Reagan	129 (58%)	93 (42%)	0

(continued)

Table 11.10.   (*continued*)

Candidate	Acclaim	Attack	Defense
1980 Carter	112 (61%)	68 (37%)	5 (3%)
1988 Bush	121 (61%)	78 (39%)	0
1988 Dukakis	206 (61%)	125 (37%)	4 (1%)
2000 Bush	101 (79%)	26 (20%)	1 (0.8%)
2000 Gore	120 (69%)	53 (30%)	1 (0.6%)
2004 Bush	135 (48%)	141 (50%)	7 (2%)
2004 Kerry	235 (55%)	202 (44%)	5 (1%)
2008 McCain	137 (38%)	224 (62%)	1 (0.3%)
2008 Obama	133 (32%)	281 (68%)	2 (0.5%)
2012 Obama	109 (27%)	278 (70%)	12 (3%)
2012 Romney	135 (32%)	214 (66%)	3 (1%)
Close Race	**2434 (54%)**	2058 (45%)	64 (1%)
	Trailed Throughout Race		
1952 Stevenson	30 (64%)	17 (46%)	0
1956 Stevenson	41 (62%)	25 (38%)	0
1964 Goldwater	98 (60%)	55 (34%)	11 (7%)
1972 McGovern	58 (39%)	90 (60%)	1 (1%)
1984 Mondale	132 (54%)	110 (45%)	2 (1%)
1992 Bush	70 (44%)	90 (56%)	0
1996 Dole	111 (37%)	185 (62%)	1 (0.5%)
Trailed Race	540 (48%)	**572 (51%)**	15 (1%)

Data from chapters 3–6
χ^2 ($df = 2$) = 42.44, $p < .0001$, $V = .08$

SOURCES OF UTTERANCES: CANDIDATES VERSUS OTHERS

Themes in presidential spots from 1952–1996 were analyzed to determine the source of each statement. Did the candidate, an announcer, or someone else acclaim, attack, or defend? There appears to be a trend over time for less reliance on candidates and more on others in presidential television spots. In presidential campaigns (primary, general, third party; 1952–1996), candidates acclaimed in 70 percent of themes and attacked in 30 percent; others acclaimed in 64 percent of themes and attacked in 36 percent). Statistical analysis confirms a difference in source and function (χ^2 [$df = 1$] = 29.8, $p < .0001$, $\varphi = .06$).

Kaid and Johnston (2001) found that 53 percent of positive ads and 14 percent of negative ads featured the candidates speaking, whereas 47 percent of positive and 86 percent of negative ads featured anonymous announcers or surrogate speakers. Although the figures are not identical, both samples found that others make a higher percentage of attacks than candidates.

Given the concerns over alienating some voters with mudslinging, it is not surprising to see an even higher percentage of attacks from others (76 percent) than from the candidate (24 percent). There is experimental evidence which suggests that attacks from spots sponsored by the candidate create more backlash than those sponsored by other organizations (e.g., Political Action Committes; see Garramone, 1985; Garramone and Smith, 1984; Kaid and Boydston, 1987). It is not clear that effects of ad *sponsor* will transfer to *source* of utterance, but these studies suggest that it might be wise for candidates to allow others to make some of the attacks.

Airne and Benoit (2005) contrasted nonpresidential ads sponsored by candidates with those from political parties. Candidate sponsored ads in their sample acclaimed more than they attacked (74 percent to 26 percent) whereas spots sponsored by political parties attacked more than they acclaimed (59 percent to 41 percent). A *chi-square* indicated that these differences were significant (χ^2 [df = 1] = 62.01, p < .0001,ϕ = .34). Benoit and Airne (2009) examined nonpresidential ads from the 2008 election. They found that candidate ads acclaimed a bit more than they attacked (52 percent to 48 percent) whereas non-candidate ads (e.g., ads from Political Action Committees) attacked four times as often as they acclaimed (80 percent to 20 percent). Statistical analysis confirms that these differences are significant (χ^2 [df =1] = 122.99, p < .0001,ϕ = .32). Again, TV spots from political candidates use more acclaims and fewer attacks than ads sponsored from others. Source of utterance within ads as well as sponsor of advertisement is related to ad function.

CONCLUSION

This book identifies and documented several trends in presidential television advertising (including greater density—more themes in thirty seconds—and increasing reliance on shorter spots). Data including presidential primary and general ads, nonpresidential ads, and non-U.S. ads are used to investigate several other facets of political advertising. In general, acclaims are more common than attacks which in turn are used more frequently than defenses. Both primary and third-party spots are less negative than general spots. There has been a gradual trend for presidential spots (both general and primary spots) to become more negative over time. Candidates discuss policy in their ads more frequently than character. Policy statements have three forms: past deeds (49 percent), future plans (14 percent), and general goals (37 percent). Character utterances take three forms: personal qualities (59 percent), leadership ability (25 percent), and ideals (16 percent). When discussing their personal qualities, TV spots talk about morality, drive, empathy, and sincerity. Candidates acclaim more than they attack when discussing general goals and ideals. Incumbents are more likely to acclaim more than challengers, who, in contrast, attack more than incumbent party candidates. More specifically, incumbents tend to acclaim more, and attack less, on past deeds and leadership ability than challengers. Challengers, on the other hand, are prone to acclaim more and attack less on future plans than incumbents. There is no significant difference in the functions of spots by winners and losers; winners address policy more, and character less, than losers. Systematic differences by position in the race occur: The most attacks originate with candidates who trail throughout the campaign; fewer attacks are made by candidates who lead throughout the campaign (and candidates in close races fall between these two groups). Candidates are more likely to acclaim, and less likely to attack, than other sources in TV spots; advertisements sponsored by candidates are less negative than ones sponsored by political parties or other groups. We have learned a great deal about political advertising. We know more about presidential ads from the general election than presidential primary ads, nonpresidential ads, or ads from races in other countries. Longitudinal research is important because that is the only way to detect trends such as ads become more negative or emphasizing policy more than in the past.

12

Development of
Political Television Spots

This chapter offers a discussion of the historical development of political advertising techniques and strategies. Discussion of presidential TV spots from 1952–1992 can be found in Diamond and Bates (1992) and Jamieson (1996). Diamond and Bates also identify three phases of presidential advertising during the general election campaign: 1992; three phases: ID spots, Argument Spots, Attack, "I see an America . . ." However, our understanding of the development of appeals in presidential television advertising is still incomplete. For example, as we have seen, one common approach to spots is to use ordinary citizens attack the opponent (or to acclaim the candidate). Testimony from citizens was used by Dwight Eisenhower to attack the incumbent Democratic administration's record in 1952, the first presidential campaign to use television spots:

MAN: Graft, corruption, and high prices. Headlines like that make me fighting mad, Mr. Eisenhower.

MAN: Food prices, clothing prices, income taxes, won't they ever go down?

WOMAN: They say we've never had it so good. But I've had to stop buying eggs, they're so expensive.

MAN: I'm a veteran, general. What's wrong down in Washington? Graft, scandal, headlines, how can you fix it?

WOMAN: My children hear so much about government graft, they think everyone is crooked.

MAN: It was extra tough paying my income tax when I read about Internal Revenue men being fired for dishonesty.

MAN: Today they say I never had it so good. Yet my pension won't even feed me and my wife.

WOMAN: I live carefully on my budget. Why can't the government do the same?

("Eisenhower Answers America," excerpts from eight spots)

Although these citizens did not refer to Stevenson directly, it is clear that their attack against the status quo was offered as a reason to prefer Eisenhower over Stevenson. McGovern's "Deep Feelings" advertisement in 1972 also used ordinary citizens to attack his opponent before Ford employed this approach.

This chapter traces the emergence of several discursive conventions in presidential advertising. I divide this account of the development of presidential television advertising into six sections. First, I discuss the origins of the three fundamental functions of presidential television advertising: acclaims (self-praise, positive spots), attacks (negative spots), and defenses (responses to attacks). Then I will discuss the use of the two basic topics for political commercials, policy and character. Third, I will discuss recurrent formats in spots. Next, I will examine the use of evidence in advertising. Fifth, I will address the use of sources, or speakers, in these commercials. Finally, I will illustrate several recurring arguments in presidential spots.

FUNCTIONS OF PRESIDENTIAL TELEVISION SPOTS

I will illustrate each of the three functions of political discourse—acclaims, attacks, defenses—and identify the earliest campaigns to employ them. Of course, I can only identify the earliest campaign *in my sample* to employ these functions (and to enact the other recurrent themes discussed in this chapter); because I could not include every spot ever used in a presidential campaign, it is conceivable that some developments occurred in earlier advertisements.

Acclaims

Acclaims were an important component of the very first presidential contest to employ television spots, between Dwight Eisenhower and Adlai Stevenson. Here is an acclaim from the Democratic candidate in that campaign:

I've decided that the man who believes the way I do is Adlai Stevenson. And he's had the courage to say so. No manmade barriers for any of us. Decent wages for us all. Security when we're too old or too sick to work. And a chance to live as a man should live, in truth and freedom. Yes sir, I've decided that on November 4, I'm voting for the man who said "The same God made us all." I'm voting for Adlai Stevenson. ("Great American")

The values of liberty or freedom and truth, the character trait of courage, the goals of equal opportunity, decent wages, and security are all offered as reasons to vote for Stevenson. That same year the Republican candidate, Eisenhower, acclaimed his desirability in this commercial: "I stand for expanded social security and more real benefits. Believe me sir: If I am president, I'll give you older folks action, not just sympathy" ("Eisenhower Answers America"). This spot acclaims Eisenhower's stand on social security: expand it and increase benefits (it also contains a swipe at the Democrats for offering sympathy without action). Thus, acclaims were a part of presidential television spots from the very beginning, and every candidate in every campaign since then has used acclaims (Benoit, 1998). As spots used to illustrate later points will make clear, acclaims are common in these television commercials.

Attacks

Like acclaims, attacks made their debut in the first presidential campaign to employ television spot. In the following spot, Eisenhower attacks the incumbent administration in 1952 for inadequate military preparedness:

> MAN: General, if war comes, is this country really ready?
>
> EISENHOWER: It is not. The Administration has spent many billions of dollars for national defense. Yet today we haven't enough tanks for the fighting in Korea. It is time for a change. ("Eisenhower Answers America")

Adding insult to injury, the current administration doesn't have enough weapons to fight the war in Korea despite spending billions of dollars on defense. On the other hand, Stevenson, his Democratic opponent, argued that if elected, Eisenhower would be a pawn of congressman Robert Taft:

> Ike. Bob. Ike. Bob. [two hearts, labeled Ike, Bob]
> We must lower taxes Bob.
> Yes Ike, we must lower taxes.
> But we have to spend more for defense Bob.
> You see Ike, we agree perfectly.
> Bob. Ike. Bob. Ike.
>
> ANNOUNCER: Will Bob give Ike the additional money for defense after Ike cuts taxes? Stay tuned for a musical interlude:
>
> [Song with hearts]: Rueben, Rueben, I've been thinking, 'bout the Gen'ral and his mob
> If you're voting for the Gen'ral, you really are electing Bob.
> Let's vote for Adlai—and John. ("Ike and Bob 2")

Our system of government is predicated on the doctrine of separation of powers. Presumably voters would not want the president to be controlled by a member of Congress. Both of these advertisements, from the first campaign to use television spots, use attacks to reduce their opponent's apparent desirability to voters. The ads used to illustrate other developments will show that attacks were quite common and come in many formats.

Defenses

Defense was not used until 1960, the third campaign using television spots. Kennedy's campaign had attacked the Eisenhower/Nixon economic record. Given that Nixon was running hard on his record as a vice president in Eisenhower's administration, it was important for him to respond to those accusations:

ANNOUNCER: Mr. Nixon, what is the truth? Is America lagging behind in economic growth?

NIXON: Certainly not. The fact is that Americans are earning more, investing more, saving more, living better than ever before. More Americans than ever before are bringing home the weekly paycheck. Sixty-eight million people are employed today. Now this is growth. The kind that ensures our strength at home, and it exceeds the economic growth in Russia today. Ours is a growth based on paying our bills, too. Not a system of reckless borrowing that will burden our children tomorrow. This is the kind of economic growth we must continue to have, in order to continue to help us keep the peace. ("Economic Growth")

Here, Nixon denies his opponent's allegation, declaring that there are more jobs, Americans are "earning more, investing more, saving more, [and therefore] living better than ever before." Notice that like Eisenhower's spots from eight years earlier, this ads use of the question and answer format suggests that Nixon is the candidate who possesses the truth.

Nixon also employed the first defense to use a surrogate to defend the candidate in his 1960 campaign:

ANNOUNCER: From Philadelphia, President Eisenhower answers the Kennedy-Johnson charges that America has accomplished nothing in the last eight years.

EISENHOWER: So I am proud of you; proud of what you have done. And proud of what has been done by America. And let no one diminish your pride and confidence in yourselves or belittle these accomplishments. My friends, never have Americans achieved so much in so short a time [applause]. Now in glib political oratory we have heard this progress called standing still [laughter]. If the great things you have done are standing still, then I say, America needs more of it [applause]. ("So Much")

Here, President Eisenhower denies (albeit rather vaguely) the attacks from Nixon's opponents. A 1964 spot used Ronald Reagan to respond to accusations that Goldwater was trigger-happy, another early example of this function. Goldwater himself also responded to charges that he was "imprudent and impulsive" in another ad from that year. In 1980, Nancy Reagan appeared in a spot for her husband to defend him against charges by Carter, the first example of a spousal defense:

I don't often speak out in campaigns. But I think this campaign now has gotten to the point, and the level, where I have to say something. I am deeply, deeply offended by the attempts of Mr. Carter to paint my husband as a man he is not at all. I am offended when he tries to portray him as a war-monger or a man who would throw the elderly out on the street and cut off their social security, when in fact he never said anything of the kind at any time. And the elderly people have enough to worry about now. They're scared to death about how they're going to make ends meet, how they're going to live without this thrown on top of them. That's a cruel thing to do. It's cruel to the people, it's cruel to my husband. I deeply, deeply, resent it as a wife, and a mother, and a woman. ("Nancy")

Note that this defense ends with an attack on Carter for being cruel.

Four years later, Reagan attacked Mondale with this spot: "Walter Mondale thinks you can squeeze some more tax money out of your household budget. What do you think? [Mother making sandwiches for her kids looks exasperated] ("Tax Vignettes"). The Mondale campaign responded to this accusation with an advertisement that began with an imitation of Reagan's attack ad:

ANNOUNCER: Walter Mondale thinks you can squeeze more tax money out of your budget—what do you think [to mother making sandwiches]?

WOMAN: I think you've got it all wrong. Mondale thinks I'm paying too much and he's right. I had to take a second job just to make ends meet. Kids please get the dog out of here. You know who ought to pay more: the fat cats who don't pay anything. I'm tired of supporting them. That's what I think. And that's why I'm for Mondale. ("Fat Cats")

This ordinary citizen explicitly denied the Reagan allegations. Thus, defenses come from the candidates, others politicians, their spouses, and ordinary citizens as well as from anonymous announcers.

One of the most famous examples of defense was "Counterpunch" from Dukakis in 1980. This commercial began with video from one of Bush's ads attacking Dukakis on national defense. Dukakis turned off the television and declared: "I'm fed up with it. Never seen anything like it in twenty-five years of public life, George Bush's negative TV ads. Distorting my record; full of lies and he knows it. I'm on the record for the very weapons systems his ads say I'm against. I want to build a strong defense." This ad denies the accusations while attacking Bush for lying. Although less common than either acclaims or attacks, defense is an option that is used by presidential candidates in their television advertisements.

TOPICS OF PRESIDENTIAL TELEVISION SPOTS

Presidential television spots can address two broad topics: policy and character. Both topics are prominent fixtures of presidential television spots, as these examples illustrate.

Policy

In 1952, both of the presidential candidates discussed policy. In this Eisenhower advertisement, he attacks the incumbent administration for inflation and taxes:

MAN: Food prices, clothing prices, income taxes, won't they ever go down?

EISENHOWER: Not with an $85 billion budget eating away on your grocery bill. Your clothing, your food, your income, yet the Democrats say you never had it so good. ("Eisenhower Answers America")

No one likes high prices or rates of taxation. Eisenhower relates inflation the impact of inflation on groceries and clothing to heighten the impact of this attack. His opponent, Stevenson, also discussed policy. Here is an acclaim of Democratic accomplishments in a 1952 presidential television spot:

ANNOUNCER: Politics? I'll tell you what politics mean to you. Open your wallet.

MAN: OK. Well?

ANNOUNCER: You've got more money than you had 20 years ago haven't you, even after taxes?

MAN: Why sure.

ANNOUNCER: See that Social Security card you have? That means security for you and your family. The Democrats made it possible.

MAN: Well. . . .

ANNOUNCER: Look there at your bank book. Your savings are insured up to 10,000, thanks to the Democrats. Is that a picture of your family?

MAN: Pretty nice, huh?

ANNOUNCER: Pretty wonderful. Nice home there too. I think the Democrats have given you the chance to do pretty well, Mister. Don't let the Republicans take all these good things away from you. Vote Democratic. ("Wallet")

Income, Social Security, insured savings accounts, and a home are all attributed to the policies of the Democrats. Thus, both candidates in 1952 discussed policy in their advertisements.

The most common form of policy arguments (58 percent) concerns past deeds. In 1952, Eisenhower used this argument to attack the incumbent (Democratic) administration, as we saw earlier. The Democrats used the "Wallet" spot just discussed to acclaim the party's accomplishments (and to attack the Republicans) as we just saw. However, the first candidate to use a television spot to acclaim his first term accomplishments was Eisenhower in 1956:

Your administration will try diligently through the next three weeks to explain its record of achievements, the problems before it, and the policies by which it proposes to solve them. You will hear your Secretary of State, John Foster Dulles, tell of the spirit that impels us in achieving peace and the record we have made as a nation in our united effort for peace. You will hear your Secretary of Treasury, George Humphrey, tell how his department has checked the galloping inflation, cut taxes, balanced the budget, and reduced the debt. You will hear your Secretary of Defense, Charles E. Wilson, tell how we have saved billions of dollars on the Armed Forces, reduced our manpower requirements, and still provided a more secure defense. You will hear your Secretary of Labor, James Mitchell, tell how employment, wages, and income have reached the highest levels in history. You will hear your Attorney General, the Secretary of our new Department of Health, Education, and Welfare, and other Cabinet officers tell what we have done to combat monopoly, to extend Social Security for seventy million Americans, and other accomplishments of this Republican administration. I am proud of the record, and I think you will be proud of it too. So let me ask you one thing. Whenever you can, listen to this series, and talk the facts over with your family and friends. Then make up your mind as to how you will vote on November 6. ("Record of Achievements")

This was a powerful reason to give Eisenhower a second term. Nixon was successful using this approach in 1972 to seek a second term as President. Reagan, with his "Morning in America" ads in 1984, and Clinton in 1996, were both successful at parlaying their past accomplishments into a second term. However, Ford, Carter, and Bush were unable to convert first term performance into a second term in office. Nixon tried unsuccessfully to run on the Eisenhower/Nixon record in 1960 (Bush did better at running on the Reagan/Bush record in 1988).

A variation on this theme argues that past accomplishments as governor are reasons to give a candidate a chance in the White House. In 1976, Jimmy Carter tried this argument:

There's one real source of our government's failings: mismanagement. We tackled this problem when I became governor of Georgia, and we beat it. We cut waste and inefficiency. And even left a surplus of $116 million. Now I'm not saying it's going to be easy to do in Washington. But we can't afford not to try. We didn't become a great country by giving up. Together we can make the effort. Let's get started. ("Get Started")

The basic argument here is that what worked in Georgia will work for America. Reagan used this approach in his 1980 bid to unseat Carter:

REAGAN: Americans are deeply concerned over the economic failures of the last four years. When I became governor of California, we solved many of the same problems America faces today, by bringing in a team of elected officials and private citizens. Working together, we cut the rate of government spending and turned a $194 million deficit into a $554 million surplus. We did it once; we can do it again.

ANNOUNCER: The time is now for strong leadership. Reagan for president. ("Economic Concerns")

The same basic assumption, that a successful governor will make a successful president, is at work here. In 1992, Clinton successfully revisited this argument:

For twelve years he's battled the odds in one of America's poorest states [Clinton working at desk] and made steady progress. Arkansas is now first in the nation in job growth. Even Bush's Secretary of Labor just called job growth in Arkansas enormous. He moved 17,000 people from welfare to work. And he's kept taxes low: Arkansas has the second lowest tax burden in the country. No wonder his fellow governors, Democrats and Republicans, have named him the nation's most effective governor. Bill Clinton: For people for a change. ("Steady")

Dukakis (1988) also tried this approach, but was unable to defeat Reagan.

Character

Once again, in the first campaign to use television spots, 1952, both candidates addressed character issues. For example, Eisenhower argues that Washington politicians are corrupt and need to be ousted from office:

MAN [Eisenhower Answers America]: I'm a veteran, general. What's wrong down in Washington? Graft, scandal, headlines, how can you fix it?

EISENHOWER: Here's how. By your votes, we'll get rid of the people who are too small for their jobs, too big for their britches. Too long in power. ("Eisenhower Answers America")

Suggesting that they are "too small for their jobs" attacks their competence whereas "too big for their britches" is a clear indictment of their character. Eisenhower promises to get rid of these unsavory people in the Democratic administration. In 1952 Stevenson used character as the basis for an acclaim in this spot:

I can't get over this man Stevenson. There's a man with real courage. When I think of what he believes in—and what he has the backbone to say. Well, for example he said that he'd resist any special privileges for pressure groups—and he told that to labor unions in Detroit. And another time, he said he wouldn't stand for special privileges for any special interests, including veterans, and the told that to the American Legion. That took real courage. And about tideland oils—Stevenson believes they belong to all of us—and he told that to the governor of Texas. Oh, he may lose Texas, but he sure stuck to his guns. He hasn't sold out for any special votes. You know, it takes courage to be a great president. But in my book, it takes even greater courage to be an honest candidate. You're right: My vote's for Stevenson. ("Resist Special Privileges")

Stevenson is portrayed as a man with the courage to stand up to special interests. Surely that is an important trait for a president to possess. So, both candidates in 1952 addressed character in their television spots. Again, other examples will illustrate the role of character in presidential spots.

An interesting twist is to use attack a candidate's policy positions and then draw a conclusion about character. The spots illustrating inconsistency discussed below point out contradictory policy stances from a candidate and then suggest that this candidate is unpredictable if not untrustworthy.

RECURRENT FORMATS FOR
PRESIDENTIAL TELEVISION SPOTS

I have identified five recurrent formats for political advertising: question and answer, biography, songs, cartoons, and the use of scrolled words in a spot. I will illustrate these formats with spots from the earliest instances I found for each.

Question and Answer

In 1952, Eisenhower developed a series of forty spots in an "Eisenhower Answers America" series of twenty second spots (Griese, 1975). These began with a question from an ordinary citizen (usually a question that attacks the incumbent Democratic administration, as the excerpts in the introduction above revealed) and Eisenhower's answer. Note that this is also the first instance of a series of thematically related spots, another durable innovation (Stevenson did run two "Ike and Bob" spots in 1952):

> MAN [Eisenhower Answers America]: Mr. Eisenhower, are we going to have to fight another war?
>
> EISENHOWER: No, not if we have a sound program for peace. And I'll add this, we won't spend hundreds of billions and still not have enough tanks and planes for Korea. (Eisenhower, 1952, "Eisenhower Answers America")

Eisenhower manages to acclaim his goals ("a sound program for peace"), to subtly remind voters of his victory in WWII, and to attack his opponents ("spend hundreds of billions and still not have enough tanks and planes"). Notice that this advertising format ("Eisenhower Answers America") suggests two key points: (1) America (and the American voter) has questions about the Democratic administration, and (2) Eisenhower is the candidate with answers. Nixon used a series of question and answer spots in 1960, "What is the truth. . . ?" In 1964, Goldwater responded to questions, sometimes under the title "The People Ask Barry Goldwater." This has become a commonplace in political advertising.

Biography

The biographical spot has become another staple in the cupboards of political campaigns. Diamond and Bates (1992) identify the ID spot. This kind of ad is traditionally used at the beginning of a campaign to help voters get to know the candidate. The first one ran in 1952 for Eisenhower: "The man from Abilene. Out of the heartland of America. Out of this small frame house in Abilene, Kansas, comes a man Dwight D. Eisenhower. Through the crucial hour of historic D-Day he brought us to the triumph and peace of V-E Day" (Eisenhower 1952, "Man from Abilene"). Eisenhower is acclaimed as a man form humble origins who rose to become the supreme commander of allied forces in WWII. This is another common advertising form. Ironically, Stevenson made several "Man from Libertyville" spots in 1956, in his *second* campaign for president (candidates often run bio spots in the primary and then again at the beginning of the general campaign). In 1992, Clinton ran a biographical spot that began with his birth in Hope, Arkansas, and Dole used a biographical spot in 1996.

Songs

Campaign songs also debuted in the initial presidential campaign to use television spots, 1952. Stevenson's "Ike and Bob" spots, discussed above, used a song. An Eisenhower commercial from 1952 had its own song.

That year the Stevenson campaign also featured several songs, including "I Love the Gov" (Stevenson was governor of Illinois) and "A White House Built for Two," sung to the tune of a bicycle built for two and revisiting the argument that Taft would control Eisenhower. One of the most famous songs was Kennedy's jingle in 1960. Nixon produced a "Nixon Now" song spot for 1972. Ford offered "Feeling Good" in 1980, and Reagan gave us "Proud" in 1984. In that same campaign, Mondale used Crosby, Stills, and Nash's song "Teach Your Children" in advertising. In 1996 the Dole campaign created a spot that used a song to accuse Clinton of cheating and lying.

Cartoons

The 1952 campaign also experimented with cartoons. Stevenson's "Ike and Bob" ads featured cartoon hearts representing Eisenhower and Taft. The "Ike for President" spot just discussed used an animated campaign parade. This format, however, has not proven to be quite as popular as many of the other innovations introduced in 1952. Jesse Venura's 1998 campaign for Minnesota governor in used what might be considered a related form, GI Joe action figure ("Action Figure").

Words in Spot Scroll on Screen

Another innovation was to display the words spoken in the commercial on the screen. Groups of words or titles (e.g., "The Man from Abilene," "Eisenhower Answers America," or the words to the song in "Ike and Bob") were used from the beginning in 1952 and became quite common in the 1990s. However, later spots displayed every word in the message. The earliest commercials that I located that scrolled every word in the advertisement occurred in 1972. The first spot is from the Republican incumbent, Nixon:

> [all words scroll on screen]: On November 7th, all America has a choice, a choice that, in this election year, is more than a choice between two men or two parties. It is a choice between Senator McGovern's plan to walk out of Vietnam now, or the

president's plan to secure the release of our prisoners first. a choice between the Sena-tor's radical tax and welfare schemes, or the president's policy of sound and sensible economic growth. Between McGovern's plan to strip the defense budget and reduce us to a second-class power, or the president's plan to keep America strong. The choice is yours—if you vote. If you don't get out and vote, you may just get outvoted. No-vember 7th: it's your choice. ("Vote Crawl")

Nixon's Democratic challenger, McGovern, used the same device in that campaign to attack the Republican candidate:

[all words scroll]: Alfred C. Baldwin, a former FBI agent, has stated this. He was hired by James McCord, security chief for both the Republican National Committee and the Nixon Campaign Committee. Mr. Baldwin was assigned to listen illegally to over two hundred private telephone conversations—calls made by Democratic Chairman Lawrence O'Brien and others from tapped telephones in Democratic headquarters at the Watergate. He sent reports on these conversations to William E. Timmons, assistant to President Nixon for congressional relations, at the White House. In 1968 Mr. Nixon said: "The president's chief function is to lead, not to oversee every detail but to put the right people in charge, provide them with basic guidance, and let them do the job." The question is, do we want the system to continue to work this way for the next four years? ("Watergate")

Notice the use of a quotation from Nixon, who debated Kennedy in 1960, to intensify the criticism. In 1968, a spot said that "Agnew for Vice President" would be funny if it weren't so serious. It used laughter, but no talking, to make its point. An interesting variation occurred in 1996. There, for the first time I could find, no one spoke in the spot. The message was displayed entirely in words shown on the screen:

[all titles, no talking; drumbeat soundtrack] Newt Gingrich. Bob Dole. Dole-Gingrich. Against Family Leave. Against a woman's right to choose. Dole. Gingrich. Cutting Vaccines for Children. Against Brady Bill and assault weapons ban. Against higher minimum wage. Cutting college scholarships. Clinton-Gore. Brady Bill signed. Higher minimum wage signed. College tuition tax deductible. Clinton-Gore. $500/child tax credit. Clean air and water. Internet access for schools. Economic growth. 10,000,000 new jobs. When it comes to America's future, which drummer do YOU want to march to? Vote. Clinton-Gore. ("Drums")

Thus, advertisements reinforce—or replace—the oral message with displays of printed words.

EVIDENCE IN TELEVISION SPOTS

Candidates at times offer evidence (graphs, statistics, testimony, or sources) to sup-port their claims. Eisenhower was the first candidate to use television spots featuring evidence from newspapers to support its claims:

Washington, 1952 [Washington Monument]: Home of the top to bottom mess. Today, all over America, patriotic men and women are jarred by the constant disclosures of graft and bribery in the Washington administration [headlines: Bribery Charged in RFC! Expose Swindle on Government Contract, 17 Tax Collectors Fired! Influence Peddling Charged to White House Aides. Mink Coat Scandal Shocks US!]. Shocked by tales of influence peddling, mink coat favors. Honest citizens, taxpayers everywhere, outraged by disclosures of crooked tax collectors, graft and bribery, speak to America's hope, Dwight D. Eisenhower. ("Mess in Washington")

These newspaper headlines are displayed so they function as (relatively) objective evidence. Eight years later, Nixon (and running mate Henry Cabot Lodge) used evidence from newspapers to argue that their experience in foreign affairs was an important qualification for office:

These are the men [picture of Nixon and Lodge; They understand what peace demands] who must lead America through the important years ahead. This is what hundreds of newspapers and magazines all over America are telling their readers [newspaper headlines and stories shown throughout]. *Christian Science Monitor*: Nixon and Lodge are best prepared to give America positive, progressive, and skilled leadership. *Philadelphia Inquirer*: They have been tested and proved worthy in the fires of national and international affairs. *Life* magazine: With Nixon and Lodge in charge of U.S. world policy, we shall feel safer and more hopeful in the enlarging struggle. We urge their election. ("Newspapers")

The Communist threat was perceived by many to be real and serious, and the Republican ticket provide evidence of their special competence in this area.

In recent years, the practice of presenting an indication of the source of supporting evidence in political spots has emerged. In 1964, the Johnson campaign used the announcer to present the date and magazine of quotations used to attack Goldwater:

In a *Saturday Evening Post* article dated August 31, 1963, Barry Goldwater said:

"Sometimes I think this country would be better off if we could just saw off the eastern seaboard and let it float out to sea" [saw cuts through wooden map; eastern seaboard floats off]. Can a man who makes statements like this be expected to serve all the people justly and fairly? ("Eastern Seaboard")

The earliest instance I found of an advertisement providing a "footnote" citation displayed on the screen occurred in a 1980 Reagan spot:

In 1966, answering the call of his party, Ronald Reagan was elected governor of California—next to president, the biggest job in the nation. What the new governor inherited was a state of crisis. California was faced with a $194 million deficit, and was spending a million dollars a day more than it was taking in. The state was on the brink of bankruptcy. Governor Reagan became the greatest tax reformer in the state's history. When Governor Reagan left office, the $194 million deficit had been transformed into a $550 million surplus. The *San Francisco Chronicle* said Governor Reagan has saved the state from bankruptcy [*San Francisco Chronicle*]. ("Record")

More recently, the "source citation" in a spot includes the date as well as the title of the publication.

ANNOUNCER: You work your whole life and hope for a secure retirement. That's why it's so wrong that Dole and Gingrich tried to slash Medicare $270 billion [Congressional Record Vote #584 11/17/95 #812 11/17/95]. Dole even voted to make it easier for corporations to raid our pension funds [Congressional Record Vote # 584 11/17/95]. Dole's risky tax scheme would balloon the deficit [*Business Week* 8/12/96], threaten Medicare cuts—again [*Business Week* 8/19/96]. Can we count on Bob Dole?

BOB DOLE [10/25/95]: "I was there, fighting the fight, voting against Medicare, one of twelve, because we knew it wouldn't work."

ANNOUNCER: Bob Dole. Wrong in the past. Wrong for our future. ("Safe")

This practice skyrocketed in presidential ads in 1992 after ad watches began checking spots for accuracy. In three campaigns—1980, 1984, and 1988—a total of four ads listed eight sources. In 1992, eighteen spots listed eighty-four sources, and in 1996, twenty-four advertisements cited one hundred and one sources (and virtually all of these, 96 percent, appeared in Democratic spots). Ad watches have not eliminated the use of false statements in advertising, but (especially for the Democratic Party) they seem to have prompted a dramatic increase in the provision of source information in contemporary television spots.

Henson and Benoit (2010) quantified the use of evidence (statements for which sources are provided) in political TV spots, analyzing presidential TV spots from 1952–2008 and nonpresidential ads (governor, U.S. Senate, U.S. House) from 2002. Sources are more likely to be used to support attacks than acclaims. In presidential ads evidence more often supported policy than character; in U.S. Senate ads evidence was more likely to address character than policy, and there was no difference in topic for evidence in presidential primary, gubernatorial, or U.S. House ads.

In 1952, the Eisenhower campaign made the first use of a graph as evidence in a presidential spot:

Today across the nation, Americans everywhere are burdened with a multitude of problems. What to do about skyrocketing prices. What to do about backbreaking taxes. What to do about the staggering national debt [chart with arrow moving up and to the right, 200 billion national debt]. ("Mess in Washington")

This graphically (no pun intended) illustrates the use of this form of visual support for a spot's claim.

Four years later, the Stevenson campaign used a graph. Stevenson's running mate, Estes Kefauver, uses a graph to illustrate corporate greed:

KEFAUVER: This is Estes Kefauver. . . . Under the Republicans, General Motor's prof-
its are up 113 percent; auto workers' income up only 14 percent [chart with two arrows].
Let's think it through. Let's get an administration that means prosperity for everybody.
("How's That Again General? 2")

So, the 1950s introduced the practice of using charts and graphs to visually present
evidence in political advertisements. Reagan offered a dramatic graph to demonstrate
how much inflation had increased under Jimmy Carter ("Everything Up"), another
example of this practice.

SOURCES FOR PRESIDENTIAL TELEVISION SPOTS

A number of different kinds of sources are utilized in presidential television spots.
First, many spots feature the candidates themselves talking. Eisenhower spoke in
his 1952 ads (e.g., "Eisenhower Answers America"), but Stevenson did not appear
in his advertising until his second presidential campaign in 1956. "Ike and Bob" by
Stevenson and "The Man from Abilene" by Eisenhower, both from 1952, illustrate
the use of anonymous announcers. Besides the candidates and anonymous announcers, presidential spots have also featured ordinary people, spouses, endorsements,
and reluctant testimony. I will discuss each of these additional sources in turn here.

Ordinary Citizens

In 1952, Eisenhower used ordinary citizens as the source of attacks (this was illustrated with several excerpts at the beginning of this chapter). However, he was also
the first candidate to use statements from ordinary citizens to acclaim during his second campaign. This excerpt from one of his spots in 1956 illustrates this approach:

WOMAN: My main reason for voting for Eisenhower is because I believe in his sincerity. I don't feel that he is furthering his own interests, but he is furthering the interests
of the country and the people. . . .

WOMAN: Inflation. We're not going to have that in the next four years if we vote
right, with Ike.

WOMAN: I'm voting for Ike because I feel that he is a God-fearing man. And I think
that's essential in any leader, and especially the leader of our country.

WOMAN: I think that Eisenhower has shown us how he feels about the average working man. He's given us the minimum wage law. The changes he's made in Social Security.
And I think in another four years he'll do even more than that for us.

WOMAN: I'm going to vote for President Eisenhower because he represents the things
in which I believe. I like his philosophy of the dignity of man. And I also believe that
he is a sincere, honest and high caliber person. ("Women Voters")

Another spot from 1956 featured students praising Eisenhower. Other spots using excerpts from multiple citizens to attack and acclaim have been employed in many campaigns. As indicated above, Mondale used an ordinary citizen to defend against an attack from Reagan in 1984.

Spouses

Although spouses often accompany candidates on the campaign trail, they rarely appear in television spots. In 1960, Jacqueline Kennedy appeared in three spots: one in which she speaks Spanish (the earliest spot I found in Spanish), one in which she asks Dr. Benjamin Spock questions about issues in the campaign, and one in which she is interviewed by Myrna Loy. In 1976, Jimmy Carter's wife was used in his campaign advertising:

ROSALYN CARTER: I have been campaigning almost continuously since April of last year. One of the things that I have learned is that people everywhere are the same. They may live in different parts of the country. They may make their living a different way. But they share the same things. They don't want anything selfish from government, but they do want government that's fair. Jimmy is honest and unselfish and truly concerned about the country. I think he'll be a great president. ("Rosalyn")

Carter also used his mother in one of his advertisements. As mentioned above Nancy Reagan defended her husband in a 1980 spot. In 1988, Barbara Bush acclaimed her husband in a television advertisement. In 1996, Elizabeth Dole spoke in two of her husband's spots (and excerpts were also used in a biographical spot).

Endorsements

Candidates make use of several sources of endorsements. Stevenson produced a spot in 1956 that featured a discussion of foreign policy with Senator John Kennedy, but Kennedy didn't really endorse Stevenson in his remarks. The earliest example of endorsements in political spots occurred in 1960. In this commercial, Nixon's former running mate, President Eisenhower, spoke on the Republican candidate's behalf:

There are four key qualities by which I believe America would like to measure the candidates in this election. They are character, ability, responsibility, experience. From eight years of intimate association, I know Richard Nixon has these qualities, and I know he shows, will use these qualities wisely and decisively and so will Cabot Lodge [applause]. This is why I trust and I believe the American people will elect this splendid team on November 8. ("Eisenhower Endorsement")

In 1980, Reagan used two spots featuring former President Gerald Ford, who was happy to acclaim Reagan in one spot and attack Carter (who defeated Ford in 1976) in the other.

In 1960, John Kennedy received an endorsement from the former first lady Eleanor Roosevelt:

> When you cast your vote for the president of the United States, be sure you have studied the record. I have. I urge you to vote for John F. Kennedy, for I have come to believe that as the president he will have the strength and the moral courage to provide the leadership for human rights we need in this time of crisis. He's a man with a sense of history. ("Eleanor Roosevelt")

Franklin Roosevelt was a very popular Democratic president, and this spot seeks to get some mileage from his first lady. Kennedy also had spots from Franklin D. Roosevelt junior. In 1980, Reagan was endorsed by Mrs. Betty Ford.

In 1968, Richard Nixon offered a host of endorsements from other politicians who were still active in government. This spot featured five such endorsers:

> ANNOUNCER: Five distinguished Americans talk about Richard Nixon.

> [SENATOR BARRY GOLDWATER]: There has never been a man in American history so thoroughly trained for the Presidency as Richard Nixon.

> [GOVERNOR RONALD REAGAN of California]: The Republican Party united behind Richard Nixon offers a chance, a return to individual freedom. a return to efforts on the part of communities and of the private sector and private groups; not just always under government domination.

> [SENATOR JOHN TOWER of Texas]: I think you have to start by putting your own house in order at home and I think Dick Nixon would do this by restoring respect for law and order in this country.

> [SENATOR HOWARD BAKER of Tennessee]: We're tired of the tired old theories of the thirties and we want answers that are relevant to the sixties and the seventies and Dick Nixon has them to offer.

> [SENATOR EVERETT DIRKSEN of Illinois]: Putting it all together, it runs in my mind that Dick Nixon would not be a good president; he would be a great president of the United States. ("Distinguished")

In this campaign Nixon used endorsements Senators (George Murphy, Hiram Fong, Jacob Javits, Charles Percy, Mark Hatfield, Hugh Scott, and Edward Brock), another governor (George Romney) and a Representative (George Bush). In 1980, Reagan relied on governors Thompson, Thornburg, Rhodes, Millikin, Dreyfus, and Alexander, Senator Baker, Congressman Jack Kemp, and former Senator McCarthy. President Ford made an ad acclaiming Reagan and one attacking Carter in 1980.

Another potential source of endorsements is the world of entertainment. In 1960, John Kennedy presented what may well be the first endorsement by an actor, Harry Belefonte, who was also a member of a minority group:

BELEFONTE: Hi. My name is Harry Belefonte. I'm an artist, and I'm not a politician. But like most Americans, I have a great interest in the political and the economic destiny of my country. I'm seated here with Senator Jack Kennedy. As a Negro, and as an American I have many questions. And I'm sure everyone does. About civil rights, about foreign policy, about the economy of the country, and about things that will happen.

KENNEDY: I want to make it very clear, Harry, that on this question of equality of opportunity for all Americans, whether it's in the field of civil rights, better minimum wages, better housing, better working conditions, jobs, I stand for these things. The Democratic party under Franklin Roosevelt stood for them.

BELEFONTE: I'm voting for this Senator. How about you? ("Belefonte")

Notice that Kennedy explicitly brings up the topic of equal opportunity and civil rights in his conversation with Belefonte. Goldwater used actor Raymond Massey in 1964. Nixon featured Pat Boone in 1968. Ford used Pearl Bailey in 1976, and Carter used Mary Tyler Moore in 1980.

In 1976 Ford reported many newspaper endorsements. Interestingly enough, the ones in this list are all from his opponent's home state, ones who "know Jimmy Carter best":

[all words scroll]: Those who know Jimmy Carter best are from Georgia. That's why we thought you ought to know: The Savannah, Georgia, *News* endorses Gerald Ford for president. The August, Georgia, *Herald* endorses President Ford. The Atlanta, Georgia, *Daily World* endorses President Ford. The Marietta, Georgia, *Journal* endorses President Ford. The Rome, Georgia, *News Tribune* endorses President Ford. The Vidalia, Georgia, *Advance* endorses President Ford. The Albany, Georgia, *Herald* endorses President Ford. The LaGrange, Georgia, *News* endorses President Ford. The August, Georgia, *Chronicle* endorses President Ford. The Brunswick, Georgia, *News* endorses President Ford. The Savannah, Georgia, *Press* endorses President Ford. The Statesboro, Georgia, *Herald* endorses President Ford. ("Georgia News—60")

Twelve repetitions are used to hammer away at this message, and each endorsement simultaneously acclaims Ford while implicitly attacking Carter. Given the fact that newspapers are often divided politically (some usually endorsing Republicans, others Democrats) it is not surprising that several newspapers in Carter's home state endorsed his opponent. Presumably many newspapers in Michigan endorsed Carter— but if so, voters did not hear about that.

Reluctant Testimony

Another fertile ground for sources in political spots is the concept of reluctant testimony, in which the source speaks against his or her own self-interests (in fact, Ford's use of newspapers from Georgia is related to this argument form). The earliest example I found of this kind of source occurred in 1960, when the Democrats used footage from an Eisenhower press conference to embarrass Nixon:

ANNOUNCER: Every Republican politician wants you to believe that he has actually been making decisions in the White House—but listen to the man who knows best, the president of the United States. A reporter recently asked President Eisenhower this question about Mr. Nixon's experience.

REPORTER: I just wondered if you could give us an example of a major idea of his that you had adopted in that role, as the, as the decider and final—

EISENHOWER [after pause]: If you give me a week, I might think of one. I don't remember. [Laughter] ("Ike's Press Conference")

Given the fact that Nixon was acclaiming his experience in the Eisenhower administration, this evidence from his president was very damning (this provoked the Nixon campaign to use Eisenhower to defend against these charges, as mentioned earlier).

Presidential candidates often must fight other members of their own party for their party's nomination. In the general election, some of these statements, from members of one's own party, can come back to haunt the nominee. In 1964, Johnson initiated this practice in the campaign against Goldwater:

Back in July in San Francisco, the Republicans held a convention. Remember him? He was there, Governor Rockefeller. Before the convention he said Barry Goldwater's positions can, and I quote, "spell disaster for the party and for the country." Or him? Governor Scranton. The day before the convention, he called Goldwaterism a quote "crazy quilt collection of absurd and dangerous positions." Or this man, Governor Romney. In June he said Goldwater's nomination would lead to the quote "suicidal destruction of the Republican Party." So, even if you are a Republican with serious doubts about Barry Goldwater, you're in good company. ("Republican Litter")

Thus, quotations from Rockefeller, Scranton, and Romney were all used against their fellow Republican, Barry Goldwater. In 1976, Carter used Reagan to attack Ford and in 1980, Reagan used Kennedy to attack Carter in an interesting turn-about.

Of course, the most damning evidence comes out of one's own mouth. The earliest example of this came in 1964 in Johnson's "Eastern Seaboard" ad, discussed above. In 1976, Jimmy Carter attacked Gerald Ford's economic record: "7.9 percent unemployment is what you arrive at when incompetent leaders follow outdated, unjust, wasteful, economic policies" ("Not Acceptable"). Four years later, an advertisement for Ronald Reagan threw these words back in Carter's face: "7.8 percent unemployment is what you arrive at when incompetent leaders follow outdated, insensitive, unjust, wasteful economic policies. Jimmy Carter did do something about unemployment—two million more people became unemployed this year alone" ("Are You Satisfied?"). As mentioned below, George Bush's "Read my lips: No new taxes" pledge was featured prominently in opponents' commercials. In 1996 Dole used Clinton's MTV interview, in which he discussed his experimentation with marijuana, against Clinton ("School"). Thus, political campaign commercials use reluctant testimony to attack their opponents.

RECURRING ARGUMENTS

In this section I will illustrate four recurrent argument forms in television spots. Presidential TV spots often argue from inconsistency, broken promises, running mates, and turnout appeals.

Inconsistency

Voters want candidates to be consistent. First, inconsistency can be evidence of confusion or outright deceit, neither desirable in a president. Second, candidates frequently make campaign proposes, but they must be consistent if we are to count on them fulfilling their promises (of course, circumstances change, so there can be good reasons for changes in policy, but still consistency is valued by voters). In 1964, Johnson attacked Goldwater for being inconsistent:

> When somebody tells you he's for Barry Goldwater, you ask him which Barry Goldwater he's for [Goldwater faces on both sides of screen; the image pans from side to side throughout the spot]. Is he for the one who said, "We must make the fullest possible use of the UN," or is he for the one who said "The U.S. no longer has a place in the UN"? Is he for the Barry who said, "I've never advocated the use of nuclear weapons anywhere in the world," or is he for the one who said "I'd drop a low yield atomic bomb on the Chinese supply lines in North Vietnam"? Is he for the Barry who said, "I seek the support of no extremist," or is he for the one who said "Extremism in the defense of liberty is no vice"? And how is a Republican supposed to indicate on his ballot which Barry he's voting for? There's only one Lyndon Johnson. ("Which Barry Goldwater?")

The argument is that we cannot know what to expect from Goldwater. It may also suggest that he is unprincipled. The argument that a candidate lacks principles, responding to the whims of public opinion, is explicit in Humphrey's attack on Nixon in 1968:

> Ever noticed what happens to Nixon when the political winds blow? [weathervane with Nixon's head, spinning in wind] Last year he said, I oppose a federal open housing law. This year he said, I support the 1968 Civil Rights Bill with open housing. Again this year he said, I just supported it to get it out of sight. Which way will he blow next? ("Weathervane")

Nixon appropriated this argument in his 1972 re-election campaign, attacking McGovern for "flip-flopping" on the issues:

> In 1967, [photo of McGovern] Senator George McGovern said he was not an advocate of unilateral withdrawal of our troops from Vietnam. Now of course he is [photo flips from facing left to right]. Last year the Senator suggested regulating marijuana along the same lines as alcohol, which means legalizing it. Now he's against legalizing it and says he always has been [photo flips back]. Last January Senator McGovern suggested a welfare plan that would give a thousand dollar bill to every man, woman, and child

in the country. [photo flips] Now he says maybe the thousand dollar figure isn't right [photo flips back]. Last year he proposed to tax inheritances over $500,000 at 100 percent [photo flips]. This year he suggests 77 percent [photo flips]. In Florida he was pro-busing [photo flips]. In Oregon he said he would support the anti-busing bill now in Congress [photo flips]. Last year, this year. The question is, what about next year [photo flips around and around rapidly]? ("McGovern Turnaround")

The flipping photos visually enact the argument advanced in the spot. In 1984, a commercial for Ronald Reagan introduced a new twist to this argument as he attacked Walter Mondale:

> How do two presidential candidates stand on the issues [How do two presidential candidates stand on the issues]? Candidate Mondale has promised to reduce government spending [smiling Mondale]. But Senator Mondale voted to increase government spending twelve years in a row [frowning Mondale]. Candidate Mondale has promised a strong national defense [smiling Mondale], but Senator Mondale voted to weaken defenses eighteen times [frowning Mondale]. Of course there's one area where they agree: They both stand for increase taxes [smiling Mondale alternates with frowning Mondale]. That's why we're voting for Reagan. ("Side by Side")

This image may have encouraged viewers to form the impression that Mondale was "two-faced." As a final example to illustrate a very durable argument, consider this advertisement from Bush attacking Clinton in 1992:

> [split screen, two candidates speaking with grey dots over faces].
>
> ANNOUNCER: The presidential candidate on the left stood for military action in the Persian Gulf, while the candidate on the right agreed with those who opposed it. He says [candidate who was on left] he wouldn't rule out term limits. While he says [candidate who was on right] he's personally opposed to term limits. This candidate [left] was called up for military service, while this one [right] claims he wasn't. One of these [split screen again] candidates is Bill Clinton [left dot removed to reveal Clinton]. Unfortunately, so is the other [other dot removed].
>
> CLINTON: There is a simple explanation for why this happened. ("Grey Dots")

Thus, candidates use their spots to accuse their opponents of inconsistency. This series of ads based on the argument of inconsistency also shows how campaigns have creatively developed innovative ways to recycle past arguments.

Broken Campaign Promises

An important variant on the theme of inconsistency is that of the broken campaign promise. This argument first emerged in this 1956 Stevenson spot:

> ANNOUNCER: How's that again, General? During the 1952 campaign, General Eisenhower promised a great crusade:

EISENHOWER: Too many politicians have sold their ideals of honesty down the Potomac. We must bring back the integrity and thrift to Washington. . . .

KEFAUVER: This is Estes Kefauver. Let's see what happened to that promise. Wesley Roberts, a Republican National Chairman, sold Kansas a building it already owned for eleven thousand dollars. He got a silver tree from Mr. Eisenhower. Hal Talbott pressured defense plants to employ a firm which paid him a hundred and thirty thousand dollars while he was Air Force Secretary. He received the General's warm wishes and an official welcome. And there are many others, like Strobel, the Public Buildings Administrator; Mansure, the General Services Administrator. ("How's That Again General? 1")

This commercial used Eisenhower's own words ("We must bring back the integrity and thrift to Washington") to indict his first term record.

Reagan combined the visual from the inconsistency spots discussed above with the charge of broken promises:

Can we afford four more years of broken promises [smiling Jimmy Carter]? In 1976 Jimmy Carter promised to hold inflation to 4 percent. Today it is 14 percent [frowning Carter]. He promised to create more jobs [smiling Carter], but now there are 8 million Americans out of work [frowning Carter]. He promised to balance the budget [smiling Carter]; what he gave us was a $61 billion deficit [frowning Carter]. Can we afford four more years? The time is now for strong leadership—Reagan for president. ("Flip-Flop Economy")

Pat Buchanan, in the 1992 Republican primary, and Bill Clinton, in the 1992 general campaign, used video clips of Bush making his famous "Read my lips: No new taxes!" pledge against him. This Reagan commercial from 1984 is unusual in that he acclaims the campaign promises that he successfully fulfilled:

Campaigning in 1980, we pledged to reduce our tax burden, stop inflation, and cut interest rates. We had to reduce spending, create jobs, and rebuild our national defense. We've started, but we haven't finished. We still have to help those who haven't shared fully in the recovery and make progress toward a balanced budget. Big jobs, but I know the American people, and together we'll get them done. ("Promises and Performance")

Although the evidence for his successes are a little vague, the argument of a fulfilled promise is clear.

Running Mate

Another source of arguments in presidential television spots is the candidate's running mate. The vice presidential candidate was first used in a television spot in 1956, when Estes Kefauver attacked Eisenhower for failing to fulfill his campaign promise ("How's That Again, General?"). Lodge appeared in some of the Nixon spots from 1960, Bush appeared in a Reagan spot in 1980, and Ferraro was featured in Mondale's advertising (1984). However, the vice presidential candidate has also been the target of attack from the opposition. In 1968, this advertisement for Humphrey contrasted his running mate (Edmund Muskie) with Nixon's ticket mate (Spiro Agnew): "[heart monitor screen]: Never before in our lives have we been so confronted with this reality [Edmund Muskie, Spiro Agnew. Who is your choice to be a heartbeat away from the presidency?" ("Heartbeats"). Stevenson made spots attacking Nixon in 1956, but according to Jamieson (1996) they did not air. Dan Quayle was subjected to attacks as well (Dukakis, 1988 "The Packaging of Dan Quayle"). Still, throughout the history of advertising, vice presidential candidates tend to have a relatively low profile.

Turnout Appeal

Another recurring argument form is the turn-out appeal. The earliest example I found of a spot urging citizens to actually go to the polls occurred in 1964: "[storm clouds, thunder, lightning, rain pouring onto sidewalk] If it should rain on November 3, please get wet. Go to the polls and vote for President Johnson. The stakes are too high for you to stay home" ("Storm").

After all, a candidate does not win simply because of a lead in the public opinion polls: Those favoring a candidate must go to the polls and cast their votes for the preferred candidate to win.

Willingness to Debate

A final recurrent argument that I wish to illustrate concerns presidential debate. The first debate between presidential candidates, of course, featured Richard Nixon and John Kennedy. Kennedy used footage from the debates in some of his spots in 1960 (I found no such spots from Nixon, however). Other candidates (especially those trailing in the polls) sometimes attempted to use political spots to prod their opponents to debate. In 1964, Democrats in Congress scuttled an attempt to suspend the FCC's "Equal Time" rule, assuring that there would be no debate in 1964. Goldwater tried to simulate a debate in this spot:

> On October 18, 1960, speaking in Shimokin, Pennsylvania, when he was running for vice president, Lyndon Johnson said: "I don't want some bearded dictator ninety miles off thumbing his nose at us." Now to debate Mr. Johnson on this statement, here is Barry Goldwater, who calls him to account for this Administration's colossal bungling on Cuba and Castro [video of Johnson, then Castro].

> GOLDWATER: The same bearded dictator is still ninety miles off, thumbing his nose at us. And the Bay of Pigs has left us not a monument to freedom, but a dark blot on our national pride. The United States must provide the leadership which will deal effectively with the problems of Cuba, and which will stop the spread of communism in the western hemisphere. ("Debate on Castro")

Humphrey explicitly called for debates with Wallace and Nixon in 1968: "I've been after Mr. Nixon and Mr. Wallace for debates or discussions, call it what you will" ("Discussion with Edward Kennedy.") In 1972, McGovern used reluctant testimony to chastise Nixon for refusing to debate:

> [all words scroll]: Presidential television debates were not designed to serve a candidate for office; they were designed to serve the public. Television debates prevent a candidate from waging a campaign based on special-interest appeals. Television debates give voters the opportunity to see the real man, not the synthetic product of public relations experts. And they contribute to four major objectives which are in the public interest: a bigger vote, better informed voters, lower campaign costs, and, in the end, a better president. The foregoing is a statement by Richard M. Nixon before he became president of the United States. Since the statement is as true today as when he wrote it, why does Mr. Nixon refuse to debate Senator McGovern? ("Debate")

Ross Perot was extremely upset when the Commission on Presidential Debates, which had invited him to debate with Bush and Clinton 1992, excluded him from the 1996 debates. He ran several spots complaining bitterly about this in his second campaign. In more recent campaigns it is assumed that candidates will engage in televised general election debates, so this argument form has disappeared.

CONCLUSION

This chapter provides insight into the historical development of presidential television spots. I identify several recurrent themes in these message forms, reveal who first developed each theme, and illustrate these themes with examples. I have also pointed to some of the many instances in which these themes were used in later campaigns. It is interesting to note that Eisenhower introduced more of the recurrent forms in presidential television spots than any other candidate (almost 40 percent; Stevenson created 25 percent of the innovations). Furthermore, 1952 alone saw the introduction by Eisenhower or Stevenson (or both, in several cases) of over 35 percent of the recurrent themes, and about 45 percent were invented by Eisenhower and Stevenson in the 1950s. This discussion contributes to our understanding of this important and pervasive form of political messages, presidential television spots. It also underlines the importance of returning to the earliest campaigns to study the history of this important political message form.

13
Conclusion

This chapter is designed to highlight some of the most important implications of this study. First, this project has demonstrated the utility of the functional approach to televised political campaign discourse. This perspective has allowed us to develop an understanding of television spots from the inception of this message form through the most recent presidential contest in 2012. Candidates produce advertising that is replete with acclaims and attacks, occasionally, defenses. Acclaims can help a candidate persuade voters that he (as mentioned earlier, all presidential candidates to this point have been men) is a desirable choice. Attacks can help reduce the apparent desirability of a candidate's opponent (or opponents, in the primary or in a multi-party election). Defenses can be used in an attempt to restore lost desirability.

Another way to look at this is to consider these three functions as aids to voters' performance of cost-benefit analysis. Although I do not consider voters to be logical or mathematical calculating machines (see Popkin, 1994), I do believe that voters use the information they possess, much of it from the candidates' discourse, to perform a very rough form of cost-benefit analysis (voters do not systematically assign numeric values to pros and cons or perform mathematical calculations such as adding or averaging). The candidates provide an indication of *their own benefits* from their acclaims of their policy and character. Candidates reveal *their opponents' costs* with attacks on opponents' policies and character. If attacked, candidates can attempt to reduce *their apparent costs* through defenses. Thus, these three functions can be seen as aids which help the voters decide between or among the competing candidates.

Furthermore, these functions occur on policy and character topics, and the functional theory of political campaign discourse analyzes each of these broad topics into useful categories (policy: past deeds, future plans, general goals; character: personal qualities, leadership ability, ideals). Although further breakdowns are possible (into topics of policy [e.g., foreign trade, national defense, taxation, the federal deficit, crime, education, transportation]) or into kinds of personal qualities (e.g., honesty, courage, compassion), this theory provides us with useful concepts for describing and understanding certain key elements of political campaign messages.

Past research on political spots has served us well. However, in my opinion, it is time to abandon the practice of classifying entire spots with a method that categorizes by themes. The traditional approach worked better when spots tended to focus on a single theme. However, candidates are likely to string together as many as six or more diverse topics in a single ad, combining both acclaims and attacks and/or both policy and character appeals. Consider this sample spot from Bush in 1992, which uses statements from ordinary citizens:

> I saw the debate last night, and I've just got one conclusion, it's all George Bush.
>
> I have, I still have a lot of confidence in my president.
>
> I think we need Bush to keep us from a big spending Congress.
>
> I don't trust Clinton.
>
> The man says one thing and does another.
>
> First he denies it and then he says well maybe it happened: you can't trust him.
>
> If Clinton gets in what we're gonna see are more taxes.
>
> One thing that's got me definitely for Bush is I remember what happened the last time we did things the way Bill Clinton wants to do 'em. ("Debate")

This commercial freely mixes acclaims of Bush (e.g., "I still have a lot of confidence in my president," "we need Bush to keep us from a big spending Congress") with attacks on Clinton (e.g., "I don't trust Clinton," "The man says one thing and does another," "If Clinton gets in we're gonna see more taxes"). This advertisement also discusses character (trust) as well as policy (taxes). Trying to categorize this spot as either acclaiming (positive) or attacking (negative), or as either policy (issue) or character (image), clearly ignores part of what voters see and hear. Even the expedient of classifying spots as "comparative" is only accurate if all spots devote an equal number of utterances to each function. The fact that spots are becoming increasingly dense (more themes per unit of time) renders the traditional approach increasingly problematic. My approach, classifying each theme in a spot (and classifying each theme according to both function and topic) is clearly superior, providing a more accurate understanding of the content of these messages.

Several trends emerged in this study. First, television spots are increasingly dense: The typical presidential advertisement crams more ideas into the same amount of time. Figure 11.1 vividly documents this trend. For example, Clinton ran this spot in 1996 ("Ignores"):

> The facts Bob Dole ignores in his negative attacks: The deficit cut 60 percent. Ten million new jobs. Family income up $1,600 [since 1993]. Health insurance you don't lose

when changing jobs. President Clinton: moving our economy ahead, helping families. Now a plan to cut taxes for college tuition: $500 per child tax credit. Break up violent gangs. Move 1 million from welfare to work. Dole resorts to desperate negative attacks. President Clinton is protecting our values.

This thirty-second spot mentions eleven topics: Dole is engaging in negative campaigning, Clinton cut the deficit, created new jobs, increased family income, made health insurance portable; Clinton is helping economy, helping families, proposing a tuition tax credit, fighting gangs, moving people from welfare to work, protecting values. This trend means that candidates address a wider range of topics in a spot; however, it also means that they spend less time on each idea. As revealed in the last chapter, in the 1996 presidential campaign (the most recent for which these data were calculated) Clinton used 8.7 themes per spot and Dole employed 5.9 themes per spot.

I believe this trend is a manifestation of several related trends in contemporary American society. As I pointed out in chapter 1, Hallin's (1992) study found that the network news quotes candidates in far shorter segments (down from an average of forty-three seconds in 1968 to only nine seconds in 1988). The news media, in my opinion, are encouraging development and use of sound bites. Furthermore, it is quite possible that the "MTV" style of videography (which is not limited to MTV), with a series of shots of short duration either encourages, or reflects, a decreased attention span. The increasing diversity of the electorate combined with the skyrocketing costs of television time may also encourage candidates to take this shotgun approach of mentioning several topics without really discussing them. However, whatever the cause, it does not seem reasonable to believe that this trend is good for the electorate or for our democracy. The issues addressed in our presidential campaigns can be very complex, and five to ten seconds (or less) is just not enough to do them justice.

The presidential debates help to offset this tendency to cram more ideas in less time to some extent, but two factors mitigate against that. First, presidential debates frequently limit candidates to one to two minutes for their statements. The hour or hour and a half devoted to a debate is chopped up by format into much smaller units of time. Second, candidates may choose to spend their minute or two discussing many topics, so that their debate answers may sound much like their television spots. The desire to appear consistent—to avoid accusations of flip-flopping—encourages repetition of ideas in ads, debates, and other campaign messages. Most of the same potential pressures (all but cost) that encourage candidates to cover many topics in a television spot exist in a presidential debate as well.

Second, and consistent with this idea, is the fact that television spots have become shorter over time. The turning point was 1976, the first time (since the experimentation of the 1950s) that thirty-second spots outnumbered sixty-second spots. Again, shorter spots mean less time for voters to learn about the candidates and their policies (remember that people obtain four times as much information from spots as from the news (Kern, 1989; Patterson and McClure, 1976).

A third pattern that emerges from this study is the fact that presidential television spots have become more negative over time (except for the highly negative campaign in 1952, acclaims were much more common in 1956). Figure 11.1 clearly reveals that campaign spots in 1956 and 1960 employed over 80 percent acclaims (and fewer than 20 percent attacks), but this gap gradually narrowed until, in the 1990s, attacks were more prevalent than acclaims. Interestingly, people often think of 1988 (and Bush's campaign in particular) as a highly negative campaign. These advertisements may have had a more vicious tone (I have not seen any content analysis of ads with "viciousness" as the dependent variable), and perhaps the 1988 ads were unusually misleading (e.g., Jamieson, 1996) than earlier commercials. However, Eisenhower in 1952 used the largest percentage of attacks of any presidential candidate in the history of televised political advertising (69 percent) until 2012 when Obama's ads had 70 percent attacks. Primary spots have also become more negative over time (see figure 9.1).

Recently, more emphasis has been placed on policy than character in presidential TV spots. As figure 11.2 demonstrates, since 1980 presidential television spots have consistently spent more time on policy than on character (although, as suggested above, they do not go into depth on these issues). They are not simply campaigning on image. Of course, these two topics are tightly intertwined. Surely candidates can attempt to influence voters' perceptions of the candidates by the policy stances attributed to candidates in their spots. As demonstrated earlier, policy attacks (e.g., inconsistent stands on policy issues) can be used to indict the candidates' character. Still, there is more of an emphasis on policy than character in recent campaigns. Although I do not believe that all character remarks are inappropriate (as I discuss below), I do think it is a good thing that candidates are clearly discussing policy in their advertisements (even if they aren't spending much time on each policy theme).

This study reveals that defenses occur in presidential television spots, but not very frequently. Some candidates never defend at all in their spots. Research reveals that defenses are more common in presidential debates than in television spots (Benoit, 2007a). Several reasons account for the infrequency of defenses in advertisements. First, candidates may not want to remind (or inform) voters of attacks against them. They surely would be reluctant to spend their own campaign funds to disseminate attacks from their opponents! Furthermore, candidates may wish to stay "on message," devoting spots to the topics that favor themselves, not the topics that favor opponents. Presidential candidates may also wish to appear active rather than reactive: They may wish to avoid creating the impression that they are on the defensive. However, some attacks are so damaging that candidates feel forced to reply. The fact remains that defenses are relatively uncommon in these spots.

We can also make comparisons among different kinds of campaigns, or of different kinds of candidates, with the data from this study. Primary spots tend to be more positive than general campaign spots. Third-party spots are often more positive than spots from the major party candidates. This may reflect a conscious desire on the part of third-party candidates to appear distinct from "politics as usual" from the major party candidates, which as we've seen, are increasingly negative.

Incumbents use acclaims often than challengers, whereas challengers use attacks more frequently than incumbents. Studies on presidential debates and acceptance addresses (Benoit, 2007a), direct mail advertising (Benoit and Stein, 2005), and Keynote Speeches (Benoit, Blaney, and Pier, 1996) all found the same pattern. Incumbents have a record in office, which serves as an important resource for acclaims by the incumbent and for attacks from the challenger.

In political television advertising, Republicans tended to be more positive than Democrats. However, this trend may not be as important as the previous one. Research on Acceptance Addresses found Republicans tend to attack more than Democrats (Benoit, Wells, Pier, and Blaney, 1999), as does research on direct mail advertising (Benoit and Stein, 2005), but our study of Keynote Speeches revealed that Democrats attacked more than Republicans (Benoit, Blaney, and Pier, 2000). It appears that situation (incumbency) is a more important influence on the functions of television spots than agent (political party).

There are no consistent differences in the functions of television spots of winners and losers. However, their position in the race may influence the nature of their spots. Candidates who led throughout the race tend to use the most acclaims (61 percent) and the fewest attacks (38 percent). Perhaps they are most concerned about alienating voters who profess to dislike mudslinging (Merritt, 1984; Stewart, 1975) and their lead in the polls decreases the importance of hammering their opponents. In contrast, candidates who trail their opponents in the polls throughout the campaign use the most attacks (51 percent) and the fewest acclaims (48 percent). They have the least to lose from a potential backlash against mudslinging, and may feel it is worth the risk created by attacking so much. Finally, candidates in close races acclaim (54 percent) and attack (45 percent) between these extremes.

SUGGESTIONS FOR CANDIDATES

This study helps us to understand what options are available to candidates. First, the functional theory of political campaigns makes it clear that candidates have three potential functions (acclaim, attack, defend) and two general topics (policy, character). It suggests that candidates can be specific (past deeds, future plans) or more general (general goals, ideals). Candidates can also discuss the past (past deeds), encouraging retrospective voting, or the future (future plans, general goals), encouraging prospective voting. Finally, candidates can discuss their leadership ability or their personal qualities in their television spots. These topics are all potential discursive resources for political candidates.

This study has also revealed that candidates have many options for their acclaims and attacks, depending upon their own (and their opponent's) circumstances. Incumbents (Eisenhower in 1956, Johnson in 1964, Nixon in 1972, Ford in 1976, Carter in 1980, Reagan in 1984, Bush in 1992, Clinton in 1996, Bush in 2004, and Obama in 2012) have a record in the office sought. Surely this is one of the best, if not the best, possible source(s) of evidence about their likely performance if re-elected. These candidates acclaimed their record, and their opponents attacked it. Candidates who are "almost" incumbents (vice presidents Nixon in 1960, Humphrey in 1968, Bush in 1988, and Gore in 2000) can attempt to take credit for current successes—but this also means that their opponents can blame them for current failures. Their opponents can also argue, as Kennedy did in 1960, that the vice president wasn't really responsible for successes of their administration. Some candidates have other governmental experience besides being president. Jimmy Carter (1976), Ronald Reagan (1980), Michael Dukakis (1988), Bill Clinton (1992), George Bush (2000), and Mitt Romney (2012) had been governors. They acclaimed their successes while their opponents attacked their failures. Bob Dole was a Senator, although as we shall Dole rarely acclaimed his past deeds. Clinton certainly attacked Dole's past deeds in the 1996 race. Other Senators who ran for president include John McCain (2008) and Barack Obama (2008). Candidates who have no governmental experience (e.g., Ross Perot, Steve Forbes, Pat Buchanan, Herman Cain) acclaim their business experience (as did George Bush in 1988 and Lamar Alexander in 1996, who both had governmental experience as well). Those who are "outsiders" (such as Ross Perot, Steve Forbes, and Pat Buchanan) can attempt to parlay this status into an advantage by attacking the Washington establishment and distancing themselves from it. If you have worked in government, stress your experience; if you have not worked in government, stress your independence and new ideas.

Candidates also have a variety of options available for source of message. The obvious first decision is whether the candidate or others should speak in spots. When others do speak there are other choices. Should an anonymous narrator or announcer be used? Should the spot use an ordinary citizen or voter to speak? Some spots use celebrity endorsers or other political figures. Bob Dole used General Colin Powell in 1996. Occasionally, the candidates' wives (e.g., Nancy Reagan in 1980) appear in a commercial. At times one candidate uses an opponent's words (or video) as "reluctant testimony" to argue for inconsistency or broken promises. Pat Buchanan attacked George Bush in 1992 for having broken his "Read my lips: No new taxes" pledge. Kennedy's "Ike's Press Conference" spot in 1960 must have embarrassed (and angered) Nixon. Sometimes one campaign (e.g., Reagan in 1980) will use clips or statements from a contested primary to get another form of reluctant testimony (e.g., Edward Kennedy attacking fellow Democrat Jimmy Carter).

Although it does not emerge in the data generated for this study, my viewing of political spots revealed that sources like charts, graphs, and video footage of criminals or polluted harbors are being used increasingly in political spots. Perot and other candidates used video "morphing" technology to have one voter transform into another in several of his commercials. Thus, as technology is increasing, candidates have more options for producing their television spots.

FUTURE RESEARCH ON POLITICAL ADVERTISING

Clearly, more work remains to be done on understanding political spots. As mentioned earlier, there has been sporadic study of primary spots (see chapter 7), of non-presidential advertisements (see chapter 10), and spots in other countries (see chapter 10). Scant research focuses on radio spots (Shapiro and Rieger, 1992). Some work has been conducted on political newspaper advertisements (Bowers, 1972; Humke, Schmitt, and Grupp, 1975). Relatively little work has been conducted on direct mail advertisements (see Benoit and Stein, 2005). In 1996, both presidential campaigns had World Wide Web pages and candidate-sponsored web sites have been standard in presidential races and more common in campaigns for other offices. It is clear that the Internet (including Facebook and twitter) has become an increasingly important part of the contemporary political campaigns (see Stromer-Galley and Sheinheit, 2012). More work could clearly be done in each of these areas.

Barbatsis (1996) examines images, or "pictorial enactment," in negative spots. Boynton and Nelson (1997) have begun to study the audio portion of political spots (voices, music, and sound effects). Hughes (1994) focused on formal logic and fallacies to examine television spots. Kaid (1996; cf. Jamieson, 1996) has analyzed spots for technological distortion that raise ethical issues. I would like to acknowledge that one limitation of my analysis is that it focused much more on verbal than nonverbal elements. I believe much remains to be done on the importance of images in political advertising (which may be informed by work like Hatcher, 1988; Lester, 1995; and Messaris, 1997). The field of political advertising is extremely rich, and very important to the modern day functioning of our democracy.

My study also revealed a trend away from candidates speaking in their ads—especially in attacks. Research has shown that sponsors can affect viewer perceptions (Garramone, 1985; Garramone and Smith, 1984; Kaid and Boydston, 1987). Clearly, this area is ripe for further inquiry.

This work focuses on the content of political advertising. It leaves unexplored the important correlate question: How do voters process political TV spot messages? Others have done important work on this question. Popkin (1994), for example, offers an interesting analysis of information short-cuts employed by voters. Lodge and Taber (2013) adopt an information processing approach. Brader (2006; see also Marcus, Neuman, and MacKuen, 2000) investigates emotional appeals in political advertising. More work remains on this key question.

Bibliography

Aden, R. C. (1989). Televised political advertising: A review of literature on spots. *Political Communication Review, 14*, 1–18.

Airne, D., and Benoit, W. L. (2005). Political television advertising in campaign 2000. *Communication Quarterly, 53*, 473–493.

Allen, M., and Burrell, N. (2002). The negativity effect in political advertising: A meta-analysis. In J. P. Dillard and M. Pfau (Eds.), *The persuasion handbook: Developments in theory and practice* (pp. 83–96). Thousand Oaks, CA: Sage.

Alvarez, R. M. (1998). *Information and elections: Revised to include the 1996 presidential election.* Ann Arbor, MI: University of Michigan Press.

Anderson, N. (2004, November 2). The race for the White House: Silence of the wolves, and their ilk, in swing states; A record-setting barrage of political ads that hit a feverish pitch in the final week is all over. *Los Angeles Times*, p. A19.

Ansolabehere, S., and Iyengar, S. (1994). Riding the wave and claiming ownership over issues: The joint effects of advertising and news coverage in campaigns. *Public Opinion Quarterly, 58*, 335–357.

Ansolabehere, S., and Iyengar, S. (1995). *Going negative: How political advertisements shrink and polarize the electorate.* New York: Free Press.

Ansolabehere, S., Iyengar, S., Simon, A., and Valentino, N. (1994). Does attack advertising demobilize the electorate? *American Political Science Review, 88*, 829–838.

Atkeson, L. R., and Partin, R. W. (2001). Candidate advertisements, media coverage, and citizen attitudes: The agendas and roles of senators and governors in a federal system. *Political Research Quarterly, 54*, 795–813.

Atkin, C. K. (1977). Effects of campaign advertising and newscasts on children. *Journalism Quarterly, 54*, 503–508.

Atkin, C., and Heald, G. (1976). Effects of political advertising. *Public Opinion Quarterly, 40*, 216–228.

Bachman, K. (2012, September 5). Analyst: Political advertising to boost TV coffers by 23% New forecast based on spending surge in August. *AdWeek*. Accessed 7/31/13: www.adweek .com/news/advertising-branding/analyst-political-advertising-boost-tv-coffers-23-143342

Barbatsis, G. S. (1996). "Look, and I will show you something you will want to see": Pictorial engagement in negative political campaign commercials. *Argumentation and Advocacy, 33*, 69–80.

Bartels, L. M. (1988). *Presidential primaries and the dynamics of public choice.* Princeton: Princeton University Press.

Basil, M., Schooler, C., and Reeves, B. (1991). Positive and negative political advertising: Effectiveness of ads and perceptions of candidates. In F. Biocca (Ed.), *Television and political advertising* (vol. 1, pp. 245–262). Hillsdale, NJ: Erlbaum.

Becker, L. B., and Doolittle, J. C. (1975). How repetition affects evaluations of and information seeking about candidates. *Journalism Quarterly, 52*, 611–617.

Benoit, P. J. (1997). *Telling the success story: Acclaiming and disclaiming discourse.* Albany: State University of New York Press.

Benoit, W. L. (1999). *Seeing spots: A functional analysis of Presidential television advertisements, 1952–1996.* Westport, CT: Praeger.

Benoit, W. L. (2000). A functional analysis of political advertising across media, 1998. *Communication Studies, 51*, 274–295.

Benoit, W. L. (2003). Topic of presidential campaign discourse and election outcome. *Western Journal of Communication, 67*, 97–112.

Benoit, W. L. (2004). Election outcome and topic of political campaign attack. *Southern Communication Journal, 69*, 348–355.

Benoit, W. L. (2007a). *Communication in political campaigns.* New York: Peter Lang.

Benoit, W. L. (2007b). Determinants of defense in political debates. *Communication Research Reports, 24*, 319–325.

Benoit, W. L. (2007c). Own party issue ownership emphasis in presidential television spots. *Communication Reports, 20*, 42–50.

Benoit, W. L. (2013d). Mudslinging: The nature of attacks in political campaigns. In C. Rountree (Ed.), *Venomous speech and other problems in American political discourse* (pp. 129–147). Westport, CT: Praeger.

Benoit, W. L. (2014). *Political election debates: Informing voters about policy and character.* Lanham, MD: Lexington Books.

Benoit, W. L., and Airne, D. (2005). Issue ownership for non-presidential television spots. *Communication Quarterly, 53*, 493–503.

Benoit, W. L., and Airne, D. (2009). Non-presidential political advertising in campaign 2008. *Human Communication, 12*, 91–117.

Benoit, W. L., and Airne, D. (2013). A functional analysis of non-presidential TV spots in campaign 2002. *Unpublished paper.*

Benoit, W. L., Blaney, J. R., and Pier, P. M. (2000). Attack, defense, and acclaiming in nominating convention keynote speeches. *Political Communication, 17*, 61–84.

Benoit, W. L., Blaney, J. R., and Pier, P. M. (1998). *Functions of campaign '96: Acclaiming, attacking, and defending discourse.* Westport, CT: Praeger.

Benoit, W. L., and Compton, J. (in press). A Functional Analysis of 2012 Republican primary TV spots. *American Behavioral Scientist.*

Benoit, W. L., Compton, J., and Phillips, B. (2013). Newspaper coverage of Prime Minister elections in Australia, Canada, and the United Kingdom. *Human Communication, 16*, 201–213.

Benoit, W. L., Delbert, J., Sudbrock, L. A., and Vogt, C. (2010). Functional analysis of 2008 senate and gubernatorial TV spots. *Human Communication, 13*, 103–125.

Benoit, W. L., Furgerson, J., Seifert, J., and Sargardia, S. (2013). Newspaper coverage of Senate, Gubernatorial, and Mayoral elections. *Human Communication, 16*, 215–229.

Benoit, W. L., and Hansen, G. J. (2002). Issue adaptation of presidential television spots and debates to primary and general audiences. *Communication Research Reports, 19*, 138–145.

Benoit, W. L., Hemmer, K., and Stein, K. (2010). *New York Times'* coverage of American presidential primary campaigns, 1952–2004. *Human Communication, 13*, 259–280.

Benoit, W. L., Leshner, G. M., and Chattopadhyay, S. (2007). A meta-analysis of political advertising. *Human Communication, 10*, 507–522.

Benoit, W. L., and McHale, J. P. (2003). Presidential candidates' television spots and personal qualities. *Southern Communication Journal, 68*, 319–334.

Benoit, W. L., and McHale, J. P. (2004). Presidential candidates' personal qualities: Computer content analysis. In K. L. Hacker (Ed.), *Presidential candidate images* (pp. 49–63). Lanham, MD: Rowman and Littlefield.

Benoit, W. L., McHale, J. P, Hansen, G. J., Pier, P. M., and McGuire, J. P. (2003). *Campaign 2000: A functional analysis of presidential campaign discourse.* Lanham, MD: Rowman and Littlefield.

Benoit, W. L., Pier, P. M., and Blaney, J. R. (1997). A functional analysis of presidential television spots: Acclaiming, attacking, and defending. *Communication Quarterly, 45*, 1–20.

Benoit, W. L., and Rill, L. A. (2012). A functional analysis of 2008 presidential primary TV spots. *Speaker and Gavel, 49*, 55–71.

Benoit, W. L., and Stein, K. A. (2005). A functional analysis of presidential direct mail advertising. *Communication Studies, 56*, 203–225.

Benoit, W. L., Stein, K. A., and Hansen, G. J. (2005). *New York Times* coverage of presidential campaigns, 1952–2000. *Journalism and Mass Communication Quarterly, 82*, 356–376.

Benoit, W. L., Stein, K. A., McHale, J. P., Chattopadhyay, S., Verser, R., and Price, S. (2007). *Bush versus Kerry: A functional analysis of campaign 2004.* New York: Peter Lang.

Benoit, W. L., and Wells, W. T. (1996). *Candidates in conflict: Persuasive attack and defense in the 1992 presidential debates.* Tuscaloosa: University of Alabama Press.

Benoit, W. L., Wells, W. T., Pier, P. M., and Blaney, J. R. (1999). Acclaiming, attacking, and defending in nominating convention acceptance addresses. *Quarterly Journal of Speech, 85*, 247–267.

Benze, J. G., and Declercq, E. R. (1985). Content of television political spot ads for female candidates. *Journalism Quarterly, 62*, 278–283, 288.

Bowers, R. A. (1972). Issue and personality information in newspaper political advertising. *Journalism Quarterly, 49*, 446–452.

Boynton, G. R., and Nelson, J. S. (1997). Making sound arguments: Would a claim by any other sound mean the same or argue as sweet? In J. F. Klumpp (Ed.), *Argument in a time of change: Definitions, frameworks, and critiques* (pp. 12–17). Annandale, VA: National Communication Association.

Brader, T. (2006). *Campaigning for hearts and minds: How emotional appeals in political ads work.* Chicago: University of Chicago Press.

Brasher, H. (2003). Capitalizing on contention: Issue agendas in U.S. senate campaigns. *Political Communication, 20*, 453–471.

Brazeal, L. M., and Benoit, W. L. (2006). On the spot: A functional analysis of congressional television spots, 1980–2004. *Communication Studies, 57*, 401–420.

Bibliography

Brazeal, L. M., and Benoit, W. L. (2008). Issue ownership in congressional campaign television spots. *Communication Quarterly, 56,* 17–28.

Breglio, V. (1987). Polling in campaigns. In L. P. Devlin (Ed.), *Political persuasion in presidential campaigns* (pp. 24–34). New Brunswick, NJ: Transaction Books.

Brewer, M. D. (2004). Tightly contested everywhere but the ballot box: The 2002 campaign for United States Senate in Maine. In L. S. Maisel and D. M. West (Eds.), *Running on empty? Political discourse in congressional elections* (pp. 199–213). Lanham, MD: Rowman and Littlefield.

Busch, A. E. (2004). Down to the wire: Colorado United States House district 7. In L. S. Maisel and D. M. West (Eds.), *Running on empty? Political discourse in congressional elections* (pp. 99–114). Lanham, MD: Rowman and Littlefield.

Center for Responsive Politics. (2009). Banking on becoming president. Accessed 1/6/09: www.opensecrets.org/pres08

Center for Responsive Politics. (2010). Most expensive [Senate] races. acccessed 4/11/10: www.opensecrets.org/bigpicture/topraces.php

Chang, C. (2000). Political advertising in Taiwan and the U.S.: A cross–cultural comparison of the 1996 presidential election campaigns. *Asian Journal of Communication, 10,* 1–17.

Christ, W. B., Thorson, E., and Caywood, C. (1994). Do attitudes toward political advertising affect information processing of televised political commercials? *Journal of Broadcasting and Electronic Media, 38,* 251–270.

Clines, F. X. (1996, June 3). Experience has colored his lessons with regret. *New York Times,* p. A12.

Cooper, C. A., and Knotts, H. G. (2004). Packaging the governors: Television advertising in the 2000 elections. In D. A. Schultz (Ed.), *Lights, camera, campaign! Media, politics, and political advertising* (pp. 101–120). New York: Peter Lang.

Cronkhite, G., Liska, J., and Schrader, D. (1991). Toward an integration of textual and response analysis applied to the 1988 presidential campaign. In F. Biocca (Ed.), *Television and political advertising* (vol. 2, pp. 163–184). Hillsdale, NJ: Erlbaum.

Crotty, W., and Jackson, J. S. (1985). *Presidential primaries and nominations.* Washington, D.C.: Congressional Quarterly Press.

Cundy, D. T. (1986). Political commercials and candidate image: The effect can be substantial. In L. L. Kaid, D. Nimmo, and K. R. Sanders (Eds.), *New perspectives on political advertising* (pp. 210–234). Carbondale: Southern Illinois Press.

Damore, D. F. (2005). Issue convergence in presidential campaigns. *Political Behavior, 27,* 71–97.

Davis, J. W. (1997). *U.S. presidential primaries and the caucus-convention system.* Westport, CT: Greenwood Press.

Descutner, D., Burnier, D., Mickunas, A., and Letteri, R. (1991). Bad signs and cryptic codes in a postmodern world: A semiotic analysis of the Dukakis advertising. In F. Biocca (Ed.), *Television and political advertising* (vol. 2, pp. 93–114). Hillsdale, NJ: Erlbaum.

Devlin, L. P. (1977). Contrasts in presidential campaign commercials of 1976. *Central States Speech Journal, 28,* 238–249.

Devlin, L. P. (1982). Contrasts in presidential campaign commercials of 1980. *Political Communication Review, 7,* 1–38.

Devlin, L. P. (1986). An analysis of presidential television commercials, 1952–1984. In L. L. Kaid, D. Nimmo, and K. R. Sanders (Eds.), *New perspectives on political advertising* (pp. 21–54). Carbondale: Southern Illinois Press.

Devlin, L. P. (1987a). Campaign commercials. In L. P. Devlin (Ed.), *Political persuasion in presidential campaigns* (pp. 208–216). New Brunswick, NJ: Transaction Books.

Devlin, L. P. (1987b). Contrasts in presidential campaign commercials of 1984. *Political Communication Review, 12*, 25–55.

Devlin, L. P. (1989). Contrasts in presidential campaign commercials of 1988. *American Behavioral Scientist, 32*, 389–414.

Devlin, L. P. (1993). Contrasts in presidential campaign commercials of 1992. *American Behavioral Scientist, 37*, 272–290.

Devlin, L. P. (1994). Television advertising in the 1992 New Hampshire presidential primary election. *Political Communication, 11*, 81–99.

Devlin, L. P. (1997). Contrasts in presidential campaign commercials of 1996. *American Behavioral Scientist, 40*, 1058–1084.

Diamond, E., and Bates, S. (1992). *The spot: The rise of political advertising on television* (3rd ed.). Cambridge, MA: MIT Press.

Donohue, T. R. (1973). Viewer perceptions of color and black-and-white paid political advertising. *Journalism Quarterly, 50*, 660–665.

Dover, E. D. (2006). *Images, issues, and attacks: Television advertising by incumbents and challengers in presidential elections.* Lanham, MD: Rowman and Littlefield.

Downs, A. J. (1957). *An economic theory of democracy.* New York: Harper and Row.

Drew, D., and Weaver, D. (1991). Voter learning in the 1988 presidential election: Did the debates and the media matter? *Journalism Quarterly, 68*, 22–37.

Elmelund-Praestekaer, C. 2010. Beyond American negativity: Toward a general understanding of the determinants of negative campaigning. *European Political Science Review, 2,* 137–156.

Enelow, J. M., and Hinich, M. J. (1984). *The spatial theory of voting: An introduction.* Cambridge: Cambridge University Press.

Ezra, M. (2004). Partisanship trumps incumbency in Maryland's 8th district. In L. S. Maisel and D. M. West (Eds.), *Running on empty? Political discourse in congressional elections* (pp. 27–39). Lanham, MD: Rowman and Littlefield.

Faber, R. J., and Storey, M. C. (1984). Recall of information from political advertising. *Journal of Advertising, 13*, 39–44.

Faber, R. J., Tims, A.R., and Schmitt, K. G. (1993). Negative political advertising and voting intent: The role of involvement and alternative information sources. *Journal of Advertising, 22*, 67–76.

Foote, J. S. (1991). Implications of presidential communication for electoral success. In L. L. Furgerson, J., Sargardia, S., Seifert, J., and Benoit, W. L. (2013). *News coverage of non-presidential campaigns.* Chicago, IL: Midwest Political Science Association.

Garramone, G. M. (1984). Voter responses to negative political ads. *Journalism Quarterly, 61*, 250–269.

Garramone, G. M. (1985). Effects of negative political advertising: The roles of sponsor and rebuttal. *Journal of Broadcasting and Electronic Media, 29*, 147–159.

Garramone, G. M., Atkin, C. K., Pinkleton, B. E., and Cole, R. T. (1990). Effects of negative political advertising on the political process. *Journal of Broadcasting and Electronic Media, 34*, 299–311.

Garramone, G. M., and Smith, S. J. (1984). Reactions to political advertising: Clarifying sponsor effects. *Journalism Quarterly, 51*, 771–775.

Geer, John G. 2006. *In defense of negativity: Attack ads in presidential campaigns.* Chicago: University of Chicago Press.

Geiger, S. F., and Reeves, B. (1991). The effects of visual structure and content emphasis on the evaluation and memory for political candidates. In F. Biocca (Ed.), *Television and political advertising* (vol. 1, pp. 125–143). Hillsdale, NJ: Erlbaum.

Ghorpade, S. (1986). Agenda setting: A test of advertising's neglected function. *Journal of Advertising Research, 26,* 23–27.

Glaser, B. G., and Strauss, A. L. (1967). *The discovery of grounded theory: Strategies for qualitative research.* Chicago: Aldine.

Gordon, B. R., and Hartmann, W. R. (2013). Advertising effects in presidential elections. *Marketing Science, 32,* 19–35.

Griese, N. L. (1975). Rosser Reeves and the 1952 Eisenhower TV spot blitz. *Journal of Advertising, 4,* 34–48.

Griffin, M., and Kagan, S. (1996). Picturing culture in political spots: 1992 campaigns in Israel and the United States. *Political Communication, 13,* 43–61.

Gronbeck, B. E. (1978). The functions of presidential campaigning. *Communication Monographs, 45,* 268–280.

Gronbeck, B. E. (1992). Negative narratives in 1988 presidential campaign ads. *Quarterly Journal of Speech, 78,* 333–346.

Hacker, K. L., Zakahi, W. R., Giles, M. J., and McQuitty, S. (2000). Components of candidate images: Statistical analysis of the issue-persona dichotomy in the presidential campaign of 1996. *Communication Monographs, 67,* 227–238.

Hallin, D. (1992). Sound bite news: Television coverage of elections, 1968–1988. *Journal of Communication, 42,* 5–24.

Henson, J. R., and Benoit, W. L. (2010). Because I said so: A functional theory analysis of evidence in political TV spots. *Speaker and Gavel, 47,* 1–15.

Hill, R. P. (1989). An exploration of voter responses to political advertisements. *Journal of Advertising, 18,* 14–22.

Himmelweit, H. T., Humphreys, P., and Jaeger, M. (1985). *How voters decide: A longitudinal study of political attitudes and voting extended over fifteen years* (rev. ed.). Milton Keynes: Open University Press.

Hitchon, J. C., and Chang, C. (1995). Effects of gender schematic processing on the reception of political commercials for men and women candidates. *Communication Research, 22,* 430–458.

Hofstetter, C. R. (1976). *Bias in the news: Network television coverage of the 1972 election campaign.* Columbus, OH: Ohio State University Press.

Hofstetter, C. R., and Zukin, C. (1979). TV network news and advertising in the Nixon and McGovern campaigns. *Journalism Quarterly, 56,* 106–115, 152.

Holtz-Bacha, C., and Kaid, L. L. (1995). A comparative perspective on political advertising. In L. L. Kaid and C. Holtz-Bacha (Eds.), *Political advertising in western democracies: Parties and candidates on television* (pp. 8–18). Thousand Oaks, CA: Sage.

Hughes, E. M. B. G. (1994). *The logical choice: How political commercials use logic to win votes.* Lanham, MD: University Press of America.

Humke, R. G., Schmitt, R. L., and Grupp, S. E. (1975). Candidates, issues and party in newspaper political advertisements. *Journalism Quarterly, 52,* 499–504.

InfoPlease. (2000). Presidential election of 2000, electoral and popular vote summary, Accessed 6/11/13: www.infoplease.com/ipa/A0876793.html

Iyengar, S., and Kinder, D. R. (1988). *News that matters: Television and American opinion.* Chicago: University of Chicago Press.

Jackson, J. S., and Crotty, W. (1996). *The politics of presidential selection*. New York: Harper-Collins.

James, K. E., and Hensel, P. J. (1991). Negative advertising: The malicious strain of comparative advertising. *Journal of Advertising, 20*, 53–69.

Jamieson, K. H. (1989). Context and the creation of meaning in the advertising of the 1988 presidential campaign. *American Behavioral Scientist, 32*, 415–424.

Jamieson, K. H. (1992a). *Dirty politics: Deception, distraction, and democracy*. New York: Oxford University Press.

Jamieson, K. H. (1992b). *Packaging the presidency: A history and criticism of presidential campaign advertising* (2nd ed.). New York: Oxford University Press.

Jamieson, J. H. (1996). *Packaging the presidency: A history and criticism of presidential campaign advertising* (3rd ed.). New York: Oxford University Press.

Jenkins, K. (1997). Learning to love those expensive campaigns. *US News and World Report* [On-line], 122 (9).

Johnson-Cartee, K. S., and Copeland, G. (1989). Southern voters' reactions to negative political ads in the 1986 election. *Journalism Quarterly, 66*, 888–893, 986.

Johnson-Cartee, K. S., and Copeland, G. (1991). *Negative political advertising: Coming of age*. Hillsdale, NJ: Erlbaum.

Johnson-Cartee, K. S., and Copeland, G. (1997). *Manipulation of the American voter: Political campaign commercials*. Westport, CT: Praeger.

Johnston, A. (1991). Political broadcasts: An analysis of form, content, and style in presidential communication. In L. L. Kaid, J. Gerstle, and K. R. Sanders (Eds.), *Mediated politics in two cultures: Presidential campaigning in the United States and France* (pp. 59–72). New York: Praeger.

Johnston, A., and White, A. B. (1994). Communication styles and female candidates: A study of the political advertising during the 1986 Senate elections. *Journalism Quarterly, 71*, 321–329.

Johnston, D. D. (1989). Image and issue political information: Message content or interpretation? *Journalism Quarterly, 66*, 379–382.

Joslyn, R. A. (1980). The content of political spot ads. *Journalism Quarterly, 57*, 92–98.

Joslyn, R. A. (1981). The impact of campaign spot advertising on voting defections. *Human Communication Research, 7*, 347–360.

Joslyn, R. (1986). Political advertising and the meaning of elections. In L. L. Kaid, D. Nimmo, and K. R. Sanders (Eds.), *New perspectives on political advertising* (pp. 139–183). Carbondale: Southern Illinois Press.

Just, M., Crigler, A., and Wallach, L. (1990). Thirty seconds or thirty minutes: What viewers learn from spot advertisements and candidate debates. *Journal of Communication, 40*, 120–132.

Kahn, K. F., and Kenney, P. J. (1999). *The spectacle of U.S. Senate campaigns*. Princeton, NJ: Princeton University Press.

Kaid, L. L. (1991). The effects of television broadcasts on perceptions of presidential candidates in the United States and France. In L. L. Kaid, J. Gerstle, and K. R. Sanders (Eds.), *Mediated politics in two cultures: Presidential campaigning in the United States and France* (pp. 247–60). New York: Praeger.

Kaid, L. L. (1994). Political advertising in the 1992 campaign. In R. E. Denton (Ed.), *The 1992 presidential campaign: A communication perspective* (pp. 111–127). Westport, CT: Praeger.

Kaid, L. L. (1996). Technology and political advertising: The application of ethical standards to the 1992 spots. *Communication Research Reports, 13*, 129–137.

Kaid, L. L. (1997). Effects of the television spots on images of Dole and Clinton. *American Behavioral Scientist, 40*, 1085–1094.

Kaid, L. L., and Ballotti, J. (1991). *Television advertising in presidential primaries and caucuses.* Paper presented at the annual conference of the Speech Communication Association, Atlanta, GA.

Kaid, L. L., and Boydston, J. (1987). An experimental study of the effectiveness of negative political advertisements. *Communication Quarterly, 35*, 193–201.

Kaid, L. L., and Davidson, D. K. (1986). Elements of video style: Candidate presentation through television advertising. In L. L. Kaid, D. Nimmo, and K. R. Sanders (Eds.), *New perspectives on political advertising* (pp. 184–209). Carbondale: Southern Illinois Press.

Kaid, L. L. ,Gerstle, J., and Sanders, K. R. (Eds.). (1978). *Mediated politics in two cultures: Presidential campaigning in the United States and France* (pp. 261–270). New York: Praeger.

Kaid, L. L., and Holtz-Bacha, C. (1995a). An introduction to parties and candidates on television. In L. L. Kaid and C. Holtz-Bacha, (Eds.) *Political advertising in western democracies: Parties and candidates on television* (pp. 1–7). Thousand Oaks, CA: Sage.

Kaid, L. L., and Holtz-Bacha, C. (1995b). Political advertising across cultures: Comparing content, styles, and effects. In L. L. Kaid and C. Holtz-Bacha (Eds.) *Political advertising in western democracies: Parties and candidates on television* (pp. 206–227). Thousand Oaks, CA: Sage.

Kaid, L. L., and Johnston, A. (1991). Negative versus positive television advertising in U.S. presidential campaigns, 1960–1988. *Journal of Communication, 41*, 53–64.

Kaid, L. L., and Johnston, A. (2001). *Videostyle in presidential campaigns: Style and content of televised political advertising.* Westport, CT: Praeger.

Kaid, L. L., Leland, C. M., and Whitney, S. (1992). The impact of televised political ads: Evoking viewer responses in the 1988 presidential campaign. *Southern Communication Journal, 57*, 285–295.

Kaid, L. L., Nimmo, D., and Sanders, K. R. (Eds.). (1986). *New perspectives on political advertising.* Carbondale: Southern Illinois Press.

Kaid, L. L., and Sanders, K. R. (1978). Political television commercials: An experimental study of type and length. *Communication Research, 5*, 57–70.

Kamber, V. (1997). *Poison politics: Are negative campaigns destroying democracy?* Cambridge, MA: Perseus.

Kelley, S., and Mirer, T. W. (1974). The simple act of voting. *American Political Science Review, 68*, 572–591.

Kendall, K. E. (2000). *Communication in the presidential primaries: Candidates and the media, 1912–2000.* Westport, CT: Praeger.

Kern, M. (1989). *30 second politics: Political advertising in the eighties.* New York: Praeger.

King, A. (2002). Conclusions and implications. In A. King (Ed.), *Leaders' personalities and the outcomes of democratic elections* (pp. 210–221). Oxford: University Press.

Lang, A. (1991). Emotion, formal features, and memory for televised political advertisements. In F. Biocca (Ed.), *Television and political advertising* (vol. 1, pp. 221–243). Hillsdale, NJ: Erlbaum.

Larson, C. U. (1982). Media metaphors: Two models for rhetorically criticizing the political television spot advertisement. *Central States Speech Journal, 33*, 533–546.

Larson, S. G. (2004). Turning a "no win" race into a win: Democrat Time Holden beats the other George W. (Gekas) in Pennsylvania's 17th. In L. S. Maisel and D. M. West (Eds.),

Running on empty? Political discourse in congressional elections (pp. 157–170). Lanham, MD: Rowman and Littlefield.

Latimer, M. K. (1984). Policy issues and personal images in political advertising in a state election. *Journalism Quarterly, 61*, 776–784, 852.

Latimer, M. K. (1989). Legislators' advertising messages in seven state campaigns in 1986. *Journalism Quarterly, 66*, 338–348, 527.

Lau, R. R., and Pomper, G. M. (2004). *Negative campaigning: An analysis of U.S. senate elections.* Lanham, MD: Rowman and Littlefield.

Lau, R. R., Sigelman, L., and Rovner, I. B. (2007). The effects of negative political campaigns: A meta-analytic reassessment. *Journal of Politics, 69*, 1176–1209.

Lee, C., and Benoit, W. L. (2004). A functional analysis of presidential television spots: A comparison of Korean and American ads. *Communication Quarterly, 52*, 68–79.

Levine, M. A. (1995). *Presidential campaigns and elections: Issues and images in the media age.* Itasea, IL: Peacock Publishers.

Lichtman, A. J. (1996). *The keys to the White House, 1996: A surefire guide to predicting the next president.* Lanham, MD: Madison.

Lodge, M., and Taber, S. S. (2013). *The rationalizing voter.* Cambridge: Cambridge University Press.

Louden, A. D. (1989). Political advertising bibliography. *Political Communication Review, 14*, 19–46.

Maisel, L. S., and West, D. M. (Eds.). (2004). *Running on empty? Political discourse in congressional elections.* Lanham, MD: Rowman and Littlefield.

Marcus, G. E., Neuman, W. R., and MacKuen, M. (2000). *Affective intelligence and political judgment.* Chicago: University of Chicago Press.

Martinez, M. D., and Delegal, T. (1990). The irrelevance of negative campaigns to political trust: Experimental and survey results. *Political Communication and Persuasion, 7*, 25–40.

McClure, R. D., and Patterson, T. E. (1974). Television news and political advertising: The impact of exposure on voter beliefs. *Communication Research, 1*, 3–21.

McCombs, M. E. (2004). *Setting the agenda: The mass media and public opinion.* Cambridge: Polity Press.

McCombs, M. E., and Shaw, D. L. (1972). The agenda setting function of the mass media. *Public Opinion Quarterly, 36*, 176–187.

Meadow, R. G., and Sigelman, L. (1982). Some effects and non-effects of campaign commercials: An experimental study. *Political Behavior, 4*, 163–175.

Menefee-Libey, D. (2000). *The triumph of campaign-centered politics.* New York: Chatham House.

Merritt, S. (1984). Negative political advertising: Some empirical findings. *Journal of Advertising, 13*, 27–38.

Miller Center, University of Virginia. (2013). *American president: A reference resource.* Accessed 11/11/13: millercenter.org/president/gwbush/essays/biography/3

Mulder, R. (1979). The effects of televised political ads in the 1975 Chicago mayoral election. *Journalism Quarterly, 56*, 335–341.

Nelson, J. S., and Boynton, G. R. (1997). *Video rhetorics: Televised advertising in American politics.* Urbana, IL: University of Illinois Press.

Nesbit, D. D. (1988). *Videostyle in senate campaigns.* Knoxville, TN: University of Tennessee Press.

New York Times. (2001). *36 days: The complete chronicle of the 2000 presidential election crisis.* New York: Times Books.

New York Times. (2008, December 1). Election 2008. Accessed 1/6/09: elections.nytimes .com/2008/president/advertising/advertisers/2-barack-obama; elections.nytimes.com/2008/ president/advertising/advertisers/8-john-mccain

Newhagen, J. E., and Reeves, B. (1991). Emotion and memory responses for negative political advertising: A study of television commercials used in the 1988 presidential election. In F. Biocca (Ed.), *Television and political advertising* (vol. 1, pp. 197–220). Hillsdale, NJ: Erlbaum.

Nie, N. H., Verba, S., and Petrocik, J. R. (1979). *The changing American voter* (enlarged ed.). Cambridge, MA: Harvard University Press.

Nowlan, J. D., and Moutray, M. J. (1984). Broadcast advertising and party endorsements in a statewide primary. *Journal of Broadcasting, 28*, 361–363.

Page, B. I. (1978). *Choices and echoes in presidential elections: Rational man and electoral democracy.* Chicago: University of Chicago Press.

Palda, K. S. (1973). Does advertising influence votes? An analysis of the 1966 and 1970 Quebec elections. *Canadian Journal of Political Science, 6*, 638–655.

Patterson, T. E. (1980). *The mass media election: How Americans choose their president.* New York: Praeger.

Patterson, T. E. (2003). *The vanishing voter: Public involvement in an age of uncertainty.* New York: Random House, Vintage Books.

Patterson, T. E., and McClure, R. D. (1973). Political advertising on television: Spot commercials in the 1972 presidential election. *Maxwell Review*, 57–69.

Patterson, T. E., and McClure, R. D. (1976). *The unseeing eye: The myth of television power in national politics.* New York: Putnam.

Payne, J. G., and Baukus, R. A. (1988). Trend analysis of the 1984 GOP senatorial spots. *Political Communication and Persuasion, 5*, 161–177.

Payne, J. G., Marlier, J., and Baukus, R. A. (1989). Polispots in the 1988 presidential primaries: Separating the nominees from the rest of the guys. *American Behavioral Scientist, 32*, 365–381.

Peterson, P. E. (1995). *The price of federalism.* Washington, DC: CQ Press.

Petrocik, J. R. (1996). Issue ownership in presidential elections, with a 1980 case study. *American Journal of Political Science, 40*, 825–850.

Petrocik, J. R. (2004). Hard facts: The media and elections with a look at 2000 and 2002. In J. A. Thurber and C. J. Nelson (Eds.), *Campaigns and elections American style* (2nd ed., pp. 129–147). Boulder, CO: Westview.

Petrocik, J. R., Benoit, W. L., and Hansen, G. L. (2003–2004). Issue ownership and presidential campaigning, 1952–2000. *Political Science Quarterly, 118*, 599–626.

Petterson, P. R. (2004). Civil discourse derailed, or the invasion of the body (politic) snatchers in Connecticut 2. In L. S. Maisel and D. M. West (Eds.), *Running on empty? Political discourse in congressional elections* (pp. 1–13). Lanham, MD: Rowman and Littlefield.

Pfau, M., and Burgoon, M. (1989). The efficacy of issue and character attack message strategies in political campaign communication. *Communication Reports, 2*, 53–61.

Pfau, M., Diedrich, T., Larson, K. M., and van Winkle, K. M. (1993). Relational and competence perceptions of presidential candidates during primary election campaigns. *Journal of Broadcasting and Electronic Media, 37*, 275–292.

Pfau, M., and Kenski, H. C. (1990). *Attack politics: Strategy and defense.* New York: Praeger.

Pfau, M., Parrott, R. and Lindquist, B. (1992). An expectancy theory explanation of political attack television spots: A case study. *Journal of Applied Communication Research, 20*, 235–253.

Pier, P. M. (2002). *He said, she said: A functional analysis of gender differences in political campaign messages.* Unpublished doctoral dissertation, University of Missouri.

Pomper, G. M. (1975). *Voters' choice: Varieties of American electoral behavior.* New York: Dodd, Mead, and Company.

Popkin, S. L. (1994). *The reasoning voter: Communication and persuasion in presidential campaigns.* Chicago: University of Chicago Press.

Popkin, S. L., Gorman, J., Smith, J., and Phillips, C. (1976). Comment: toward an investment theory of voting behavior: What have you done for me lately? *American Political Science Review, 70*, 779–805.

Prisuta, R. H. (1972). Broadcast advertising by candidates for the Michigan legislature: 1970. *Journal of Broadcasting, 16*, 453–459.

Procter, D. E., and Schenck-Hamlin, W. J. (1996). Form and variations in negative political advertising. *Communication Research Reports, 13*, 147–156.

Prysby, C. (2004). A civil campaign in a competitive state: The 2002 North Carolina U.S. Senate election. In L. S. Maisel and D. M. West (Eds.), *Running on empty? Political discourse in congressional elections* (pp. 215–228). Lanham, MD: Rowman and Littlefield.

Reinemann, C., and Maurer, M. (2005). Unifying or polarizing? Short-term effects and postdebate consequences of different rhetorical strategies in televised debates. *Journal of Communication, 55*, 775–794.

Roberts, M., and McCombs, M. (1994). Agenda setting and political advertising: Origins of the news agenda. *Political Communication, 11*, 249–262.

Roddy, B. L., and Garramone, G. M. (1988). Appeals and strategies of negative political advertising. *Journal of Broadcasting and Electronic Media, 32*, 415–427.

Rose, E. D., and Fuchs, D. (1968). Reagan vs. Brown: A TV image playback. *Journal of Broadcasting, 12*, 247–260.

Rotheld, M., and McGreevy, P. (2010, March 22). Meg Whitman sets record spending pace in campaign for governor. *LA Times.* Accessed 4/15/10: articles.latimes.com/2010/mar/22/local/la-me-money23-2010mar23

Rountree, J. C. (1995). The president as God, The recession as evil: *Actus, status,* and the president's rhetorical bind in the 1992 election. *Quarterly Journal of Speech, 81*, 325–352.

Rudd, R. (1986). Issues as image in political campaign commercials. *Western Journal of Speech Communication, 50*, 102–118.

Rudd, R. (1989). Effects of issue specificity, ambiguity on evaluations of candidate image. *Journalism Quarterly, 66*, 675–682, 691.

Sabato, J. L. (1981). *The rise of political consultants: New ways of winning elections.* New York: Basic Books.

Salamore, S. A., and Salamore, B. G. (1985). *Campaigns, parties, and campaigns: Electoral politics in America.* Washington, DC: Congressional Quarterly Press.

Schleuder, J., McCombs, M., and Wanta, W. (1991). Inside the agenda-setting process: How political advertising and TV news prime viewers to think about issues and candidates. In F. Biocca (Ed.), *Television and political advertising* (vol. 1, pp. 265–309). Hillsdale, NJ: Erlbaum.

Schultz, D. A. (Ed.). (2004). *Lights, camera, campaign! Media, politics, and political advertising.* New York: Peter Lang.

Shapiro, M. A., and Rieger, R. H. (1992). Comparing positive and negative political advertising on radio. *Journalism Quarterly, 69,* 135–145.

Sheckels, T. F. (1994). Mikulski vs. Chavez for the Senate from Maryland in 1986 and the "rules" for attack politics. *Communication Quarterly, 42,* 311–326.

Shockley, J. S. (2004). A three-peat in the 2nd congressional district race in Minnesota. In L. S. Maisel and D. M. West (Eds.), *Running on empty? Political discourse in congressional elections* (pp. 41–55). Lanham, MD: Rowman and Littlefield.

Shyles, L. (1983). Defining the issues of a presidential election from televised political spot advertisements. *Journal of Broadcasting, 27,* 333–343.

Shyles, L. (1984). The relationships of images, issues, and presentational methods in televised spot advertisements for 1980's American presidential primaries. *Journal of Broadcasting, 28,* 405–421.

Shyles, L. (1986). The televised political spot advertisement: Its structure, content, and role in the political system. In L. L. Kaid, D. Nimmo, and K. R. Sanders (Eds.), *New perspectives on political advertising* (pp. 107–138). Carbondale: Southern Illinois Press.

Shyles, L. (1991). Issue content and legitimacy in 1988 televised political advertising: Hubris and synecdoche in promoting presidential candidates. In F. Biocca (Ed.), *Television and political advertising* (vol. 2, pp. 133–62). Hillsdale, NJ: Erlbaum.

Sigelman, L., and Buell, E. H. (2004). Avoidance or engagement? Issue convergence in U.S. presidential campaigns, 1960–2000. *American Journal of Political Science, 48,* 650–661.

Simon, A. F. (2002). *The winning message: Candidate behavior, Campaign discourse, and democracy.* Cambridge: Cambridge University Press.

Sinclair, J. (1995). Reforming television's role in American political campaigns: Rationale for the elimination of paid political advertisements. *Communications and the Law [On-line], 17(1).*

Smith, C. A. (1990). *Political communication.* San Diego, CA: Harcourt Brace Jovanovich.

Smith, C. A. (2005). Candidate strategies in the 2004 presidential campaign: Instrumental choices faced by the incumbent and his challengers. In R. E. Denton (Ed.), *The 2004 presidential campaign: A communication perspective* (pp. 131–151). Lanham, MD: Rowman and Littlefield.

Smith, C. A., and Mansharamani, N. (2002). Challenger and incumbent reversal in the 2000 election. In R. E. Denton (Ed.), *The 2004 presidential campaign: A communication perspective* (pp. 91–116). Westport, CT: Praeger.

Smith, L. D., and Johnston, A. (1991). Burke's sociological criticism applied to political advertising: An anecdotal taxonomy of presidential commercials. In F. Biocca (Ed.), *Television and political advertising* (vol. 2, pp. 115–31). Hillsdale, NJ: Erlbaum.

Splaine, J. (1995). *The road to the White House since television.* Washington, DC: C-SPAN.

Steele, C. A., and Barnhurst, K. G. (1996). The journalism of opinion: Network news coverage of U.S. presidential campaigns, 1968–1988. *Critical Studies in Mass Communication, 13,* 187–209.

Stein, R. M. (1990). Economic voting for governor and U.S. senator: The electoral consequences of federalism. *Journal of Politics, 52,* 29–53.

Stewart, C. J. (1975). Voter perception of mud-slinging in political communication. *Central States Speech Journal, 26,* 279–286.

Stromer-Galley, J., and Sheinheit, I. (2012). On line campaigning. *Oxford Bibliographies On-line.* DOI: 10.1093/OBO/9780199756841-0059

Sullivan, J., and Sapir, E. V. 2012. Modeling negative campaign advertising: Evidence from Taiwan. *Asian Journal of Communication, 22,* 289–303.

Tak, J., Kaid, L. L., and Lee, S. (1997). A cross-cultural study of political advertising in the United States and Korea. *Communication Research, 24*, 423–430.

Thurber, J. A., Nelson, C. J., and Dulio, D. A. (2000). *Crowded airwaves: Campaign advertising in elections.* Washington, DC: Brookings.

Thorson, E., Christ, W. G., and Caywood, C. (1991). Effects of issue-image strategies, attack and support appeals, music, and visual content in political commercials. *Journal of Broadcasting and Electronic Media, 35*, 465–486.

Tidmarch, C. M., Hyman, L. J., and Sorkin, J. E. (1984). Press issue agendas in the 1982 congressional and gubernatorial election campaigns. *Journal of Politics, 46*, 1226–1242.

Tinkham, S. F., and Weaver-Lariscy, R. A. (1995). Incumbency and its perceived advantage: A comparison of 1982 and 1990 congressional advertising strategies. *Political Communication, 12*, 291–304.

TNS, (2004, November 1). U.S. Political advertising spending reaches $1.45 billion reports TNS Media Intelligence/CMR. Accessed 8/7/05: www.tns-mi.com/news/11012004.htm

Trent, J. D., and Trent, J. S. (1995). The incumbent and his challengers: The problem of adapting to prevailing conditions. In K. E. Kendall (Ed.), *Presidential campaign discourse: Strategic communication problems* (pp. 69–93). Albany: State University of New York Press.

Trent, J. S., and Friedenberg, R. V. (1995). *Political campaign communication: Principles and practices* (3rd ed.). Westport, CT: Praeger.

Trent, J. S., and Friedenberg, R. V. (2000). *Political campaign communication: Principles and practices* (4th ed.). Westport, CT: Praeger.

Trent, J. S., and Trent, J. D. (1974). The rhetoric of the challenger: George Stanley McGovern. *Central States Speech Journal, 25*, 11–18.

Tucker, D. E. (1959). Broadcasting in the 1956 Oregon senatorial campaign. *Journal of Broadcasting, 3*, 225–243.

Walter, A. S., and Vliegenthart, R. (2010). Negative campaigning across different communication channels: Different ball games? *International Journal of Press/Politics, 15*, 441–461.

Wanat, J. (1974). Political broadcast advertising and primary election voting. *Journal of Broadcasting, 18*, 413–422.

Wattenberg, M. P. (1991). *The rise of candidate-centered politics: Presidential elections of the 1980s.* Cambridge, MA: Harvard University Press.

Wattenberg, M. P. (1998). *The decline of American political parties, 1952–1996.* Cambridge, MA: Harvard University Press.

Weaver, D., and Drew, D. (1993). Voter learning in the 1990 off-year election: Did the media matter? *Journalism Quarterly, 70*, 256–268.

Weaver-Lariscy, R. A., and Tinkham, S. F. (1987). The influence of media expenditure and allocations strategies in congressional advertising campaigns. *Journal of Advertising, 16*, 13–21.

Weaver-Lariscy, R. A., and Tinkham, S. F. (1996). Advertising message strategies in U.S. congressional campaigns, 1982, 1990. *Journal of Current Issues and Research in Advertising, 18*, 53–66.

Weisberg, H. F., and Kimball, D. C. (1993). *The 1992 presidential election: Party identification nd beyond.* Paper presented at the American Political Science Association, Washington, D.C. (quoted in M. A. Levine, (1995). *Presidential campaigns and elections: Issues and images in the media age.* Itasea, IL: Peacock Publishers.)

Wen, W-C., Benoit, W. L., and Yu, T-H. (2004). A functional analysis of the 2000 Taiwanese and US presidential spots. *Asian Journal of Communication, 14*, 140–155.

West, D. M. (1993). *Air wars: Television advertising in election campaigns, 1952–1992.* Washington, DC: Congressional Quarterly. West, D. M. (1997). *Air wars: Television advertising in election campaigns, 1952–1996* 2nd ed. Washington, DC: Congressional Quarterly.

West, D. M. (1997). *Air wars: Television advertising in election campaigns, 1952–1996* (2nd ed.). Washington, DC: Congressional Quarterly.

West, D. M. (2014). *Air wars: Television advertising in election campaigns, 1952–2000* (6th ed.). Washington, DC: CQ Press.

Wilson, R. (2012, November 2). Obama and Romney teams top $1 billion in ad spending: The Romney side is outspending Obama, and both sides are now emptying their coffers at an unprecedented pace. *National Journal.* Accessed 3/31/13: www.nationaljournal.com/politics/obama-and-romney-teams-top-1-billion-in-ad-spending-20121102

Wisconsin Public Television. (2001). *The: 30 second candidate.* Accessed 3/8/05: www.pbs.org/30secondcandidate/timeline

Zaller, J. R. (1992). *The nature and origins of mass opinion.* New York, NY: Cambridge University Press.

Zhao, X., and Bleske, G. L. (1995). Measurement effects in comparing voter learning from television news and campaign advertisements. *Journalism and Mass Communication Quarterly, 72,* 72–83.

Index of Topics

Index of Authors

About the Author

William L. Benoit (Ph.D., Wayne State University, 1979) is a professor of communication studies at Ohio University; before that he spent twenty-five years at the University of Missouri. He has published fifteen books including eight on political campaigns. His most recent book (also published in 2014) is *Political Election Debates: Informing Voters About Policy and Character*. He has published over ninety journal articles and book chapters on political campaigns, including articles in *Communication Monographs*, *The Journal of Communication*, *Human Communication Research*, *Journalism and Mass Communication Quarterly*, and *The Quarterly Journal of Speech*. He collects rock and roll and blues music. Recently he has started painting in the style of Mondrian.

DATE DUE	RETURNED